365: AIGA YEAR IN DESIGN 22

IS THE AUTHORITATIVE

CHRONICLE OF

NORTH AMERICAN DESIGN

FOR THE YEAR 2001.

IDENTIFIED BY THIRTEEN

SPECIALIZED JURIES

THE SELECTED WORK

REPRESENTS THE BEST

COMMUNICATIONS DESIGN

ACROSS ALL DISCIPLINES.

365

contents

The year 2001 was a year of forces in transition even before it became epochal. For nearly half a decade, the design economy had demonstrated a permissiveness that nourished irony as well as clarity. As the economy stumbled in early 2001, the demand for design also changed. And after September 11, public interest gravitated toward clear, simple, truthful and effective communication.

Now, after a period in which design and style may have become confused in the popular mind, the quest for effective design is more evident than ever in the values of the profession and the artifacts it creates.

365: AIGA Year in Design 23 is a collection of exemplars, demonstrating the role of design in adding economic, cultural and aesthetic value. Each featured piece is characterized by the designer's statement and the observation of a juror, making this book »

a means of communicating the process, as well as the outcome, of designing.

The process of designing may be the competitive advantage designers of all disciplines bring to projects in the future, particularly as projects become more complex, strategic, multidisciplinary and conceptual. AIGA is adapting to this "post-disciplinary" dynamic—finding ways to communicate the value of designing, emphasizing the special role of the designer in addressing complex problems and reinforcing professional standards for the designer-client relationship.

The selections in *365: AIGA Year in Design 23* and the annotation of each piece provide a benchmark for the changes that are occurring as designers adapt to the needs of business and society in the 21st century. □

Richard Grefé, executive director

the medal of aiga

THE MEDAL OF AIGA, THE MOST DISTINGUISHED IN
THE FIELD, IS AWARDED TO INDIVIDUALS IN
RECOGNITION OF THEIR EXCEPTIONAL ACHIEVEMENTS,
SERVICES OR OTHER CONTRIBUTIONS TO THE FIELD
OF GRAPHIC DESIGN AND VISUAL COMMUNICATION.

THE AIGA MEDAL HONORS INDIVIDUALS FOR CONTRIBUTIONS IN THE PRACTICE OF
GRAPHIC DESIGN, TEACHING, WRITING OR LEADERSHIP OF THE PROFESSION.
SIMILARLY, THE DESIGN LEADERSHIP AWARD HONORS CORPORATIONS
AND ORGANIZATIONS FOR THEIR ACHIEVEMENTS IN DESIGN.
MEDALS HAVE BEEN AWARDED SINCE 1920 TO INDIVIDUALS WHO HAVE
SET STANDARDS OF EXCELLENCE OVER A LIFETIME OF WORK, OR HAVE MADE
INDIVIDUAL CONTRIBUTIONS TO INNOVATION WITHIN THE PRACTICE OF DESIGN.
MEDALISTS MAY BE HONORED POSTHUMOUSLY.
ALTHOUGH MEDALISTS HAIL FROM MANY COUNTRIES, THE CONTRIBUTIONS FOR
WHICH THEY ARE RECOGNIZED HAVE HAD A SIGNIFICANT
IMPACT ON GRAPHIC DESIGN PRACTICE WITHIN THE UNITED STATES.

the medal of aiga
aiga 1920—2002 medalists

1920 NORMAN T.A. MUNDER
1922 DANIEL BERKELEY UPDIKE
1924 JOHN C. AGAR, STEPHEN H. HORGAN
1925 BRUCE ROGERS
1926 BURTON EMMETT
1927 TIMOTHY COLE, FREDERIC W. GOUDY
1929 WILLIAM A. DWIGGINS
1930 HENRY WATSON KENT
1931 DARD HUNTER
1932 PORTER GARNETT
1934 HENRY LEWIS BULLEN
1935 RUDOLPH RUZICKA, J. THOMPSON WILLING
1939 WILLIAM A. KITTREDGE
1940 THOMAS M. CLELAND
1941 CARL PURINGTON ROLLINS
1942 EDWIN AND ROBERT GRABHORN
1944 EDWARD EPSTEAN
1945 FREDERIC G. MELCHER
1946 STANLEY MORISON
1947 ELMER ADLER
1948 LAWRENCE C. WROTH
1950 EARNEST ELMO CALKINS, ALFRED A. KNOPF
1951 HARRY L. GAGE
1952 JOSEPH BLUMENTHAL
1953 GEORGE MACY
1954 WILL BRADLEY, JAN TSCHICHOLD
1955 P. J. CONKWRIGHT
1956 RAY NASH
1957 DR. M. F. AGHA
1958 BEN SHAHN
1959 MAY MASSEE
1960 WALTER PAEPCKE
1961 PAUL A. BENNETT
1962 WILHELM SANDBERG
1963 SAUL STEINBERG
1964 JOSEF ALBERS
1965 LEONARD BASKIN
1966 PAUL RAND
1967 ROMANA JAVITZ
1968 DR. GIOVANNI MARDERSTEIG
1969 DR. ROBERT R. LESLIE
1970 HERBERT BAYER
1971 WILL BURTIN
1972 MILTON GLASER
1973 RICHARD AVEDON, ALLEN HURLBURT, PHILIP JOHNSON
1974 ROBERT RAUSCHENBERG
1976 BRADBURY THOMPSON, HENRY WOLF, JEROME SNYDER
1977 CHARLES AND RAY EAMES
1978 LOU DORFSMAN
1979 IVAN CHERMAYEFF AND THOMAS GEISMAR
1980 HERB LUBALIN
1981 SAUL BASS
1982 MASSIMO AND LELLA VIGNELLI
1983 HERBERT MATTER
1984 LEO LIONNI
1985 SEYMOUR CHWAST
1986 WALTER HERDEG
1987 ALEXEY BRODOVITCH, GENE FEDERICO
1988 WILLIAM GOLDEN, GEORGE TSCHERNY
1989 PAUL DAVIS, BEA FEITLER
1990 ALVIN EISENMAN, FRANK ZACHARY
1991 COLIN FORBES, E. McKNIGHT KAUFFER
1992 RUDOLPH DE HARAK, GEORGE NELSON, LESTER BEALL
1993 ALVIN LUSTIG, TOMOKO MIHO
1994 MURIEL COOPER, JOHN MASSEY
1995 MATTHEW CARTER, STAN RICHARDS, LADISLAV SUTNAR
1996 CIPE PINELES, GEORGE LOIS
1997 LUCIAN BERNHARD, ZUZANA LICKO AND RUDY VANDERLANS
1998 LOUIS DANZIGER, APRIL GREIMAN
1999 STEVEN HELLER, TIBOR KALMAN, KATHERINE McCOY
2000 P. SCOTT MAKELA AND LAURIE HAYCOCK MAKELA, FRED SEIBERT, MICHAEL VANDERBYL
2001 SAMUEL ANTUPIT, PAULA SCHER
2002 ROBERT BROWNJOHN, CHRISTOPHER PULLMAN

THE DESIGN LEADERSHIP AWARD
1980–1999

1980 IBM CORPORATION
1981 MASSACHUSETTS INSTITUTE OF TECHNOLOGY
1982 CONTAINER CORPORATION OF AMERICA, CUMMINS ENGINE COMPANY, INC.
1984 HERMAN MILLER, INC.
1985 WGBH EDUCATIONAL FOUNDATION
1986 ESPRIT
1987 WALKER ART CENTER
1988 THE NEW YORK TIMES
1989 APPLE AND ADOBE SYSTEMS
1990 THE NATIONAL PARK SERVICE
1991 MTV, OLIVETTI
1992 SESAME STREET, CHILDREN'S TELEVISION WORKSHOP
1993 NIKE, INC.
1998 CHAMPION INTERNATIONAL CORPORATION
1999 ALFRED A. KNOPF

robert brownjohn
aiga 2002 medalist

robert brownjohn: from bj with love

WRITTEN BY MICHAEL WORTHINGTON

For many years, Robert Brownjohn, or BJ, as he was known, has been the best-kept secret in graphic design. In the 1950s in New York and in the 1960s in London, he had a powerful influence on those who worked with him, or even briefly encountered him. His death at the age of 44 cut short his brilliant, though turbulent, career, leaving behind an afterimage of an intense personality as well as an array of glittering fragments from a body of work, only now being reassembled and fully appreciated for its importance in design history.

I first came across Brownjohn's work in 1988 when, as a student rummaging through the Central Saint Martin's college library in London, I found his contribution to issue number 10 of Herbert Spencer's publication, *Typographica*. Both the unorthodox title of his article ("Sex and Typography") and the seductive images of his work—all of which featured the abstracted female form in combination with typography—stopped me in my tracks. One particularly striking example was a poster for the art exhibition "Obsession and Fantasy,"[1] for the Robert Fraser Gallery, featuring a woman's breasts with the word "OBSESSION" written across them, her nipples taking the place of the "Os."

PG[1]24

Beneath the cunning title of Brownjohn's "Sex and Typography," there lurked an appealing wit and intellect, as well as an impish desire to shock and an understanding of graphic design's most simple and immediate methods of communication. I was immediately captivated by the freshness, impudence and energy in the work of a designer who seemed to me to be conspicuous in his absence from the design canon.

Brownjohn's work is infused with the experimental and multidisciplinary tradition of the European avant-garde. In many ways he was a generalist; his body of work and his interests encompassed motion graphics, print, photography (especially photo-essays), design education, film and the collecting of found design ephemera. His ability to engage with a wide range of disciplines came from his belief that concept was everything, and could be the foundation of a good solution in any medium. Despite being a man of contradictions—witty, enthralling and awe-inspiring at one moment, outrageous and intimidating in another—the most common word BJ's friends, peers and colleagues use to describe him is "genius." He seems to have touched the lives of everyone he met.

Brownjohn was born in Newark, New Jersey in 1925. He grew up with his mother and 3 sisters; his father, who was a bus driver, died when Brownjohn was 12. One of his early art teachers recognized his precocious talent and pointed him in the direction of the Chicago Institute of Design, where he studied architecture starting in 1944. »

The Institute's director, Laszlo Moholy-Nagy, became somewhat of a father figure to the young Brownjohn; BJ even lived for a short while with Moholy-Nagy and his wife Sibyl. Both Moholy-Nagy's design philosophy and his advocacy of formal experimentation—especially apparent in his Light Workshop for Advertising Arts— were extremely influential to Brownjohn. BJ's first published piece of design was almost certainly a graphic chart, made of bent clear plastic, included in Moholy-Nagy's *Vision in Motion* (Paul Theobald, 1947).

Although BJ never completed his architectural training, the principles of the Foundation course had a lasting influence on how he thought about time, space and light. Talking about the titles he designed for *Goldfinger* [2] in 1965, he stated: "Architecture is the greatest catalyst in design… it provides the structural sense of discipline to your composition. I like working with film because it is a very architectonic medium. Making a movie is building in space just like architecture."

PG 2 35

After graduating, Brownjohn spent a few years freelancing in architecture and advertising offices in Chicago before moving to New York City in 1951. Here, he worked for agencies including George Nelson and Betolucci Cato Associates (with his friend Robert Cato) and taught at Cooper Union and Pratt Institute. Then, in 1957, Brownjohn formed a company with Ivan Chermayeff—the son of Serge Chermayeff, Brownjohn's teacher and close friend from Chicago—and Tom Geismar.

BJ wrote to Herbert Spencer to introduce BC&G's work in 1960, when Spencer was just starting the second series of *Typographica*. "I've not been at our office regularly in the past few weeks, I've just now come into possession of your letter…. I've included stats of the inset we designed for the German publication *Der Druckspiegel*. We, and a number of other designers were asked to do something experimental. And I chose New York as a theme… the cover of this inset as well as the other lines of type being used in a currently appearing ad are much like some of Grignani's solutions. It is very refreshing to arrive at independent solutions and have another designer you respect highly arrive at similar solutions at a great distance and in a much different culture." BJ's comment concerns Franco Grignani, the Italian graphic designer whose op-art typographic experiments echo BJ's own typographic distortions, and whose work Alan Bartram had written about in the first issue of *Typographica*.

The included work shows BC&G clearly defining their formal vocabulary through playful typography. Compared to the European experimental work also showcased in *Typographica*, the work of BC&G remains essentially American: »

21

robert brownjohn
aiga 2002 medalist

OBSESSION AND FANTASY POSTER FOR A POP ART EXHIBITION
AT THE ROBERT FRASER GALLERY, LONDON, EARLY 1960s.

Brownjohn, Chermayeff & Geismar
An Exhibition of Graphic Design
The Composing Room: Gallery 303
130 West 46th St., New York City
Showing: July 15th to July 31st

ANNOUNCEMENT FOR EXHIBITION AT THE COMPOSING ROOM, JULY 1959.

PRINTED ON VELLUM AND MAILED UNFOLDED.
DESIGNED WITH IVAN CHERMAYEFF AND TOM GEISMAR.

1
FLYER FOR GRILLER QUARTET, 1958.
DESIGNED WITH IVAN CHERMAYEFF AND TOM GEISMAR.
2
CHRISTMAS CARD, CIRCA 1958.
DESIGNED WITH IVAN CHERMAYEFF AND TOM GEISMAR.

commercial in application; full of "big ideas"; aggressive, brash and immediate; a perfect expression of the New York world that was the designers' cultural environment. In the accompanying essay, Gene Federico says of BC&G: "they are well versed in this 'language' of today, and they use it with virtuosity. Moreover, there is more than a suggestion that they have already perceived some of tomorrow's 'sounds.'"

One of the most significant pieces designed by BC&G is *That New York*,[3] a booklet produced under the sponsorship of Dr. Robert L. Leslie's Composing Room and *Der Druckspiegel*. The clientless freedom gave BC&G a chance to merge language and form in a more complex fashion, pre-empting the computer and its ability to tweak, repeat, irregularly space, distort, splice and anthropomorphize type. The most apt synopsis of BJ's formal skills and the sly wit that inform the work comes from Eugene M. Ettenberg, who wrote in 1959: "The essence of Robert Brownjohn's design is the dry chuckle. Brownjohn gets his fun in working chiefly with letterforms, finding in their shapes, stripped of their symbolic meaning, a wondrous jungle of contours and textures, all things no matter how mundane come out of his 'thinkmill' of little jokes, smiles and twinkles in the eye."

PG [3] 33

The work created by BC&G in the late 1950s was always credited to all three partners and a collaborative spirit permeated the studio. Co-founder Tom Geismar recalls: "The idea was to base the office on an architectural office: a collaboration—just the three of us. BJ and I shared a room together and we sat facing each other. It was a great experience; I looked up to him. It was my first job. He was so smart and tough-minded. Ideas were always the most important thing for him; BJ's way was concepts and ideas. He was brilliant in his own way, recognizing as well as developing amazing ideas."

Despite their commercial and critical success as a team, Brownjohn left BC&G in 1960, and headed for swinging London. Here, BJ and Herbert Spencer continued to maintain an active relationship throughout the 1960s, sharing an obsession with typographic ephemera and photographing type in its natural environment, as shown in photo-essays published in *Typographica*: Brownjohn's "Street Level," and Spencer's "Fishing Figures" and "Mile-A-Minute Typography." BJ's photo-essay was awash with humor and was built around a constraint of his own making—the photographs were all taken while walking through London in one day. The resulting crop of images in "Street Level" was spontaneous and quirky, embracing the vernacular of the street, celebrating its joyous dirt and decay. BJ himself described the factors that drew him to the human and the accidental in typography: "They show what weather, wit, accident, lack of judgment, bad taste, bad spelling, necessity and good loud repetition can do »

to put a sort of music into the streets where we walk."
BJ used his own work and the work of his peers (especially
his close friends, designers Alan Fletcher and Bob Gill)
to compare the ideas existing in the vernacular world
with parallels in the sophisticated design world.
The resulting pages are rich in formal and verbal wordplay;
in characteristic fashion Brownjohn and his peers close the
gap between thinking and formmaking, the ideas-man and the
image-maker, the wordsmith and the typographer.

Brownjohn's primary legacy may well be that he was the
bridge between the European experimental tradition
epitomized by Moholy-Nagy on one hand, and American/
English "pop" culture on the other. Throughout his career
he chose not to focus on the formal attributes of the
idealized world that Modernism came to embody in the
1950s; instead, he opted for the experimental attitudes
and conceptually based solutions of the early pioneers of
European avant-garde. The lineage is clear as he talks
about the inspiration for his titles for *From Russia With
Love*:[4] "I remembered that many years ago Moholy-Nagy had   PG 4 34
proposed projecting advertisements onto clouds at night—
perhaps having London in mind as the most suitable
place." For BJ the "suitable place" ended up being
the body of a dancing woman, upon which he projected
typographic slides for the Bond titles. The projected
images distort over the surface of the dancer's flesh as
she moves beneath them. BJ forces the viewer to be
conscious of the typography's existence in the physical
world—the "real" world represented by the body—rather
than the confining "graphic" world from which it has
escaped: the sheet of paper.

Every design project that BJ worked on seemed to have been
an exercise in encouraging the unexpected. Trevor Bond,
assistant title designer, worked with BJ on both the Bond
titles he made, and tells how "BJ was always fascinated by
the way the pictures projected against your body when one
stood in front of the projector when getting up from the
seat in a small cinema. So he had the idea to use the belly
dancer from the film. It was to be a live action production,
quite a change; we hired a photographer's studio in
Marylebone and made the whole thing in three weekends.
The final title has three dancers. An exotic snake dancer
did most of the film, she handled the projected lettering
like a snake…and ate bananas all day to give her stomach
something to grip." The story of how BJ sold this idea for
the titles to Producer Albert "Cubby" Broccoli is typical of
BJ's humor and his ostentatious character. According to film
critic Tony Crawley, BJ borrowed a projector, removed his
jacket and gave an on-the-spot demonstration of what he
wanted to do.

As well as the titles for *From Russia With Love*, Brownjohn
designed those for the subsequent Bond movie, *Goldfinger.* »

This time he used a moving image, rather than a static one, projected onto the gold-painted body of Margaret Nolan. The sequence's brilliance lies in the playful relationships between the images projected and the body itself: the Aston Martin's revolving license plates cover the mouth; a golf ball rolls the length of the arm heading for the armpit; Bond himself runs across the landscape of the figure, seemingly scared of falling from the edge of the giant body.

In print BJ used the signifiers of typography and composition to create simple and powerful messages. Throughout the 1960s in London, BJ tried to apply these strategies to work that would reach a mass audience, (usually through advertising agencies, such as J. Walter Thompson and McCann Erickson) but often the idea would eclipse the opportunity for typographic experimentation. The notable exceptions were BJ's forays into motion graphics. For a Midland Bank cinema advertisement he created a purely typographic animation that uses simple shifts in scale, space and visibility. This multi-award-winning piece, *Money Talks, Money Walks*, has a clear lineage back to a small booklet produced for *Typographica* by BC&G, called *watching words move*, which uses the same strategies in a static medium, and clearly indicates that BJ was thinking in filmic terms even in his New York period. The animated typography conveys a complex and specific narrative through whimsical form and double meaning, and uses the tools of the typographer—scale, spacing, leading, kerning, hierarchy—to their full effect.

One of BJ's last pieces of graphic design was a poster for the New York peace campaign[5] made in 1970. The poster features a playing card—the ace of spades—preceded by the handwritten letters "PE" and followed by a question mark. The image is signed in the lower left: "love—Bj." This final piece of design seems to contain the characteristics present throughout BJ's body of work—directness, intelligence and wit—yet the uncertainty implied by the question mark, the image of the death card (antithetical to peace) and the intimate sign-off are an eerie premonition of BJ's own death later the same year.

PG[5] 36

As time has passed, Robert Brownjohn gradually has become a design icon of the times he lived in. His work has proven to be of the best of the post-war period, when graphic design was evolving from the ashes of commercial art, when graphic designers' role as shapers of culture beyond the notion of a service profession was gaining momentum. BJ had a talent for communicating concepts using typography as the vehicle, without the use of extraneous form. He packed powerful punches, but always delivered them in a poetic fashion, and more often than not, with a wry smile. BJ remembered Moholy-Nagy suggesting projecting images onto clouds at night, and that's just what BJ did. He took his witty and playful designs and, for a fleeting moment, broadcast them in an exuberant and fantastic manner for the world to see. □

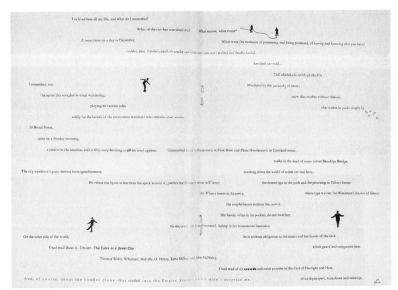

SPREADS FROM *THAT NEW YORK*, 1959.

PRODUCED WITH THE SPONSORSHIP OF DR. ROBERT L. LESLIE'S COMPOSING ROOM AND *DER DRUCKSPIEGEL*. DESIGNED WITH IVAN CHERMAYEFF AND TOM GEISMAR.

CREDIT SEQUENCE FOR *FROM RUSSIA WITH LOVE*, 1963.
COURTESY OF MGM CLIP+STILL

CREDIT SEQUENCE FOR *GOLDFINGER*, 1964.
COURTESY OF MGM CLIP+STILL

PEACE? POSTER, 1970.

christopher pullman
aiga 2002 medalist

christopher pullman : a life in design

WRITTEN BY JESSICA HELFAND

Chris Pullman is describing a finger puppet: a hand-crocheted, Guatemalan trinket he found some years ago in a pushcart at Boston's Faneuil Hall. He chooses his words carefully, his deep, raspy voice—one is reminded of the self-effacing, somewhat patrician tones of Harrison Ford—steeped in specificity. Pullman tells stories the same way he does everything: with an almost scientific intention. He aptly describes himself as a person who likes to describe things (he once drew a storyboard to explain a bandage on his head, the consequence of a surprise encounter with a speed bump while bikeriding), a skill which perhaps more than anything, characterizes his deep appreciation for—and lifelong pursuit of—clarity in communication.

At the same time, Pullman is quick to note the evocative subtleties of the handmade, the loopy idiosyncrasies of found objects. "There's something delicious about all those little things that lie around the house," he observes. He talks about quilts and teapots, fishing lures and photographs, flags and kimonos and Eskimo tusk carvings. I am suddenly reminded of the astonishing degree to which everything becomes inspirational fuel for his tireless imagination. ("He's a sponge," notes his wife of 35 years, Yale classmate and photographer Esther Pullman, "with no limit to what he can absorb or how much he can give back.") What's more, Pullman not only amasses such far-flung miscellany but also curates his treasures, circulating selected items between home and office. "Just yesterday I brought in a blue Amish child's dress covered in patches of red and white," he tells me, "and a little doll's dress made out of calico from the mid-19th century—covered with a pattern of wood screws."

I am momentarily puzzled by the idea that no-nonsense Chris Pullman has brought in a calico-clad doll to display to his staff, a 50-plus person team that designs approximately one-third of the graphics seen on public television around the country. The fact that this doesn't immediately square with my sense of Pullman's tough-as-nails demeanor soon gives way to the more profound realization that such tensions lie at the core of his infinitely paradoxical personality. And therein lies his charm: Pullman's a serious guy with a wicked penchant for hitting the funny bone. He's a principled classicist and a committed modernist, a demanding critic and a devoted friend, at once deeply opinionated yet disarmingly humble. And he is, perhaps more than anything else, supremely capable of offering the most penetrating insights with an unparalleled—and frequently monosyllabic—simplicity. »

("Goofy!" he once remarked in response to a solution I'd come up with as a graduate student, in his studio at Yale. I later realized it was possibly the greatest compliment he could have paid me.)

As vice president for design at WGBH-TV Boston since 1973, Pullman has designed books, advertisements, posters, maps, animations, newspapers, brochures, station breaks, series openers, multimedia programs, classroom guides and press materials. Pullman has also designed a host of promotional gimmicks (among them, a series of die-cut cardboard pools of blood that he "paid off the bellboy" to fling under the hotel room doors of PBS sales convention attendees as a way to introduce "Mystery!" in its premiere 1980 season). Pullman is equally comfortable with serious content. His program guide for **"Vietnam: A Television History"**[1] (1983-84) is a striking example of thoughtful readability and typographic restraint, while a *Morning Pro Musica* poster series, produced at about the same time, introduces an elegant graphic idiom for a classical music station. Pullman's non-WGBH professional work has involved stints in the office of George Nelson as well as at Universal Limited Art Editions, and a freelance practice that has tackled such diverse projects as **Social Security training manuals,**[2] MoMA greeting cards and the **1978 13-cent Quilt Stamp.**[3] He was selected for the inaugural "ID40" by *I.D.* magazine in 1993, named AIGA Boston's first fellow in 1999 and, with WGBH, received AIGA's Design Leadership Award in 1985. For nearly four decades, he has held court as one of a handful of senior critics in Yale's graduate program in Graphic Design and he continues to participate in numerous professional organizations: Pullman is a former board member of AIGA, the American Center for Design and the Design Management Institute, and currently serves as a trustee to the Corporate Design Foundation.

PG[1] 46
PG[2] 57
PG[3] 57

Pullman's on-air credits range from series openers for **"Masterpiece Theatre"**[4] to "Mystery," "Rock & Roll: An Unruly History" to "Commanding Heights: The Battle for the World Economy." He is also responsible for considerable amounts of in-house screen, print and experimental work. Besides, in the spirit of what many call his "quiet generosity," there is perhaps no single designer who has groomed more young talent. Together with WGBH design director and fellow Yale senior critic Doug Scott, Pullman has, over the years, created a kind of informal think-tank for emerging designers at WGBH, spawning such innovative teams as The Design Lab (founded in 1990 by Wendy Richmond and Paul Souza as one of the first design offices to look at the visual»

PG[4] 46

implications of the then-embryonic "new" media) and featuring a long list of accomplished alumni, many of them former Yale students.

In addition to sustaining this considerable level of professional achievement, Chris Pullman also makes things. He sews: shapes and collages in the form of bags, flags, bibs and purses. He paints: watercolors and more recently, oils. He sails: keeping his 16-foot, locally designed wooden sailboat at his summer cottage in Annisquam, Massachusetts. (In a characteristic display of Pullmanesque multitasking, longtime friend Joe Moore recalls a recent boating trip during which Pullman managed to paint and sail at the same time.) He writes: reflective essays on design pedagogy, pithy pronouncements on design practice and the 1975 tagline for "Crockett's Victory Garden"—"Weed it and Reap"—that managed at once to capture the freewheeling spirit of the network and the folksy character of the program. Ever the collaborator, Pullman is quick to note the support of then-vice president for Promotion, Sylvia Davis, who spearheaded the cross-disciplinary brainstorming that ultimately begat hundreds of these witty one-liners. Many of them— "Channel 2" in a "Chanel No. 5" bottle with the tagline, "For those unforgettable evenings," for example—are unmistakably Pullman's. (The "Two-mobile," a head-turner as it wheeled around Boston, grew out of the same collaboration.)

And he bakes: for years at Christmastime, Pullman would stay up all night before the WGBH Christmas party creating **individual, highly personalized, gingerbread cookies**[5] for his staff. After several years, he opted instead to give out the recipe. The year he did so, Pullman's co-workers reciprocated, in turn, by each baking a letter of his name. (The dozen-and-a-half letters have been lovingly preserved and currently hang in the office of longtime WGBH designer Jack Foley.) But cookies were just the beginning. Since the 1980s, Pullman has produced a **series of watercolors, one for each staff member,**[6] each a variation on a theme—one year trains, the next year teapots—and typically skewed to reflect something personal about the recipient: an initial, a favorite pastime or recent project. The small, five- by seven-inch paintings combine keen observation with kooky inspiration, merging Pullman's passion for clarity with his proclivity for fun. The results, shown together for the first time last year at the Art Institute of Boston Fellows' exhibit, are a superb mix of compositional sophistication and pictorial playfulness. And though painterly in form, this notion of variation on a theme has, in a conceptual sense, everything to do with graphic design. And everything to do with Chris Pullman. »

PG 58

PG 58

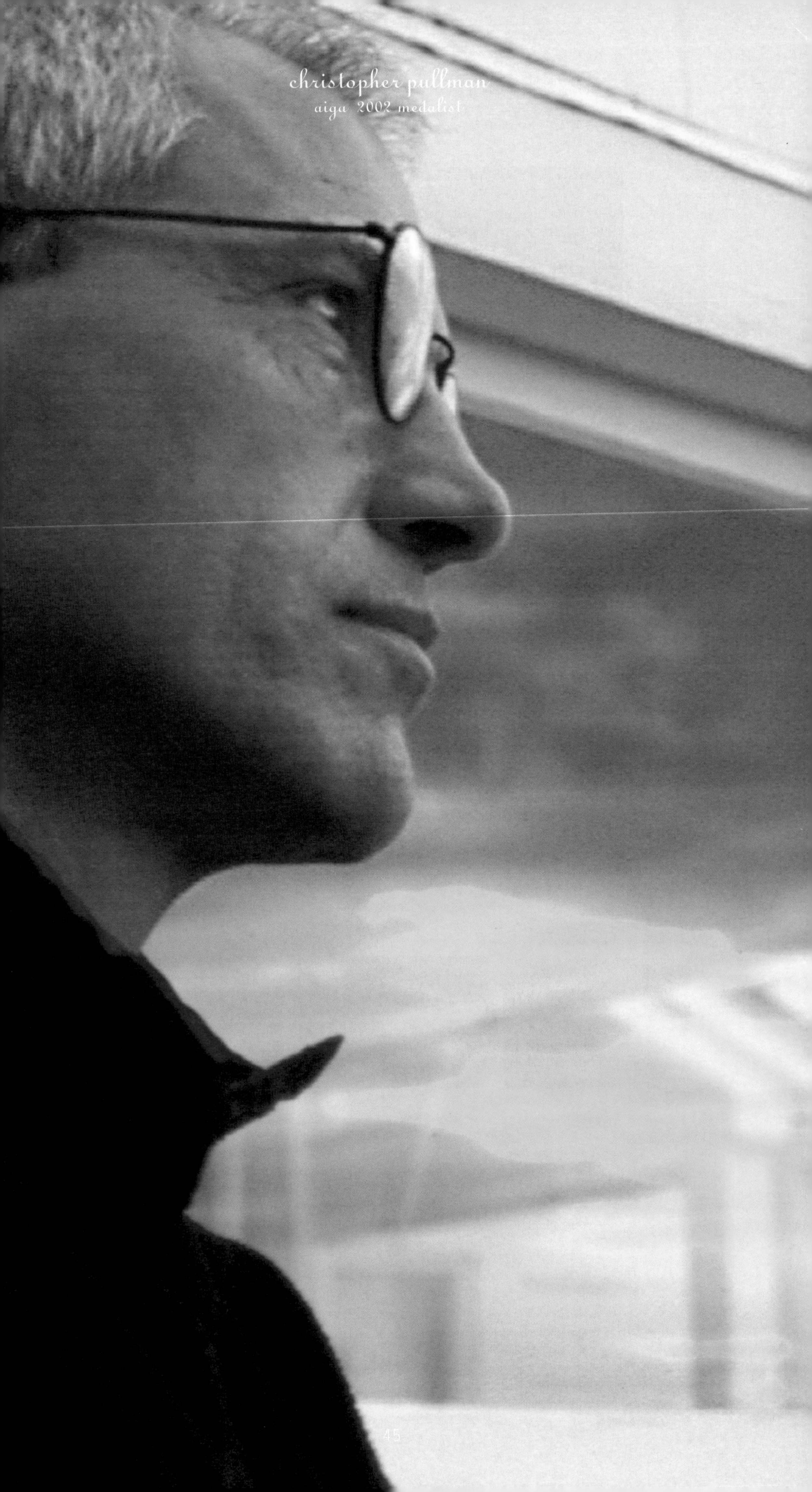
christopher pullman
aiga 2002 medalist

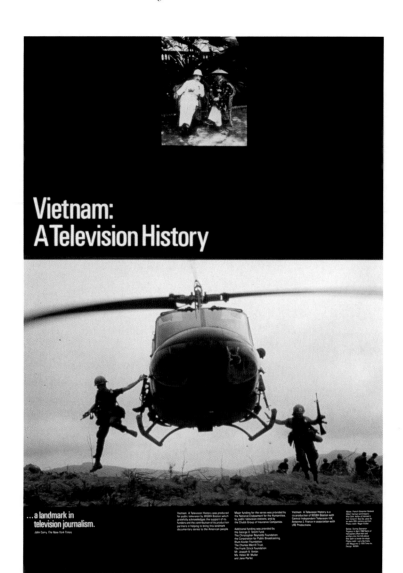

1

VIETNAM: A TELEVISION HISTORY, POSTER FOR WGBH BOSTON, 1983.

THIS PBS SERIES MARKED THE FIRST MAJOR
DOCUMENTARY CHRONICLING THE VIETNAM WAR EXPERIENCE.
PHOTOGRAPHY BY LARRY BURROWS.
DESIGNED WITH DENNIS O'REILLY.

2

"MASTERPIECE THEATRE," TITLE SEQUENCE FOR WGBH BOSTON, 1993.

A NOSTALGIC TRIP THROUGH A LIBRARY OF MEMORABILIA, SET TO A FAMILIAR THEME,
IDENTIFIES THIS LONG-RUNNING PBS SERIES OF BRITISH DRAMAS.
MOTION CONTROL CAMERA AND SPECIAL EFFECTS BY R/GA.
DESIGNED WITH ALISON KENNEDY AND KYLE COOPER.

1

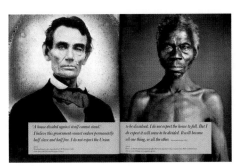 

2

1

*PRODUCED IN BOSTON, SHARED WITH THE NATION,
POSTER/TRADE AD FOR WGBH BOSTON, 1997.*

WGBH BOSTON HAS BEEN A MAJOR FORCE IN PUBLIC BROADCASTING FOR MORE THAN
50 YEARS, NOW PRODUCING MORE THAN ONE THIRD OF THE PBS PRIME-TIME PROGRAMMING
AND THE BULK OF THE WEB CONTENT ON PBS.ORG.

2

AFRICANS IN AMERICA, FUNDING PROPOSAL FOR WGBH BOSTON, 1994.

THIS PROPOSAL FOR A SERIES ON AMERICA'S MORAL DILEMMA WITH SLAVERY
USED EVOCATIVE WORD/IMAGE JUXTAPOSITIONS TO SUGGEST THE EDITORIAL INTENT
AND ATTITUDE OF THE PROGRAM WELL BEFORE ANY FOOTAGE WAS SHOT.
DESIGNED WITH ALISON KENNEDY.

1

WGBH ON-AIR SIGNATURE FOR WGBH BOSTON, 1975.

THIS 3-SECOND ANIMATED SOUND SIGNATURE HAS IDENTIFIED EVERY WGBH PROGRAM ON PBS SINCE 1975. FILM ANIMATION BY IF STUDIOS. DESIGNED WITH GENE MACKLES.

2

3-DIMENSIONAL "2"s, FOR WGBH BOSTON, 1974–1978.

AN ANTHROPOMORPHIZED CHANNEL NUMBER WAS USED FOR YEARS TO PROMOTE WGBH. THE DIGIT'S CONTINUALLY CHANGING PERSONA WAS AN APT REFERENCE TO THE ECLECTIC AND ENERGETIC CHARACTER OF THE STATION'S PROGRAMMING. BASED ON AN IDEA PROPOSED BY CHERMAYEFF & GEISMAR.

3

2-TOY, FOR WGBH BOSTON, 1977 AND 2-MOBILE, FOR WGBH BOSTON, 1975.

THE 3-DIMENSIONAL "2" THEME LED TO MANY EXPRESSIONS. THIS WOODEN PULL-TOY SOLD BRISKLY AS A FUNDRAISING PREMIUM. FABRICATION BY CONCEPT INDUSTRIES.

The fact that Pullman chooses to exercise this form-and-content relationship as a painter transposes, for a moment, those kinds of negotiations that typically take place between client and designer, on paper and on screen, in identity systems and across collateral programs. (They also fulfill a somewhat more personal need: "I can do in a painting what I either can't or choose not to do in person," Pullman reflects, "which is to be emotionally up-front with the people that I work with.") To look at this body of work is to understand that while such orchestrations may be facilitated by certain methods and materials, they succeed best when conceived by a particular kind of mind. Flexible, yet focused. Penetrating, yet playful. Deeply analytical, yet never inaccessible. This is Pullman's approach both to design and to life, and it is evident in everything he does from coordinating large-scale design programs for public television to creating small-scale watercolors for friends. In this context, trains and teapots are really not so different after all.

"In the big picture," Pullman notes, "as my role as a manager increased, I found painting to be more and more important as a 'making' opportunity." Indeed, his compositions benefit greatly from his formal design training, sometimes too much so: the wedding paintings, a series of elegantly composed collages, read more like a didactic classroom exercise than an opportunity for personal expression, whereas the looser, more illustrative examples reflect both the designer's indelible sense of comedy and his fine-tuned talent for distilling a message. Wide-ranging in representational content, the watercolors feature everything from boats to birdhouses, dogs to cameras, nests and clocks to letterforms, fish and flags. Of these, a set of insect paintings for Joe Moore and his family are a particular delight, gesturing at once to the classical proportions of 19th-century botanical engravings and to the muted color palette of contemporary artists like Dugald Stermer. But here, too, Pullman exhibits considerable stylistic range: a series of bird paintings features a white owl carved out of an inky blue field that recalls the minimalist silkscreens of Alex Katz. This same series includes silhouetted songbirds, a pair of high-heeled foot-flippers and a watery, digitized duck. As a group, these paintings are united not by form but by content, allowing the artist enormous flexibility to experiment with varying formal evocations, a panoply of visual iterations connected by a single, unifying theme.»

Tom Strong, one of Pullman's closest friends since their days as graduate students at Yale in the 1960s, calls this "vintage Pullman": "This ability to reflect a deeply principled sense of what belongs—the sense of a grid here, or a particular alignment there—and then just do something that's simply magical." Indeed, like the watercolors, Pullman's early student work already reveals a particular sensitivity with regard to combining formal elements (grids, typography) with playful ones (image, composition) to create work with a clear message that is skewed in some subtle, often humorous way. A poster for a student production of *West Side Story* shows a grainy image of a boy's high-top sneaker floating over a switchblade, while a red, hand-scrawled heart floats, like a graffiti dingbat in the negative space between image and information. For *Bolero*,[7] Pullman fashions a modern sampler that loosely approximates the vocabulary of the type specimen; a distilled visual evocation of *Bolero's* metred, hauntingly repetitive musical theme. For Verdi's *Requiem*,[8] a dramatically cropped three-quarters profile of a screaming man (it's actually Pullman) is surprinted with a red rectangle creating an unusual juxtaposition of geometry and anatomy, restrained Swiss typography sharing space with a highly gestural photograph.

PG 7 56

PG 8 56

This interest in balancing tensions lies not only at the core of Pullman's design methodology (and arguably, of his personality) but characterizes his approach to teaching as well. It's another take on theme and variation: "see you and raise you one," as Pullman calls it. Put simply, just when one of his students thinks she's nailed it, Pullman adds a complication, often a "real world" factor to make the student work that much harder. As an undergraduate at Yale in the early 1980s, I participated in one of his graduate studios in which he proposed a seemingly plausible exercise that involved creating a series of seasonal interstitial bumpers for a small public television affiliate in New Hampshire. Our first assignment began, simply enough, with a Christmas greeting. As the weeks progressed, Pullman introduced more obscure holidays (I remember Passover in particular) thereby making the immediate designation of a recognizable mark that much more difficult to achieve. As we tried to pay attention to the emerging integrity of our own work, we were quickly stymied by yet another hefty dose of reality. "Switch with the person to your left," Pullman announced one afternoon, "and continue where that person left off. Since you've inherited someone else's body of work, you want to continue to evolve the idiom. But now you're the boss," he added pointedly. "So make it better." »

Pullman-the-boss, as it turns out, is unequivocally credited with giving his designers enormous independence. (Former student and WGBH director of Interactive Design, Julia Whitney, calls him a "design champion.") At the same time, Pullman has long been known as a merciless critic. Recalls former WGBH designer and friend, Tom Sumida (Yale MFA 1976): "We were always totally terrified of him because he was Mr. Tough Guy. He was there, essentially, to tell you the truth about your work." Hired by Alvin Eisenman to teach in the graduate program at Yale shortly after completing his MFA there in 1966 (he received a BA in History from Princeton just three years earlier), Pullman was initially not much older than his students. In those early years, he was close to them—perhaps too close. Today, he chalks this up to a "flawed instinct" that being buddies with the students was a good thing. "I think that my subsequent return to teaching from my position as design director at WGBH gave me a kind of much-needed distance and credibility that I didn't exactly have before," Pullman confesses, even if, as many former students have suggested, the empathy pendulum has, at times, swung too far in the opposite direction. This fundamental edge—part skepticism, part street smarts—may explain why he is so good in the classroom, however. Pullman never stops asking questions of himself—consequently, he expects nothing less (and anticipates considerably more) from his students.

As a designer and painter, critic and mentor, thinker and maker, Chris Pullman's stamina is nothing short of remarkable. "He is unfailingly committed to things that matter," notes friend and former student Deri Noyes, offering a summary of his unique sense of appropriateness, his keen and impeccable eye. But more commendable even than this, it is Pullman's intellectual curiosity that continues to astonish, his generosity of spirit that remains so indelibly written on those who have had the good fortune to know and work with him over the years. Pullman's undergraduate thesis at Princeton, as it turns out, was on the visual manifestations of American character. Looking back, it seems to have been a rather prophetic (and indeed, poetic) blueprint for what lay ahead: a prolific life in design, anchored in thoughtfulness, in clarity, in humor and, most of all, by a profound sense of self. Chris Pullman is unquestionably a design champion. And there is nothing paradoxical about that. □

POSTERS FOR THE BOSTON CHAPTER OF AIGA, 1980s–1990s.

THESE POSTERS WERE PRODUCED TO PROMOTE AIGA BOSTON CHAPTER EVENTS
(MANY OF WHICH PULLMAN ORGANIZED). THE *VOTE* POSTER WAS PART OF A NATIONAL
CAMPAIGN TO PROMOTE PARTICIPATION IN THE PRESIDENTIAL ELECTION.

BOLERO AND *VERDI: REQUIÉM*, CONCERT POSTERS FOR YALE SYMPHONY ORCHESTRA, 1967–74.

TWO OF A SERIES OF LOW-BUDGET SILK SCREENED POSTERS
FOR YALE UNIVERSITY'S STUDENT ORCHESTRA.

christopher pullman
aiga 2002 medalist

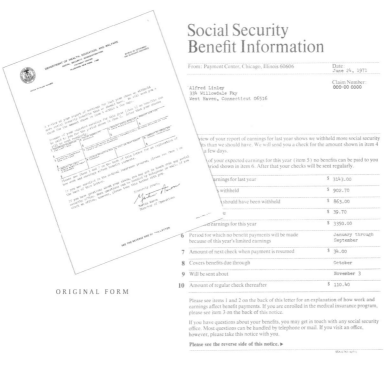

ORIGINAL FORM

REVISED FORM

1

GRAPHIC STANDARDS FOR SOCIAL SECURITY ADMINISTRATION, 1970–1971.

DESIGNED TO INCREASE USER COMPREHENSION AND REDUCE ERROR (AND SYSTEM COST),
THIS SERIES OF SIMPLIFIED, HUMANIZED FORMS AND COMPUTERIZED FORM LETTERS
ANTICIPATED LATER FORM- AND LANGUAGE-SIMPLIFICATION PROGRAMS FOR GOVERNMENT
AND INDUSTRY. DESIGNED WITH GEORGE NELSON.

2

AMERICAN FOLK ART: QUILTS, 13C STAMP FOR US POSTAL SERVICE, 1978.

THIS STAMP GREW OUT OF PULLMAN'S PERSONAL INTEREST IN AMERICAN GEOMETRIC
PIECED QUILTS. IT WAS ORIGINALLY PROPOSED AS A FULL QUILT ON A SHEET WITH EACH
STAMP A DIFFERENT VARIATION OF THE "BASKET" PATTERN.

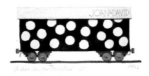

STAFF COOKIES AND PAINTINGS, 1980–PRESENT.

EACH YEAR, PULLMAN HAS MADE SOMETHING FOR EVERY MEMBER OF HIS DESIGN
DEPARTMENT AT WGBH. FIRST, THERE WERE GINGERBREAD COOKIES, THEN, STARTING IN 1983,
SMALL WATERCOLORS. EACH YEAR THERE IS A THEME (TEAPOTS, TRAINS, BIRDS), WITH A
VARIATION EXPRESSING AN ATTRIBUTE OF EACH RECIPIENT.

365

2001: It was an awful year for business, opening as it did with the dawning awareness that history's longest, wildest economic party was really over and ending with the confused anguish of September 11 and its aftermath. Creative caution characterized the state of design early in the year, as Americans collectively shrugged off the excesses of boom times. By year's end many designers were openly questioning the value—even the relevance—of their work. Questions of style and strategy (how "good" is our work?) were replaced with questions of context and meaning: in the largest sense, are we engaged in work that matters? This volume represents neither the best nor the worst show in AIGA's venerable history. What it does is capture an industry in the act of quietly asking itself bigger, harder questions than it's ever had to before.

Lana Rigsby, show chair

01

illustration

SELECTED WORKS DEMONSTRATE THE YEAR'S BEST
ILLUSTRATIONS AND ANIMATED ILLUSTRATIONS IN ALL MEDIA.

JURORS
LEANNE SHAPTON, LONDON;
DJ STOUT, PENTAGRAM DESIGN INC., AUSTIN

01

illustration

WRITTEN BY ANDREA CODRINGTON

In a year notorious for its cataclysmic news events, visual storytellers have played a vital role in public commentary. "Artists are now part of the intellectual conversation," observed DJ Stout, of illustrators who are able to place their work in editorial contexts without separate text. "There are places that allow illustrators to provide the content," said fellow juror Leanne Shapton.

The most shining example of this editorial generosity is *The New York Times Magazine*, which often features stand-alone visual commentaries like Christoph Niemann's "How to Please Elise,"[1] a witty information graphic that shows—using a diagram of a keyboard, a pair of hands and a series of directional arrows—how to play the theme song to *Jaws*, "Yankee Doodle" and Beethoven's "Für Elise." Another *Times* stand alone, "How to Stop Telemarketers,"[2] is an illustrated grid of tried-and-true methods by Ivan Brunetti sure to crush any hapless disturber of the evening peace. (Method #1 suggests guilt-inducing false-hoods; #5 advocates Manson-like insanity.)

PG 72[1]

PG 79[2]

Although the visual styles selected in AIGA's illustration competition are widely divergent—from a strangely suggestive digital portrait of the deceased pop singer Aaliyah[3] to a scritchy-scratchy blood-and-guts illustration for an article on the band Alien Ant Farm[4]—they share a largely conceptual strength. "We're looking for illustration that goes beyond having an interesting style or a good grasp of the medium," said Stout. "The big question was, 'Is there a nice idea behind it?'"

PG 80[3]

PG 81[4]

As could be expected, there were several illustrations that picked up the theme of the destruction of the World Trade Center—an event that was itself experienced graphically through an endless barrage of televised images. Praised for its quiet resonance was »

01

illustration

Christoph Niemann's illustration for a *Times* article called "2011: Ten Years From Now,"[5] which shows a PG 5 78 Japanese-woodcut-reminiscent Tsunami with two ripples reflecting the twin towers. "It seemed perfect and of the moment," noted Stout, "and this at a time when a lot of stuff that came out wasn't subtle."

Shapton called out a Robert Grossman illustration for *Rolling Stone* called "Plan to Rebuild the WTC"[6] for its biting PG 6 77 commentary: two new anthropomorphic buildings that brandish middle fingers to the world. In an unintentional echoing a *Rolling Stone* illustration for an article on Ralph Nader called "The Sign of the Times"[7] offers up another one-finger PG 7 76 salute. "Talk about instant impact," noted Shapton. "Somebody should be publishing really pissed-off artists," said Stout.

It takes a very savvy art director to give illustrators the latitude to realize their own visions. Or it just takes somebody who is as madly in love with the non-photo graphic visual medium as *McSweeney's* editor Dave Eggers is. *McSweeney's*, the shape-shifting literary journal[8] known PG 8 82 for its quirky use of type and art, was chosen for the way in which various illustrators were given short story pamphlets to create covers for. "He even lets the artist illustrate Garamond on the cover instead of using type," enthused Shapton. "It's beyond nerdcore!"

Conspicuous in its absence was Art Spiegelman's now-famous cover for the *New Yorker* following the events of September 11. Eschewing dramatic depictions of the World Trade Center's towering infernos, Spiegelman— and the *New Yorker*'s powers that be—made the bold decision to run an all-black cover on which the two towers were faintly visible because of a spot varnish overlay. "That," concluded Shapton, "is communication through the power of illustration." □

04
illustration

DESIGN FIRM: MASS™, NEW YORK

CREATIVE DIRECTORS: STEPHAN VALTER, KAI ZIMMERMANN
DESIGNER: STEPHAN VALTER
ILLUSTRATORS: STEPHAN VALTER, KAI ZIMMERMANN
ANIMATORS: STEPHAN VALTER, KAI ZIMMERMANN
SOUND DESIGN: HUMAN
TYPEFACE: MASS ABC™
CLIENT: GRAND MARNIER

NEW YORK FILM FESTIVAL/GRAND MARNIER TRAILER

We took the sentence "The Film Society of Lincoln Center Presents the 39th New York Film Festival, Proudly Sponsored by Grand Marnier," broke it into sections, animated the words and interspersed them with mini scenes in different illustration and animation styles. In the resulting mini movie, the main scene, New York, is illustrated as a crowd of abstract humanoids running up and down a surreal street, each one in their own style and movement. The Flash-animated trailer, which also doubled as a commercial, naturally integrates the sponsor. Because we were the designers as well as the filmmakers, the design was not compromised.

DESIGN FIRM: *THE NEW YORK TIMES MAGAZINE*, NEW YORK

ART DIRECTOR: JANET FROELICH
DESIGNERS: ANDREA FELLA, NANCY HARRIS
ILLUSTRATOR: CHRISTOPH NIEMANN
CLIENT: *THE NEW YORK TIMES MAGAZINE*

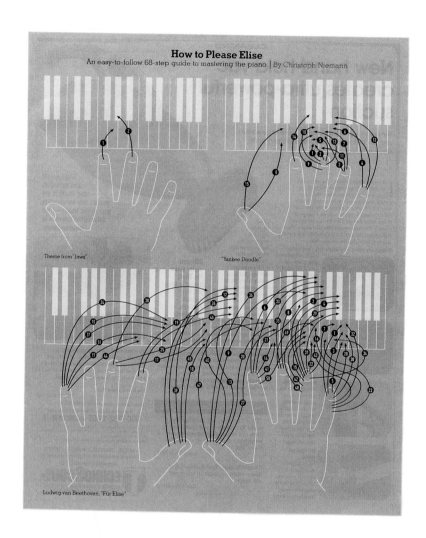

"HOW TO PLEASE ELISE" ILLUSTRATION

For this special issue of *The New York Times Magazine*, entitled "How to: A User's Manual for Modern Living," we asked Christoph Niemann to propose an illustrated story in which he would instruct the reader to accomplish something complex. Niemann, who had been learning to play the piano, proposed visualizing the playing of "Für Elise," which is the classic piece in every piano student's repertoire. Niemann diagrammed it like dance notation, and the difficulty of playing this complex composition became instantly apparent.

JURORS' COMMENTS

"The *Times* hires illustrators as contributors. It seems that these were stand-alones in terms of space and authorship." "The *Times* lets the illustrator provide the content. It's communication through pure illustration as opposed to the pure editorial model."

DESIGN FIRM: *THE NEW YORK TIMES MAGAZINE*, NEW YORK

ART DIRECTOR: JANET FROELICH
DESIGNER: NANCY HARRIS
ILLUSTRATOR: DUGALD STERMER
WRITER: JAMES BENNET
CLIENT: *THE NEW YORK TIMES MAGAZINE*

"C.E.O. U.S.A." SPREAD

The New York Times Magazine art director, Janet Froelich, and designer Nancy Harris asked me to do a portrait of George W. Bush in the style of a 19th-century paper cut-out silhouette. In fact, that's just what I did: cut his likeness out of a piece of black paper.

JURORS' COMMENTS

"Silhouettes are part of presidential heritage. This is purely graphical, and I like it. It doesn't have a big idea, but there is something about his face."

DESIGN FIRM: *FAST COMPANY* MAGAZINE, BOSTON

DESIGN DIRECTOR: PATRICK MITCHELL
DESIGNER: KRISTIN FITZPATRICK
ILLUSTRATOR: R.O. BLECHMAN
WRITER: JOHN ELLIS
CLIENT: *FAST COMPANY* MAGAZINE

DIGITAL MATTERS JOHN ELLIS

IN MY HUMBLE OPINION So what happens next in Adland? A couple of years ago, people in the advertising community looked out across the horizon and saw the Internet bearing down on them like an ugly tornado. They were terrified. The more they read about what was coming—TiVo, permission marketing, wireless technology—the more frightened they became. The question loomed: How does advertising's push model "work" in a networked, peer-to-peer world? THE INITIAL ANSWER, to Adland's complete surprise: Better than your wildest dreams! When the tornado touched down, it didn't rattle windows and tear down walls. It showered money on every agency from California to New York. All of those new dotcom companies wanted to advertise during the Super Bowl and the Academy Awards and the Grammys and ER! And on the radio. And in all of the new magazines. The tornado turned into a money tree. BETTER YET, the whole dotcom business model was premised on something called "mindshare." It was a term that most folks in Adland had never heard before but one that they quickly adopted as a sexy new mantra. The Adlanders got very good at all the lingo—"first movers," "monetized eyeballs"— very fast. Before long, they had it down cold. Their answer to every dotcom marketing challenge was a ton of traditional advertising—

July 2001

Illustration by R.O. BLECHMAN

"IN MY HUMBLE OPINION" SPREAD

JURORS' COMMENTS

"R.O. Blechman is still relevant, still deft and works with a beautiful palette. He knows how to make content speak."

DESIGN FIRM: KBDA, LOS ANGELES

CREATIVE DIRECTOR: KIM BAER
DESIGNER: KATE RIVINUS
ILLUSTRATOR: ROBERT NEUBECKER
WRITERS: LEW GRONER, STACEY YOUNG
TYPEFACES: FILOSOFIA, FRUTIGER, REQUIEM, ROTIS, TRADE GOTHIC
PRINTER: COSTELLO BROTHERS LITHOGRAPHERS, INC.
PAPER: SUNDANCE ULTRA WHITE 70 LB. TEXT
CLIENT: THE JEWISH COMMUNITY FOUNDATION

THE JEWISH COMMUNITY FOUNDATION 2000 ANNUAL REPORT

Our goal was to produce a series of thought-provoking essays in the form of a tabloid and in the tone of something you might find in the *New Yorker* or *The New York Times Magazine*. Focused on the "changing face of philanthropy," we wanted to position our client, The Jewish Community Foundation, as an organization that reports on current trends, and that is a problem-solver responding to today's donors and their needs.

Working within a very tight production budget, we commissioned black-and-white illustrations from renowned editorial illustrator Robert Neubecker to highlight the text. Large-scaled, richly colored trend statements and key statistics put the major point of each spread prominently in front of the reader.

DESIGN FIRM: *ROLLING STONE* MAGAZINE, NEW YORK

ART DIRECTOR: FRED WOODWARD
ILLUSTRATOR: DAVID PLUNKERT
CLIENT: *ROLLING STONE* MAGAZINE

"RALPH NADER" SPREAD

JURORS' COMMENTS

"Talk about instant impact. Bam! Right on target. The timing is great.
It's a simple idea pulled off nicely and graphically."

01

illustration

DESIGN FIRM: *ROLLING STONE* MAGAZINE, NEW YORK

ART DIRECTOR: FRED WOODWARD
ILLUSTRATOR: ROBERT GROSSMAN
CLIENT: *ROLLING STONE* MAGAZINE

"PLAN TO REBUILD THE WTC" ILLUSTRATION

DESIGN FIRM: *THE NEW YORK TIMES MAGAZINE*, NEW YORK

ART DIRECTOR: JANET FROELICH
DESIGNER: NANCY HARRIS
ILLUSTRATOR: CHRISTOPH NIEMANN
CLIENT: *THE NEW YORK TIMES MAGAZINE*

2011

Ten years from now, historians will look back and see the events of Sept. 11 as mere ripples in a tidal wave of terrorism and political fragmentation.

By Niall Ferguson

TAKE THE LONG VIEW. What will New York be like on Sept. 11, 2011? It's not difficult to imagine a rather wretched future. You need only visit one of those cities — Jerusalem or Belfast — that have been fractured by terrorism and religious strife to get a glimpse. Imagine a segregated city, with a kind of Muslim ghetto in an outer borough that non-Muslims can enter only — if they dare — with a special endorsement on their ID cards. Imagine security checkpoints at every tunnel and bridge leading into Manhattan, where armed antiterrorist troops check every vehicle for traces of explosives and prohibited toxins.

Does that mean you also have to count on even worse gridlock on the Van Wyck Expressway? No, because you also need to imagine a decline in the number of cars on the road. For by 2011, the third and final oil shock will have heralded the end of the internal-combustion era.

Still, there will be some comfort to be found downtown. There, rising like a phoenix from the rubble of the World Trade Center, will be that gleaming monument to American resilience: the twin towers of the Nafta Center. Even if world trade couldn't be rebuilt after the Great Depression of 2002-03, at least the city's beloved landmark could. And the new towers will be even taller — thanks to the antiaircraft turrets on top.

IN ITS IMMEDIATE AFTERMATH, the destruction of the World Trade Center looked like one of those events — the assassination at Sarajevo, the bombing of Pearl Harbor — that set history on a new course. Some excitable commentators began talking about "World War III" almost the same day the twin towers fell. That's one possible future. Much more likely, however, is the nightmare scene sketched above. That's because this outcome could arise out of already discernible trends, all of which predated Sept. 11, 2001. Tragic and spectacular though it was, that

event was far less of a turning point than is generally believed.

We should be wary, in fact, of ever attaching too much importance to any single event. It was not Gavrilo Princip alone who started World War I. In his great novel, "The Man Without Qualities," Robert Musil dismissed the idea that history moves in a straight line like a billiard ball, changing direction only when struck. For Musil, history was more like "the passage of clouds," constantly in flux, never predictable. That quality is what makes it impossible to predict where exactly we will be 10 years from now.

Yet Musil's analogy of history and clouds illuminates something else. Though the weather is hard to forecast, the range of possible weathers is not infinitely large. It may not rain tomorrow, but we know that if it does, it will rain water, not boiling oil. It may not be quite as warm as yesterday, but we know that it will not be minus 52 degrees.

In other words, Sept. 11 was the historical equivalent of a violent and unpredictable storm. But the storm did not alter the fact that summer was slowly shading into fall. In just the same way, the attacks on New York and Washington, however shocking, did not alter the direction of several underlying historical trends. In many respects the world will not be so very different in 2011 from the world as it would have evolved under the influence of those trends, even had the attacks not happened.

THE FIRST DEEP TREND is obvious enough: the spread of terrorism — that is to say the use of violence by nonstate organizations in the pursuit of extreme political goals — to the United States. This kind of terrorism has been around for quite a while. Hijacking planes is certainly not new: since the late 1960's, when the tactic first began to be used systematically by the Palestine Liberation Organization and its sympathizers, there have been some 520 hijackings. As for the tactic of flying planes directly at populous targets, what else were the 3,913 Japanese pilots doing

76

Illustrations by Christoph Niemann

The Ferguson essay presents a vision of the world ten years hence—a world reeling from the effects of more than just one act of terrorism. It cautions attaching too much importance to a single event and suggests that the destruction of the Twin Towers is only one part of a rippling effect which began before September 11 and which would continue after. Christoph Niemann created an image of a tidal wave that contains a small reflection of the Twin Towers. The editors wrote the headline in response to his solution.

JURORS' COMMENTS

"This seemed perfect, of the moment. We were looking for illustration that goes beyond having an interesting style or a good grasp of the medium. We asked, 'Is there a nice idea behind it?'"

DESIGN FIRM: *THE NEW YORK TIMES MAGAZINE*, NEW YORK

ART DIRECTOR: JANET FROELICH
DESIGNER: NANCY HARRIS
ILLUSTRATOR: IVAN BRUNETTI
CLIENT: *THE NEW YORK TIMES MAGAZINE*

"HOW TO STOP TELEMARKETERS" ILLUSTRATION

The New York Times Magazine published a special issue entitled "How to: A User's Manual for Modern Living." We asked several comic artists to identify a modern problem that could be visually narrated or explained. Ivan Brunetti proposed the piece "How to Stop Telemarketers" as a humorous riposte to one of the great contemporary annoyances, the telemarketer's phone call. His graphically charming drawings and perfectly pitched dialogue offered a light-hearted aspect to our issue.

DESIGN FIRM: *ROLLING STONE* MAGAZINE, NEW YORK

ART DIRECTOR: FRED WOODWARD
ILLUSTRATOR: FAIYAZ JAFRI
CLIENT: *ROLLING STONE* MAGAZINE

"AALIYAH" ILLUSTRATION

JURORS' COMMENTS

"Given all the handcrafted stuff that *Rolling Stone* usually has, this moves along into what an 18-year-old is going to love. It's a great portrait." "It's very futuristic. She was a beautiful woman, and they could have done a sexy photo. Instead, they chose an almost obscene, odd-looking illustration."

DESIGN FIRM: *ROLLING STONE* MAGAZINE, NEW YORK

ART DIRECTOR: FRED WOODWARD
DESIGNER: SIUNG TIGA
ILLUSTRATOR: TED JOUFLAS
CLIENT: *ROLLING STONE* MAGAZINE

"ALIEN ANT FARM" ILLUSTRATION

JURORS' COMMENTS

"It's just a satisfying drawing. There's a lot out there that I've seen that is deliberately alternative. This seems to be genuine—juicy and insane."

01
illustration

DESIGN FIRM: *MCSWEENEY'S*, SAN FRANCISCO

ART DIRECTORS: DAVE EGGERS, ELIZABETH KAIRYS
DESIGNER: DAVE EGGERS
ILLUSTRATORS: MELINDA BECK, TIM BOWER, ELIZABETH KAIRYS, SHARON LEONG,
KATHERINE STREETER, CHRIS WARE, ERIC WHITE
TYPEFACE: GARAMOND 3
CLIENT: *MCSWEENEY'S*

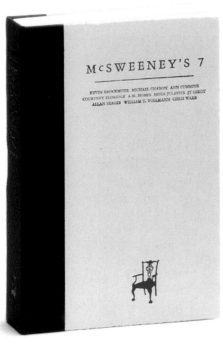

MCSWEENEY'S 7 LITERARY JOURNAL

Giving each story in this issue of *McSweeney's* its own binding and
cover is a great way to work with lots of artists at once and to make
ten books when you're supposed to be making one. The outer cover is just
raw board with the type letter-pressed into it. We wanted to have a thick
rubber band holding the booklets together, but the printer, Oddi Printing
of Reykjavik, felt they might buckle within the band, and recommended
using a hardcover shell with the books slipped inside. We love the result:
it looks like a book in mid-process, before binding—very raw. As always,
it was a true collaboration between the authors, Elizabeth Kairys
(who commissioned all the illustrations) and Oddi Printing.

JURORS' COMMENTS

"Even when he puts Garamond on the cover, he has the artists do it."

01
illustration

DESIGN FIRM: VISUAL ARTS PRESS, NEW YORK

CREATIVE DIRECTOR: SILAS H. RHODES
ART DIRECTOR: JAMES D. McKIBBEN
ILLUSTRATOR: THOMAS WOODRUFF
TYPEFACE: BERTHOLD BODONI ANTIQUA
CLIENT: SCHOOL OF VISUAL ARTS

ART IS… AND THEN… POSTER

Art is…And then… is one of three posters created for the School of
Visual Arts. I attempted to describe aspects of the art making process:
the fear and concentration of the first charge (Suddenly); the
elaborately ridiculous effort involved (Meanwhile); and the delicate
research, study and gathering of hybrid information (And Then). I did
color studies of the compositions and photographed my main character
for reference. The original paintings were larger than the reproduced
size (approximately three and a half by five feet).

JURORS' COMMENTS

"This illustration is so bizarre. There's a point to be made about
when artists have a style and a world of their own, you just have to
buy into it. This is definitely Woodruff. It's crazy, buggy, flowery.
It's really *not* cool."

85

leanne shapton

DRAWING FOR THE "AVENUE" SECTION, *NATIONAL POST*, 1999.

LEANNE SHAPTON, LONDON
LEANNE SHAPTON IS AN ILLUSTRATOR AND ART DIRECTOR FROM TORONTO, CANADA.
BEFORE ART-DIRECTING *SATURDAY NIGHT* MAGAZINE, IN ITS INCARNATION AS
A WEEKLY IN 2000, LEANNE EDITED AND ART-DIRECTED THE "AVENUE" SECTION IN CANADA'S
DAILY NEWSPAPER, *NATIONAL POST*. SHE IS ONE-HALF OF THE PUBLISHERS J&L,
WHO HAVE PUBLISHED SUCH TITLES AS *DANCING PICTURES* AND *J&L ILLUSTRATED #1*,
AND WAS COEDITOR OF *SKID ATTENTI AL CANE*, A JOURNAL OF DRAWINGS.
SHAPTON RESIDES IN LONDON, ENGLAND.

01

illustration

juror

dj stout

LANDS' END CATALOGUE REDESIGN, LANDS' END, INC., 2002.

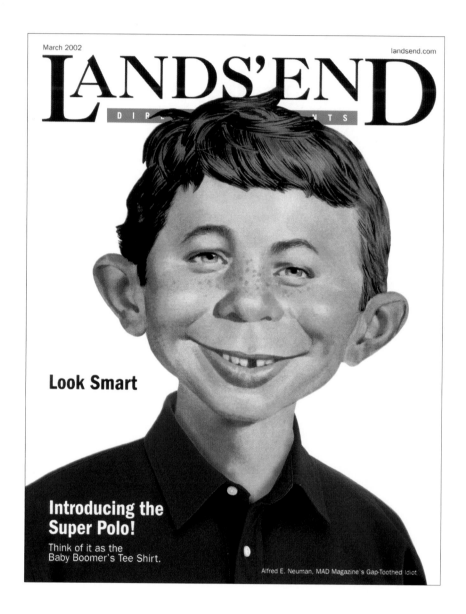

DJ STOUT, PENTAGRAM DESIGN INC., AUSTIN

DJ STOUT, A SIXTH-GENERATION TEXAN, JOINED PENTAGRAM DESIGN'S AUSTIN OFFICE
AS PRINCIPAL IN 2000. PRIOR TO THAT, HE ART-DIRECTED THE MAGAZINE *TEXAS MONTHLY* FOR
13 YEARS. DURING STOUT'S TENURE, THE MAGAZINE WAS NOMINATED FOR
10 NATIONAL MAGAZINE AWARDS AND WON 3. STOUT, WHO ONCE PLANNED TO BE AN
ILLUSTRATOR HIMSELF—BEFORE BEING STEERED TOWARD ART DIRECTION BY DALLAS
ILLUSTRATOR JACK UNRUH—HAS ALWAYS CHAMPIONED THE USE OF ILLUSTRATION.
SAYS DJ OF HIS RELATIONSHIP WITH ILLUSTRATORS: "I TRY NOT TO TELL THEM WHAT TO
DO UNLESS THEY ASK FOR MY INPUT. WHEN YOU HIRE AN ILLUSTRATOR, IT'S NOT LIKE
YOU'RE HIRING A DRAFTSMAN. YOU'RE REALLY HIRING A CONCEPTUAL ARTIST."

02

typographic design

SELECTED WORKS DEMONSTRATE BOTH EXCELLENCE AND
EXPERIMENTATION IN THE DESIGN AND USE OF TYPOGRAPHY.

JURORS
BARBARA GLAUBER, HEAVY META, NEW YORK; LUKE HAYMAN, *TRAVEL + LEISURE*, NEW YORK;
ERIK SPIEKERMANN, BERLIN, LONDON, SAN FRANCISCO

02
typographic design

WRITTEN BY ANDREA CODRINGTON

"Millenniums are always difficult," said Erik Spiekermann about what he saw as a very subdued time in typographic experimentation. "We're all still waiting for the new century to begin, and the design shows it." As a result, the dominant theme in AIGA's typographic design competition was modesty: simple ideas perfectly executed.

The most challenging—and conceptually rigorous—project in the competition was the Harbourfront Centre World Leaders Award,[1] a typographic, thin metal wall hanging that definitively breaks the statuette tradition of most awards. "What's lovely about it," noted Barbara Glauber, "is it's turning type into something material." A token of admiration to such world creative leaders as architect Frank Gehry, the emphatically two-dimensional award is comprised of recipients' names rendered calligraphically and connected by a web of delicate lines—as if the bulky trappings of the usual trophy had melted away, leaving only the lettering as artifact. The jurors also admired the mailing label used for the award: a printed rendering of the lines that connect the names—an almost Japanese woodprint abstraction that cleverly references the award itself. "It's incredible art," concluded Spiekermann. PG 99[1]

Appropriately enough, the design for a book titled *On the Sublime*[2] also emphasized a subtle conceptual approach rather than typographic bombast. Created to accompany an exhibition at the Guggenheim Berlin on the sublime in contemporary art, the catalogue is an exercise in control and pacing. "It's unconventionally beautiful," said Glauber of the type, which is a grayish-green and appears on every other page perfectly kerned and ragged in blocks that echo the subtle color-field paintings that accompany it. "It's not something that's overtly fashionable," agreed Spiekermann of the book. "It's a kind of softened Eurostyle." PG 100[2]

One of the more visually outspoken selections in this competition was the identity system for the New 42nd Street,[3] which cleverly riffs on the area's past and present by using a motif that is a hybrid between the flashing » PG 95[3]

black-and-white light bulbs of the old-style Times Square and the LED "zippers" of its current incarnation. "I like the fact that it's based on a matrix of circles but that they didn't do the typography in it," said Luke Hayman. "There's a simple device that's used in a blunt, straightforward way. It's crudely commercial and garish in a tongue-in-cheek kind of way."

"I love bravado," enthused Glauber while considering the Letraset starbursts, retina-popping colors and general baroqueness of the *Byproduct: Deviation from Design exhibition catalogue.*[4] In contrast to the controlled perfection of the majority of this year's selections, this multipart catalogue in a Ziploc bag referenced "stuff you find at really cheap stationery stores," as Spiekermann described it. Particularly appealing to the jurors were the carefully orchestrated fades in color—"as if they had been sitting out in the sun," said Hayman of the pinks and yellows that subtly shifted over the pages.

PG 4 103

While the jurors enjoyed these rare instances of exuberance, the general consensus was that the year in typographic design was less than adventuresome. Spiekermann, however, was emphatic that change was on the horizon. "Something's going to happen politically and economically," he said. "We were at the end of an age, even before September 11." One possible explanation, he maintained, is that designers are simply frozen by the "anything-goes" nature of design today. Historical graphic styles and typefaces coexist cheek-to-jowl with contemporary subversive experiments. Without stricture or structure, design becomes tame. Another reason might be that there have been no major software breakthroughs since Flash, which engendered a new typographic direction.

Whatever the reason may be, the jurors recognized that time's pendulum—and the public's fickle taste—swings on. "I'd like to see design be a little further out on the edge," agreed Glauber. "These are all forward dives with one-and-a-half twists. I guess I'd like to see the degree of difficulty go up in the future." □

DESIGN FIRM: PENTAGRAM DESIGN INC., NEW YORK

ART DIRECTOR: PAULA SCHER
DESIGNERS: SEAN CARMODY, PAULA SCHER
TYPEFACES: CUSTOMIZED, TRADE GOTHIC
CLIENT: THE NEW 42ND STREET

THE NEW 42ND STREET IDENTITY SYSTEM

This identity was created for a non-profit group dedicated to the restoration and reuse of historic theaters and playhouses on New York's West 42nd Street. The design conveys the color and intensity of Times Square, its marquees and "spectaculars."

JURORS' COMMENTS

"I like the fact that it's a matrix of circles, but they didn't do the typography out of it. It's very carefully planned out in terms of overprinting and use of colors." "It's not too pretty. There's a simple device that's used in a blunt, straightforward way. It's restrained but strong. Not too cute or pretty. The palette is somehow surprising. It's crudely commercial in a tongue-in-cheek way. Garish."

02
typographic design

DESIGN FIRM: DOYLE PARTNERS, NEW YORK

DESIGNER: STEPHEN DOYLE
PHOTOGRAPHER: STEPHEN DOYLE
TYPEFACE: BUREAU GROTESQUE
CLIENT: *THE NEW YORK TIMES*

"TRUTH" PHOTO ILLUSTRATION

"Truth" illustrates an op-ed piece in *The New York Times* by Stanley Fish that attempts to understand terrorism and relativism. Entitled "Condemnation without Absolutes," it was about looking at truth from different points of view.

JURORS' COMMENTS

"It's an obvious metaphor that's almost redundant. It's unusual to use a photographic image for an op-ed piece rather than an arts-related illustration." "This could have been done in illustration. The fact that it's truth photographed adds another layer, makes it surreal." "It's translated elegantly and simply. It's effective."

02

typographic design

DESIGN FIRM: IA COLLABORATIVE, CHICAGO

CREATIVE DIRECTOR: DAN KRAEMER
DESIGNERS: JASON EPLAWY, DAN KRAEMER
WRITER: NICOLE WILSON
TYPEFACE: BULMER MT
CLIENTS: SCOTT AND NICOLE WILSON

"SAVE THE DATE" WEDDING INVITATION

Scott and Nicole Wilson asked us to design an announcement for their wedding. We designed the invitation to display all pre- and post-wedding locations on one map. The invitation was produced using one-color letterpress on Bible paper, which z-folded into an elegant square envelope. Because the groom is a contemporary product designer, we focused heavily on both form and function to create a classic yet contemporary invitation.

JURORS' COMMENTS

"What a great map—letter-pressed and folded into a square. It doesn't use any of the trappings of romantic correspondence. There's nice detailing that changes enough, and it delivers Midwestern tough information. A nicely spiced sausage!"

DESIGN FIRM: MICAH LEXIER AND LISA NAFTOLIN, NEW YORK

DESIGNERS: MICAH LEXIER, LISA NAFTOLIN
TYPEFACE: HANDWRITTEN
CLIENT: HARBOURFRONT CENTRE

"HARBOURFRONT CENTRE 2001 WORLD LEADERS PRIZE" AWARD

The assignment was to create a unique object for the "Harbourfront Centre 2001 World Leaders Prize" that would be presented to 14 of the world's creative visionaries—including Issey Miyake, Pina Bausch and Frank Gehry. We used a metal etching process to create a paper-thin lace work of the recipients' names joined by a web of tiny lines. The award was sewn with red thread to a clear acrylic sheet for the presentation and packaged in a custom-made cardboard case for travel.

JURORS' COMMENTS

"It's turning type into something material, and taking textured, hand-rendered letterforms and making them machine-like. It's counter to a traditional engraving." "It's not overly designed or tricky. It has a purity and delicacy to it." "It's a really intricate piece of totally relaxed-looking calligraphy. It's spontaneous. It's incredible art. Crude handwriting meets high-tech, and it's still modest."

02
typographic design

DESIGN FIRM: STUDIO BLUE, CHICAGO

CREATIVE DIRECTORS: KATHY FREDRICKSON, CHERYL TOWLER WEESE
DESIGNERS: KAYO TAKASUGI, SUE WALSH, CHERYL TOWLER WEESE
AUTHORS: TRACEY BASHKOFF, THOMAS McEVILLEY, FRANCES RICHARD, ROBERT ROSENBLUM
TYPEFACE: MONOLINE
CLIENT: GUGGENHEIM MUSEUM

ON THE SUBLIME: MARK ROTHKO, YVES KLEIN, JAMES TURRELL BOOK

On the Sublime accompanied a small exhibition of minimalist works by Mark Rothko, Yves Klein and James Turrell. The exhibit included color-field paintings and light installations that are quietly captivating, and we tried to evoke the same spirit in this simple book. The cover is delicate and evanescent; pages are thick and sober; transparent tints separate chapters; and the typography is (we hope) both retiring and monumental.

JURORS' COMMENTS

"It is sublime. It's very minimal. There's just such gorgeous, elegant type. It's unconventional and lovely, and I really appreciate that it's not black type." "It's 1960s-evocative with a subtle 1980s book design. It's not using something that's overtly fashionable. It's very modest." "Somebody looked at that rag. They worked very hard on the details. It's exquisite."

DESIGN FIRM: AVI HALTOVSKY, GIVAT-SHMUEL, ISRAEL

DESIGNER: AVI HALTOVSKY

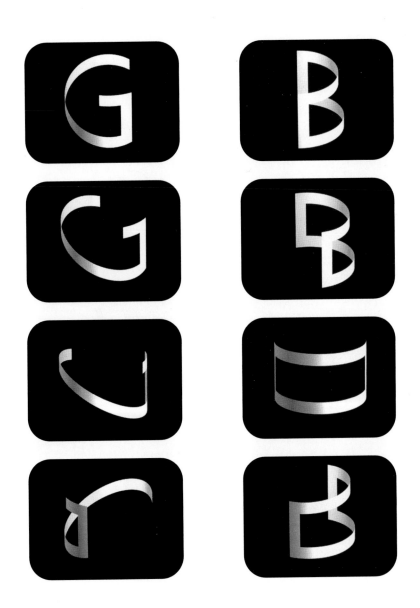

PAPERCUT, A 3D FONT

Papercut is a modern font designed specifically for use in three-dimensional environments. Instead of taking an existing font and giving it three-dimensional characteristics, Papercut is carved out of a physical shape. The resulting letterforms are all recognizable when viewed from a particular angle. Each letter's rotation is an important feature of this font, although the designer who uses it has the freedom to use any rotation they want.

JURORS' COMMENTS

"It's an unusual premise, and it's surprising. It comes out with some amazing results. It's an end to itself—there's no application to it. It's intriguing and worthwhile. Every character has a critical shape. Very interesting." "It's really lovely to see it happen in front of your eyes."

02

typographic design

DESIGN FIRM: PENTAGRAM DESIGN INC., SAN FRANCISCO

CREATIVE DIRECTOR: KIT HINRICHS
DESIGNERS: BRIAN COX, BRIAN JACOBS, DOUGLAS McDONALD, HOLGER STRUPPEK
ANIMATORS: BRIAN COX, BRIAN JACOBS, DOUGLAS McDONALD, MATT ROGERS, HOLGER STRUPPEK
WRITER: DELPHINE HIRASUNA
TYPEFACE: NEWS GOTHIC
CLIENT: POTLATCH PAPER

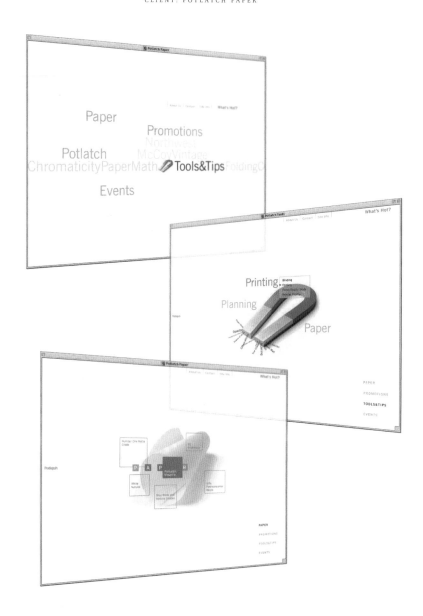

POTLATCH PAPER WEBSITE

The Potlatch Paper website, orientated toward the sensibilities of those who work in or around the graphic design industry, makes use graphically of two of the industry's core tools: type and paper. These elements are used in an innovative, elegant and sometimes whimsical manner as a central part of the site and the site navigation.

JURORS' COMMENTS

"It's liberated type. The lack of gimmicks in the interface is refreshing. It's effortless, like leafing through a book. It's also useful, not in-your-face." "There are some really charming ways of animating typography—like when it becomes magnetic-seeming, sticking to the type. It's a lovely and sweet idea." "There's a very light touch to it."

DESIGN FIRM: EFRAT RAFAELI DESIGN, SAN FRANCISCO

DESIGNER: EFRAT RAFAELI
WRITER: STEPHANIE SYJUCO
TYPEFACE: UNIVERS
CLIENT: SOUTHERN EXPOSURE

BYPRODUCT: DEVIATION FROM DESIGN EXHIBITION CATALOGUE

A "coupon-style" 11-card catalogue—printed in 2-color and inserted into a Ziploc bag—was produced on a shoe-string budget to accompany "Byproduct: Deviation from Design." The exhibition featured nine commercial artists and posed questions about the utility, need, aesthetics and impetus of the design process. The catalogue, which looks at the gimmickry of design and marketing and its associated pop iconography, was sold for $6.99.

JURORS' COMMENTS

"It's so charming and executed really well. It's about theme and variation. It uses really choice type that seems pared down from something baroque." "I love the subtle fades that look like they've been sitting out in the sun." "If this were from Europe, it would come out of East Germany. Everything is considered. It combines Letraset starbursts with desktop publishing themes."

02
typographic design
juror

barbara glauber

1
CHAIN REACTION: RUBE GOLDBERG & CONTEMPORARY ART, TANG MUSEUM, 2002.

2
*THE SMOKING GUN: A DOSSIER OF SECRET, SURPRISING, & SALACIOUS DOCUMENTS
FROM THE FILES OF THESMOKINGGUN.COM*, THE SMOKING GUN, 2001.

3
DETAIL, *PARADISE NOW: PICTURING THE GENETIC REVOLUTION*, TANG MUSEUM, 2001.

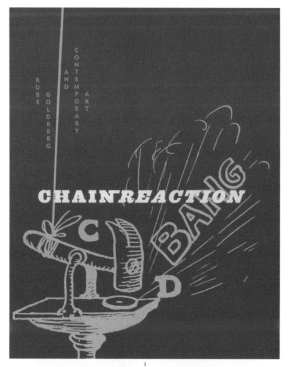

1

2   3

BARBARA GLAUBER, HEAVY META, NEW YORK
BARBARA GLAUBER IS THE PRINCIPAL OF HEAVY META, A GRAPHIC DESIGN STUDIO
THAT FOCUSES ON THE DESIGN OF PUBLICATIONS, EXHIBITION AND
INFORMATION GRAPHICS, IDENTITIES AND OTHER PROJECTS FOR CLIENTS IN THE ARTS
AND ENTERTAINMENT INDUSTRIES.
SHE CURATED THE 1993 EXHIBITION "LIFT AND SEPARATE: GRAPHIC DESIGN AND
THE QUOTE UNQUOTE VERNACULAR" AT THE COOPER UNION, NEW YORK,
AND EDITED THE ACCOMPANYING PUBLICATION. SHE SERVED AS THE CHAIR FOR
THE 18TH ANNUAL AMERICAN CENTER FOR DESIGN "100 SHOW" AND FROM 1999-2001
WAS ON THE BOARD OF AIGA NEW YORK. SHE TEACHES AT YALE UNIVERSITY.

02
typographic design
juror

luke hayman

THE FOLIO: SHOW PROMOTIONAL MATERIAL, *FOLIO:* MAGAZINE, 2001.

LUKE HAYMAN, *TRAVEL + LEISURE*, NEW YORK

LUKE HAYMAN IS THE CREATIVE DIRECTOR OF *TRAVEL + LEISURE* MAGAZINE. PREVIOUS POSITIONS
HAVE INCLUDED CREATIVE DIRECTOR OF MEDIA CENTRAL AND BRILL MEDIA HOLDINGS,
PARTNER AND ASSOCIATE CREATIVE DIRECTOR IN THE BRAND INTEGRATION GROUP IN THE
NEW YORK OFFICE OF OGILVY & MATHER AND DESIGN DIRECTOR FOR *I.D.* MAGAZINE.
A GRADUATE OF CENTRAL SAINT MARTIN'S SCHOOL OF ART IN LONDON, HAYMAN HAS JUDGED
COMPETITIONS FOR THE SOCIETY OF PUBLICATION DESIGNERS. HIS OWN WORK HAS BEEN
RECOGNIZED AND AWARDED BY SUCH ORGANIZATIONS AS AIGA, ASME, THE SOCIETY
OF PUBLICATION DESIGNERS, *FOLIO:* MAGAZINE AND THE ART DIRECTORS CLUB, WHICH FEATURED
HIS WORK IN ITS "YOUNG GUNS II" EXHIBITION.

02
typographic design
juror

erik spiekermann

FF META PROMOTIONAL BROCHURE, FF META, 1991.

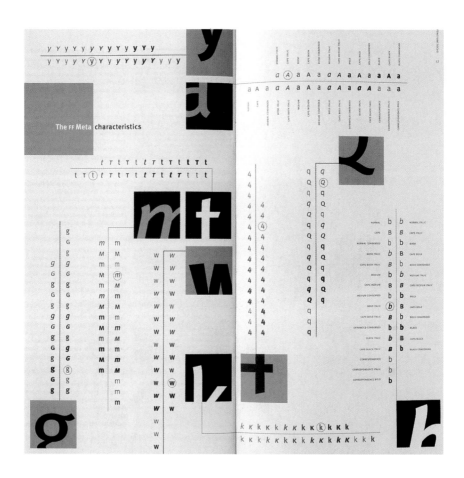

ERIK SPIEKERMANN, BERLIN, LONDON, SAN FRANCISCO
ERIK SPIEKERMANN'S TYPEFACE DESIGNS INCLUDE FF META, ITC OFFICINA, FF INFO,
LOTYPE AND BERLINER GROTESK. HE IS THE AUTHOR OF BOOKS AND ARTICLES ON TYPE AND
TYPOGRAPHY. HIS BOOK STOP STEALING SHEEP (ADOBE PRESS, 1993) HAS JUST APPEARED
IN A SECOND EDITION. IN 1979, HE FOUNDED METADESIGN, GERMANY'S LARGEST DESIGN FIRM,
WITH OFFICES IN BERLIN, LONDON AND SAN FRANCISCO. IN 1988, HE STARTED FONTSHOP,
A COMPANY FOR PRODUCTION AND DISTRIBUTION OF ELECTRONIC FONTS.
IN 2000, SPIEKERMAN WITHDREW FROM THE MANAGEMENT OF METADESIGN BERLIN.
HE RECENTLY DESIGNED A NEW CORPORATE TYPEFACE FOR NOKIA AND IS CURRENTLY DESIGNER
A FAMILY OF FACES FOR DEUTSCHE BAHN, GERMANY'S STATE RAILWAYS.

03

editorial design

SELECTED WORKS EXHIBIT EXCELLENCE IN THE DESIGN OF
PERIODICAL PUBLICATIONS AND THEIR ONLINE COUNTERPARTS.

JURORS
LUKE HAYMAN, *TRAVEL + LEISURE*, NEW YORK; LISA NAFTOLIN, NEW YORK;
DJ STOUT, PENTAGRAM DESIGN INC., AUSTIN

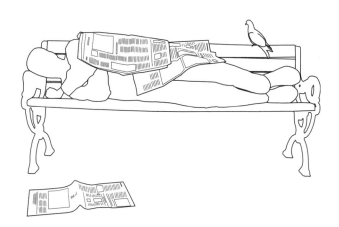

03
editorial design
WRITTEN BY ANDREA CODRINGTON

The inherently combative relationship between art directors and editors was well hidden in this year's selections for AIGA's editorial design competition, which featured magazine covers, articles and entire issues that seamlessly blended form and content. Once again, *The New York Times Magazine* garnered the most kudos for several projects: the post-September 11 "Remains of the Day" cover[1] that showed the then-conceptual towers of light sculpture; a blood-soaked bandage that formed a Red Cross;[2] and special issues on "Women Looking at Women"[3] and "The Year in Ideas."[4]

PG 115 [1]
PG 124 [2]
PG 119 [3]
PG 125 [4]

"Teams at *The New York Times Magazine* are working together in a really intelligent way," noted juror DJ Stout. "The images seem to be conceived before or in conjunction with the story rather than as an after-thought"—a stark contrast to so many publications in which the art department plays a wholly subordinate role.

With this year's horrifying events, it became very clear that imagery and design can, at their best, tell a unique and complementary story—maybe even a more visceral one. The jurors spent considerable time poring over the special issue of *Time*[5] that came out an astonishing two days after the World Trade Center disaster. "This was really well designed and edited at a time when people were starving for this information," commended Lisa Naftolin. "They put together a really great historical document in magazine form." Details that might seem subtle in a more flamboyantly designed magazine—like running full-bleed multi page images rather than containing them within borders, as *Time* usually does—were clear indications that extreme situations call for different criteria. Even *Time's* hallmark red border on the cover, the jurors noted, was changed to black to commemorate the event.

PG 128 [5]

Not every selection in this year's competition had the somber tone of world events, however. *Big* magazine's special "Iceland" issue[6] was remarkable for the silence it evoked among the jurors, who were too busy devouring its cheeky editorial tone and deadpan design to summon much commentary. (Particularly popular was one comparative photo essay of flabby Icelandic bellies.) "There's very little going on when it comes to typography," »

PG 122 [6]

said juror Luke Hayman, "but it still has an edge to it. There's personality there—such minimal means, but it's not at all boring."

In a similar vein was *BEople*, a magazine that focuses on Belgium[7] and its contemporary culture using, in Stout's opinion, "real content, not just photographic masturbation." The jurors particularly enjoyed the magazine's visual sense of humor, which was evident in such flourishes as having the masthead—a circle with the title "BEople," short for "Belgian people"—obscuring the face of a model, who is assumedly a Belgian person; or an article about a town famous for its castle accompanied by a photo that shows just the top of the building and the rest only an expanse of grass. "It's not so much minimal as it is a clever visual economy," said Naftolin.

7
PG 116

An artful pairing of editorial content and art was also found, somewhat surprisingly, in an in-house promotional magazine called *Red*,[8] which is published for, and by, the ad firm Ogilvy & Mather. An outsized publication that can be folded for distribution, *Red* impressed the jurors by the expertly written text and carefully considered design of its contents, which mostly concerns case studies of recent Ogilvy projects. "As opposed to a lot of large-scale publications, this one actually takes advantage of its scale," noted Naftolin. "Normally nobody embraces these in-house things as real projects because they're too busy making advertising," added Stout. "But this really seems like somebody cared about it. It gives nice insight into the thought process behind their various campaigns."

8
PG 120

The jurors were disappointed to note that two categories of editorial design were completely missing: fashion magazines and newspapers. "I feel guilty when I pick up *W* because it's so beautiful," confessed Hayman. "And *Jane* pops. It's got such an attitude." The two magazines conspicuous in their absence, given their stunning success in an otherwise abysmal economic atmosphere, were Oprah's *O* and Conde Nast's *Lucky*—representing opposite, albeit similar, posts on the consumer magazine horizon. And if mainstream spirituality and obsessive shopping are the rule of the day, then it looks like there's increasingly less room for an already shrinking design press. □

03

editorial design

DESIGN FIRM: *THE NEW YORK TIMES MAGAZINE*, NEW YORK

ART DIRECTOR: JANET FROELICH
DESIGNERS: JOLENE CUYLER, JANET FROELICH
ARTISTS: JULIAN LAVERDIERE, PAUL MYODA
PHOTOGRAPHER: FRED R. CONRAD
PICTURE EDITOR: KATHY RYAN
EDITOR: ADAM MOSS
TYPEFACES: HELVETICA LIGHT, STYMIE
CLIENT: *THE NEW YORK TIMES MAGAZINE*

"REMAINS OF THE DAY" COVER

For the cover of the September 23, 2001 issue of *The New York Times Magazine* we wanted to present a sense of moving forward. Julian LaVerdiere and Paul Myoda—artists who had spent the previous year as artists-in-residence in the Twin Towers—conceived of the two beams of light, which would emanate from the site. We imposed these towers of light upon a photograph of the skyline. The idea had such force in the New York community that it eventually became an actual (temporary) memorial.

JURORS' COMMENTS

"This cover played against the dailies. It was the only one that was vaguely hopeful." "In some ways, it's a more powerful image than *Time*'s. It captures graphically the mood of the country, as far as a photo and an idea."

DESIGN FIRM: BASE DESIGN, NEW YORK

CREATIVE DIRECTION: BASE DESIGN
DESIGN: BASE DESIGN
PHOTOGRAPHER: JAN WELTERS
EDITOR: HILDE BOUCHEZ
TYPEFACES: 65 HELVETICA MEDIUM, SABON
CLIENT: *BEOPLE* MAGAZINE

BEOPLE MAGAZINE

BEople was launched in one of the most difficult magazine markets of the last two decades. We therefore made design decisions to attempt to have it attract attention in a crowded newsstand: first, the dot on the cover, a simple idea to place emphasis on the magazine's title; second, an indeterminate grid that shifts according to the subject matter. But perhaps most importantly, we strove for an overall aesthetic that blends classicism and modernism, allowing the magazine to appear rich but uncluttered and to evolve with every new issue.

JURORS' COMMENTS

"We love that they stuck the masthead over the face of a person, and that it's a magazine called 'Belgian People.'" "I like the pacing and the use of white space."

03
editorial design

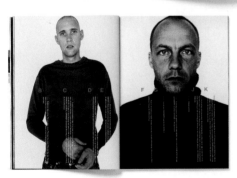

03

editorial design

DESIGN FIRM: *FAST COMPANY* MAGAZINE, BOSTON

CREATIVE DIRECTOR: PATRICK MITCHELL
DESIGNER: EMILY CRAWFORD
PHOTOGRAPHER: GEOF KERN
EDITORS: BILL TAYLOR, ALAN WEBBER
WRITER: CHARLES FISHMAN
CLIENT: *FAST COMPANY* MAGAZINE

In a land that gave birth to fairy tales and conquerors, there is a peaceful village that seems unfazed by the impatience of the modern world. For almost 70 years, the people of this village have specialized in one thing: making toys. At first, there were only two toymakers: a carpenter and his son. Now the carpenter's grandson is the chief toymaker, and he has thousands of others working for his global company. Lego has a history that most companies only dream about. Yet its efforts to grow with the times haven't worked out. Here's a story—a fable, really—of a noble company and its difficult encounters with a fickle, fast-moving world.
Why Can't Lego Click?
By Charles Fishman
Photographs by Geof Kern

"LEGO" ARTICLE

JURORS' COMMENTS

"The choice of Geof Kern is great. There's a great simplicity to using the Lego colors in pull quotes."

DESIGN FIRM: *THE NEW YORK TIMES MAGAZINE*, NEW YORK

ART DIRECTOR: JANET FROELICH
DESIGNER: JOELE CUYLER
PHOTOGRAPHERS: NAN GOLDIN, LAUREN GREENFIELD, JUSTINE KURLAND, GILLIAN LAUB, SALLY MANN, MARY ELLEN MARK
PICTURE EDITOR: KATHY RYAN
EDITOR: ADAM MOSS
TYPEFACE: STYMIE
CLIENT: *THE NEW YORK TIMES MAGAZINE*

"WOMEN LOOKING AT WOMEN" ISSUE

Every year *The New York Times Magazine* publishes an issue devoted entirely to pictures. This year the magazine sent 23 women photographers to cover a variety of women whose lives embodied the idea of power and its opposite. The complexity and contradictions of power are apparent in many of the photographs. The design is respectful of the images, presenting them in clearly defined layouts with typography in shades of black, white and gray helping to convey the photographic message of the magazine.

JURORS' COMMENTS

"The power of this is photography linked with intelligent content. Teams are working together in a really intelligent way. I feel that the images are conceived before, or in conjunction with, the story rather than as an afterthought."

03
editorial design

DESIGN FIRM: BRAND INTEGRATION GROUP, OGILVY & MATHER, NEW YORK

CREATIVE DIRECTORS: RICK BOYKO, BRIAN COLLINS
DESIGNER: DAVID ISRAEL
EDITOR: TONICE SGRIGNOLI
WRITER: TONICE SGRIGNOLI
CLIENT: OGILVY & MATHER

RED, ISSUES 1 AND 2

RED is the first and only in-house publication for the North American region of Ogilvy & Mather Worldwide, the eighth-largest communications agency in the world. *RED* was created in 2001 to showcase the best creative work in the region and to increase communication between Ogilvy's 2,100 employees in North America.

Each issue of *RED* is 12 pages; 4 pages of every issue are dedicated to case studies that highlight Ogilvy's best work—breakthrough campaigns that typically appear in a variety of media, including television, print, outdoor, interactive and direct marketing.

JURORS' COMMENTS

"As opposed to a lot of large publications, this one actually takes advantage of its scale." "It's so well written. There's a real marriage of editorial and art."

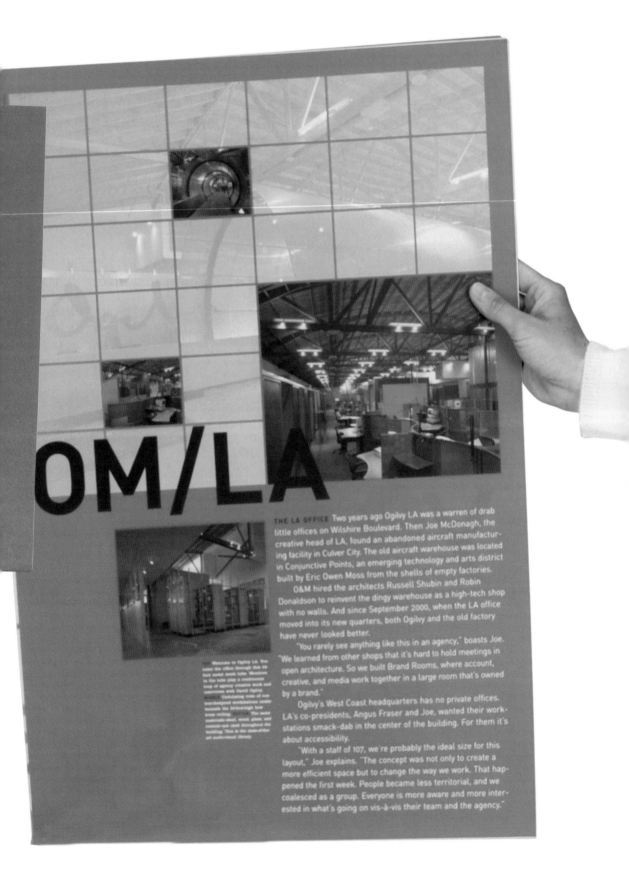

OM/LA

THE LA OFFICE Two years ago Ogilvy LA was a warren of drab little offices on Wilshire Boulevard. Then Joe McDonagh, the creative head of LA, found an abandoned aircraft manufacturing facility in Culver City. The old aircraft warehouse was located in Conjunctive Points, an emerging technology and arts district built by Eric Owen Moss from the shells of empty factories.

O&M hired the architects Russell Shubin and Robin Donaldson to reinvent the dingy warehouse as a high-tech shop with no walls. And since September 2000, when the LA office moved into its new quarters, both Ogilvy and the old factory have never looked better.

"You rarely see anything like this in an agency," boasts Joe. "We learned from other shops that it's hard to hold meetings in open architecture. So we built Brand Rooms, where account, creative, and media work together in a large room that's owned by a brand."

Ogilvy's West Coast headquarters has no private offices. LA's co-presidents, Angus Fraser and Joe, wanted their workstations smack-dab in the center of the building. For them it's about accessibility.

"With a staff of 107, we're probably the ideal size for this layout," Joe explains. "The concept was not only to create a more efficient space but to change the way we work. That happened the first week. People became less territorial, and we coalesced as a group. Everyone is more aware and more interested in what's going on vis-à-vis their team and the agency."

DESIGN FIRM: THE FOLD, NEW YORK

ART DIRECTORS: JOHN CODLING, DARREN CRAWFORTH
DESIGN: THE FOLD
EDITOR: THE SNORRI BROS.
TYPEFACES: CLASSICAL GARAMOND, ROSEWOOD
CLIENT: *BIG* MAGAZINE

BIG MAGAZINE "ICELAND" ISSUE

Based on our response to the images of Icelandic landscapes, the design of the "Iceland" issue of *Big* was kept spacious, clean and covered in snow.

JURORS' COMMENTS

"This is not just an art magazine. This actually has really interesting, quirky stuff about Iceland. There are ideas behind the photo essays." "There's very little going on when it comes to typography, but it still has an edge to it."

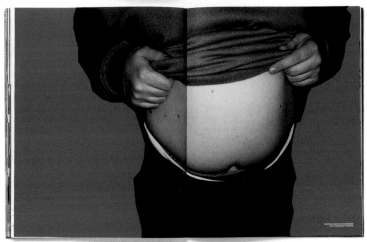

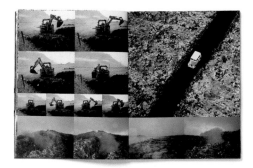

DESIGN FIRM: *THE NEW YORK TIMES MAGAZINE*, NEW YORK

ART DIRECTOR: JANET FROELICH
DESIGNER: JANET FROELICH
PHOTOGRAPHER: MIKAKO KOYAMA
PICTURE EDITOR: KATHY RYAN
EDITOR: ADAM MOSS
TYPEFACES: CHELTENHAM NYT, STYMIE
CLIENT: *THE NEW YORK TIMES MAGAZINE*

"RED CROSS" COVER

The New York Times Magazine's cover story was a portrait of the Red Cross as an agency in deep trouble. The story centered on Bernadine Healy, the Red Cross's embattled president, but our editor felt that a photograph of her would not be the most compelling cover. There are few symbols with the graphic power of the Red Cross, and from there it was pretty clear how to go—a cross, made of gauze, dipped in blood-red paint and fraying, photographed against a clean white background. Photographer Mikako Koyama's clean, modern aesthetic translated the idea beautifully.

JURORS' COMMENTS

"When I saw this cover, I couldn't help but imagine the meeting where it was conceived. It's so well conceived, designed and photographed. Everything there is in service of the message—and it's beautiful."

DESIGN FIRM: *THE NEW YORK TIMES MAGAZINE*, NEW YORK

ART DIRECTOR: JANET FROELICH
DESIGNER: JOELE CUYLER
PHOTOGRAPHERS: EIKA AOSHIMA, DAVIES AND STARR, RODNEY SMITH
ILLUSTRATORS: MOONRUNNER DESIGN, NATASHA TIBBOTT
PICTURE EDITOR: KATHY RYAN
EDITOR: ADAM MOSS
TYPEFACE: CHELTENHAM NYT
CLIENT: *THE NEW YORK TIMES MAGAZINE*

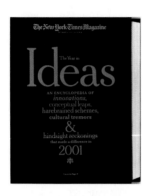

"THE YEAR IN IDEAS" ISSUE

This special issue of *The New York Times Magazine*, called "The Year in Ideas," viewed the year 2001 as the latest volume in the encyclopedia of human innovation. The issue was designed to resemble a classic dictionary. The cover was made in cloth binding and photographed as a trompe l'oeil to include the three-dimensional texture of the cloth cover and the depth of the inside pages. All the stories were presented in alphabetical order, with the dictionary tabs on the left and right. The illusion of page depth was preserved throughout to create the perception of being in an actual encyclopedia. Photography and illustration were commissioned to reflect the diagrammatic and explanatory form of 19th-century illustration.

JURORS' COMMENTS

"This is really inventive magazine design. You just can't get enough of it."

03

editorial design

DESIGN FIRM: *WIRED* MAGAZINE, SAN FRANCISCO

DESIGN DIRECTOR: SUSANA RODRIGUEZ DE TEMBLEQUE
DESIGNERS: FEDERICO GUTIERREZ, BECKY HUI, CHAD KLOEPFER
EDITOR: ADAM FISHER
WRITERS: WILLIAM GIBSON, FRANK ROSE
TYPEFACE: HELVETICA ROUNDED
CLIENT: *WIRED* MAGAZINE

"JAPAN PACKAGE" ARTICLE

Wired's Japan package consists of 4 stories—a total of 22 pages. The stories vary greatly from each other but the overarching idea is that Japan still represents the future.

We hired avant-garde Japanese photographers and illustrators to document the innovation we were describing. We researched hundreds of different books, magazines, films and advertisements to fully capture the essence of Japan's visual language.

JURORS' COMMENTS

"It's just crazy and very Japanese in its colors and detailing of icons and logos. It's ugly, but knowingly ugly. Tokyo intensity." "It's design that really looks like what it's about."

DESIGN FIRM: *WIRED* MAGAZINE, SAN FRANCISCO

DESIGNER: SUSANA RODRIGUEZ DE TEMBLEQUE
GRAPHICS: LOST IN SPACE
TYPEFACE: CHOLLA
CLIENT: *WIRED* MAGAZINE

"BEES" INTRODUCTION

This four-page introduction to *Wired* provides a visual interpretation of a key idea from the issue. The quote that was given to us describes how to fight a diffuse network of opponents like Al Qaeda. As a metaphor for the network, we chose a swarm of yellowjackets—attacking on the first spread, and harmlessly isolated on the second. We hired the English firm Lost in Space to illustrate them using three-dimensional rendering software We simultaneously attempted a photographic version using real-bees. The bees refused to pose as dramatically as the computer generated yellowjackets, and that version was quickly scrapped.

JUROR'S COMMENTS

"We're used to seeing overdone graphics in *Wired*, and suddenly there's this single, huge image. It's a four-page op-ed piece, and it looks so menacing."

03
editorial design

DESIGN FIRM: *TIME* MAGAZINE, NEW YORK

ART DIRECTOR: ARTHUR HOCHSTEIN
PHOTOGRAPHERS: LYLE OWERKO (COVER); ROBERT CLARK, TIMOTHY FADEK, ANGEL FRANCO, RUTH
FREMSON, JUSTIN KANE, TORSTEN KJELLSTRAND, STEVE LISS, JAMES NACHTWEY, SPENCER PLATT,
SUZANNE PLUNKETT, GULNARA SAMIOLAVA, DAVID SUROWIECKI, DAVE ZAJAC, HARRY ZERNIKE
PHOTO EDITOR: MARYANNE GOLON
INFORMATION GRAPHICS: ED GABEL, *TIME* GRAPHICS
EDITOR: JAMES KELLY
WRITERS: NANCY GIBBS, JAMES KELLY, LANCE MORROW, *TIME* MAGAZINE
CLIENT: *TIME* MAGAZINE

"SEPTEMBER 11" ISSUE

Produced in 36 hours, with 7 million copies sent to newsstands and
subscribers, the *Time* September 11 issue is a vivid chronicle of the
tragic day's events. It features photographs that people will return
to in years to come to immediately understand the scope and impact
of September 11.

JURORS' COMMENTS

"This was really well designed and edited at a time when people were
starving for this information. They put together a really great
historical document in magazine form." "It's amazingly well done—a very
truthful presentation."

luke hayman

1

TRAVEL + LEISURE MAGAZINE SPREAD, MAY 2002.

2

BRILL'S CONTENT QUARTERLY COVER, FALL 2002.

The Art of It. At the very core of its Baroque center, Vienna unveils an ultra-modern museum complex. With more than 20 arts institutions, it would seem to herald a cultural apotheosis. But, as DANIEL MENDELSOHN discovers, the more things change ...

1

2

LUKE HAYMAN, *TRAVEL + LEISURE*, NEW YORK
LUKE HAYMAN IS THE CREATIVE DIRECTOR OF *TRAVEL + LEISURE* MAGAZINE. UNTIL JANUARY 2002,
HE WAS THE CREATIVE DIRECTOR OF MEDIA CENTRAL AND BRILL MEDIA HOLDINGS, RESPONSIBLE
FOR A RANGE OF PUBLICATION AND CONFERENCE PROJECTS INCLUDING THE RE-DESIGN OF
BRILL'S CONTENT MAGAZINE, *FOLIO:* MAGAZINE AND KAGAN WORLD MEDIA. PRIOR TO JOINING BRILL'S,
HAYMAN WAS SENIOR PARTNER AND ASSOCIATE CREATIVE DIRECTOR IN THE BRAND INTEGRATION
GROUP IN THE NEW YORK OFFICE OF OGILVY & MATHER. HAYMAN HAS ALSO SERVED AS
DESIGN DIRECTOR FOR *I.D.* MAGAZINE, WHERE HE LED THE MAGAZINE TO A NUMBER OF ACCOLADES,
INCLUDING GOLD AWARDS FROM THE SOCIETY OF PUBLICATION DESIGNERS. PREVIOUS TO HIS
APPOINTMENT TO *I.D.*, HE WAS A SENIOR DESIGNER AT DESIGN WRITING RESEARCH.

03
editorial design
juror

lisa naftolin

1
MICAH LEXIER: BOOK SCULPTURES, OAKVILLE GALLERIES, 1993.
DESIGNED WITH MICAH LEXIER.

2
ANN HAMILTON: TROPOS, DIA CENTER FOR THE ARTS, 1995.
DESIGNED WITH HAHN SMITH DESIGN.

1

2

LISA NAFTOLIN, NEW YORK
LISA NAFTOLIN IS AN ART DIRECTOR WHOSE PRACTICE HAS BEEN DIVIDED BETWEEN CULTURAL
AND EDITORIAL PROJECTS. HER WORK HAS RECEIVED NUMEROUS DESIGN AWARDS FROM
INSTITUTIONS INCLUDING THE AMERICAN CENTER FOR DESIGN ("100 SHOW"),
THE SOCIETY OF PUBLICATION DESIGNERS AND THE ART DIRECTORS CLUB OF NEW YORK.
NAFTOLIN HAS BEEN A VISITING CRITIC IN GRAPHIC DESIGN AT YALE AND A GUEST LECTURER AT
THE UNIVERSITY OF TORONTO DEPARTMENT OF ARCHITECTURE LANDSCAPE AND DESIGN.
MOST RECENTLY SHE WAS THE ART DIRECTOR OF *ARCHITECTURE* MAGAZINE.

dj stout

THE AMERICAN QUARTER HORSE JOURNAL REDESIGN,
THE AMERICAN QUARTER HORSE ASSOCIATION, JUNE 2001.

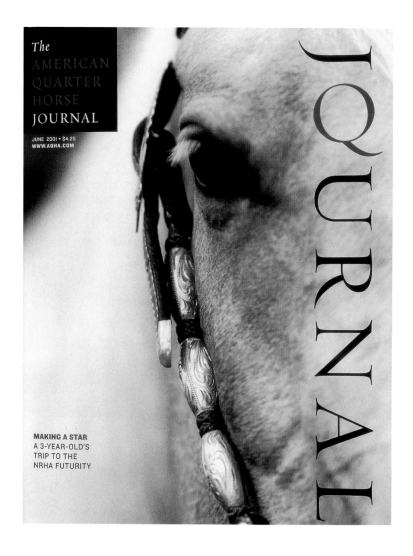

DJ STOUT, PENTAGRAM DESIGN INC., AUSTIN

DJ STOUT, A SIXTH-GENERATION TEXAN, JOINED PENTAGRAM DESIGN'S AUSTIN OFFICE
AS PRINCIPAL IN 2000. PRIOR TO THAT, HE ART-DIRECTED THE MAGAZINE
TEXAS MONTHLY FOR 13 YEARS. DURING STOUT'S TENURE, THE MAGAZINE WAS NOMINATED
FOR 10 NATIONAL MAGAZINE AWARDS AND WON 3, FOR PHOTOGRAPHY AND FOR
GENERAL EXCELLENCE IN 1990, AND AGAIN FOR GENERAL EXCELLENCE IN 1992. IN A SPECIAL
1998 ISSUE, *AMERICAN PHOTO* MAGAZINE SELECTED STOUT TO BE INCLUDED ON THEIR
LIST OF "THE 100 MOST IMPORTANT PEOPLE IN PHOTOGRAPHY."

04

corporate communications design

SELECTED WORKS DEMONSTRATE THE BEST OF
CORPORATE COMMUNICATIONS DESIGN IN ALL MEDIA.

JURORS
JOHN BIELENBERG, C2, BELFAST, MAINE; LEE GREEN, IBM, SOMERS, NEW YORK;
LANA RIGSBY, RIGSBY DESIGN, HOUSTON

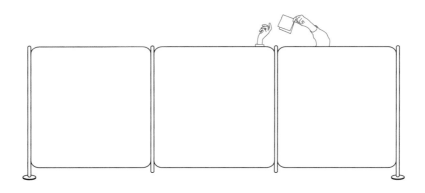

corporate communications design

Employing an economy of means to cope with a mean economy was the theme of many of the 777 entries to AIGA's corporate communications design competition this year. "Compared with last year, we're seeing smaller formats, less foil stamping and less extravagant production," noted juror Lana Rigsby. "Overall the entries seem to be very conservative. A lot of pieces are about how to respond to a small photography budget, or the need to do a 10K wrap." With glitzy production values stripped away, conceptual weaknesses become all the more obvious, she added. "There's not a lot of new design thinking going on."

The jury, which also included John Bielenberg and Lee Green, looked for work that stayed away from trends. The jurors have grown tired of annual reports in which a single sans-serif word floats over a photo, and of pages of blocky, boldfaced text bleeding to the edges of pages. "The little, bitty fat book is big," Rigsby reported, attributing the shrinking size of corporate publications to a need for economy. Bielenberg, however, saw a "coolness factor" as the inspiration for these chubby little tomes: "It goes back to *S, M, L, XL*," he said, referring to Rem Koolhaas and Bruce Mau's back-breaking oeuvre. "But to get that feeling of weightiness, a lot of things had to go small. In their ultimate expressions, these books become dysfunctional from being so fat."

Print documents that made self-conscious references to digital tools and techniques were quickly shown the door. Likewise digital projects that offered no reason to exist in that medium, for all their Flash animation tricks and musical riffs, turned the jurors' eyes into glassy pools of boredom. "People are so used to watching TV and movies, there's an expectation that we'll be entertained by seeing things move," Bielenberg said, "but so much Flash is elementary in its storytelling." "These text-heavy, interactive applications are part of an evolutionary process," added Green, comparing the growing pains of digital media to the many messy experiments with Photoshop 15 years ago.

The jurors placed a high premium on verbal content as well, tossing out skillfully rendered but poorly written communications. "If designers aren't influencing content, they're not doing their whole jobs," Rigsby said.

What was left after the dust cleared? Fourteen finalists, including two interactive works that had strong concepts bolstered, but never outstripped, by their production values. The annual reports of Cahan & Associates, »

SamataMason Inc. and VSA Partners continued to dominate the category, as they have done on the design-competition circuit for years. SamataMason's books for Swiss Army Brands[1] and Tupperware[2] revealed a fruitful partnership between designer and client that has weathered the recent bad times. VSA Partners' work for IBM[3] and Harley-Davidson[4] won kudos for distilling complicated corporate entities into elegant narratives. And Cahan & Associates' three annual reports were applauded for distinctive approaches, ranging from Silicon Valley Bank's[5] plain-speaking minimalism to Maxygen's[6] vivid illustrations to Aspect Communications'[7] use of domestic couples to tell the story of relationship-management software for workplaces. About this last, Bielenberg marveled, "This company could never approach thinking about itself the way the designer thought about it." Rigsby added: "Cahan's pieces are like really good pop music; each one has a little hook."

PG 1 145
PG 2 149
PG 3 152
PG 4 153
PG 5 144
PG 6 142
PG 7 146

Together, these three firms produced half of the finalists. The other half comprised venerable creative forces as well, such as Herman Miller's[8] in-house design department. This year's annual report for the contract furniture company delicately balanced clarity and abstraction, with black lines of text appearing and melting away through vellum pages. Williams-Sonoma[9] returned to the fore again, with an annual report designed by Eleven, Inc.—a celebration of the comforts of home, whose poignancy was unwittingly redoubled after September 11. And Tolleson Design stole the jury's hearts with a Shiseido brochure[10] that wrung distinction out of stock photography.

PG 8 148
PG 9 143
PG 10 156

Pentagram was represented by one of the category's few effective digital submissions: a website for Potlatch[11] (before it was acquired by Sappi). And a typographically inventive poster for Boston Consulting Group,[12] by Siegelgale, might have taken Best of Show had the jurors formally designated that honor. According to Rigsby, the poster possessed the highest intellectual content of all.

PG 11 154
PG 12 141

The sleeper in the crowd was an animated fundraising presentation piece for Harlem's Apollo Theatre,[13] by Broadstreet. The jury was charmed by the jazz soundtrack that accompanied the melting graphics.

PG 13 158

"What we come back to here is good, solid, classic design, where design doesn't get in the way," Green said of all the finalists. Bielenberg hammered home the importance of the works' conceptual strengths: "It's not just about images and typography and paper and color." □

DESIGN FIRM: SIEGELGALE, NEW YORK

DESIGNERS: CHRIS ALLEN, CHAUNDA TAN
WRITER: SUE MONTGOMERY
TYPEFACE: HELVETICA NEUE
PRINTER: COLAHAN SAUNDERS CORPORATION
PAPER: MOHAWK OPTIONS TRUE WHITE 65 LB. COVER
CLIENT: THE BOSTON CONSULTING GROUP

THE BOSTON CONSULTING GROUP RECRUITMENT POSTER

SiegelGale was asked to create a recruitment campaign for The Boston Consulting Group that positions the company as the employer of choice among prospective recruits, undergraduates, graduates and post-graduates. Our solution was to visualize BCG's creative approach to problem solving. The message ("Can you see it?") embedded in the background pattern invites its audience to look beyond the status quo and see possibilities others cannot.

The poster was produced in black and white so that it could be published in newsprint, student publications and posters."

JURORS' COMMENTS

"It's always a challenge to find stimulating intellectual content in corporate design. This does it—and it was produced with economy.

DESIGN FIRM: CAHAN & ASSOCIATES, SAN FRANCISCO

CREATIVE DIRECTOR: BILL CAHAN
DESIGNER: GARY WILLIAMS
PHOTOGRAPHERS: ANN GIORDANO, ESTHER HENDERSON
ILLUSTRATOR: JASON HOLLEY
WRITER: JEANNINE MEDEIROS
TYPEFACES: MINION, TRADE GOTHIC
PRINTER: COLORGRAPHICS
PAPER: VISION 60 LB. TEXT, HAMMERMILL ACCENT OPAQUE WARM WHITE 65 LB. COVER
CLIENT: MAXYGEN

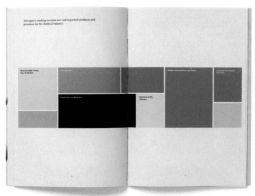

MAXYGEN 2000 ANNUAL REPORT

Maxygen, a biotechnology company, wanted its annual report to focus on Maxygen products this year. My first thought was to create a book with the look and feel of a 19th-century scientific journal. Visually, the theme of the book rested on the idea of nature as a metaphor. The size and scope of the book emphasized the credibility of Maxygen as the leader in their industry.

JURORS' COMMENTS

"Beautifully done—almost an artifact. The illustrations are wonderful. Shows some fresh thinking in the annual report business."

DESIGN FIRM: ELEVEN, SAN FRANCISCO

CREATIVE DIRECTORS: PAUL CURTIN, ROB PRICE
DESIGN AND ART DIRECTION: ROBERT KASTIGAR
PHOTOGRAPHER: WILLIAM ABRANOWICZ
WRITER: ROB PRICE
TYPEFACE: BASKERVILLE
PRINTER: GEORGE RICE AND SONS
PAPER: MEAD PRIMA DULL 80 LB. AND 100 LB. TEXT,
FRENCH CONSTRUCTION WHITEWASH 80 LB. TEXT,
FRENCH CONSTRUCTION SLATE BLUE 80 LB. TEXT,
MOHAWK SUPERFINE ULTRAWHITE EGGSHELL 100 LB. TEXT,
FRENCH FROSTONE FROSTBRITE 70 LB. TEXT AND 100 LB. COVER
CLIENT: WILLIAMS-SONOMA, INC.

WILLIAMS-SONOMA, INC. 2000 ANNUAL REPORT

The challenge was to communicate the concept of Williams-Sonoma as a true lifestyle brand in a way that was heartfelt and honest, without being boastful.

We chose a random moment in time—9:26 on a particular Sunday morning—for a glimpse at how Williams-Sonoma has influenced people's lifestyles across the country. Each of the company's six brands was highlighted by a combination of lifestyle photography and a narrative vignette—in the form of small page inserts printed on contrasting stock—about the lives of the people shown.

JURORS' COMMENTS

"Since September 11 there has been a celebration of the home, and that's what this annual report is all about." "The photography and the sensitivity to the environment are really nice."

corporate communications design

DESIGN FIRM: CAHAN & ASSOCIATES, SAN FRANCISCO

CREATIVE DIRECTOR: BILL CAHAN
DESIGNER: GARY WILLIAMS
PHOTOGRAPHER: ROBERT SCHLATTER
WRITER: BRENDAN SMITH-BENTLEY
TYPEFACE: ADOBE CASLON
PRINTER: WOODS LITHOGRAPHICS
PAPER: FRENCH CONSTRUCTION SLATE BLUE 70 LB. TEXT,
FRENCH SMART WHITE 70 LB. AND 100 LB. TEXT
CLIENT: SILICON VALLEY BANK

SILICON VALLEY BANK 2001 ANNUAL REPORT

Silicon Valley Bank's 2001 annual report was designed in response to a year that shook the confidence of investors and challenged the determination of entrepreneurs. We chose to start the Stockholder Letter on the cover because it was the most direct and compelling way to address these issues. Our goal was to keep the book simple, clean, direct and forthright, reflecting the bank's leadership style in these difficult times.

JURORS' COMMENTS
"A fine example of representing financial information on a reduced budget."

DESIGN FIRM: SAMATAMASON, DUNDEE, ILLINOIS

CREATIVE DIRECTOR: DAVE MASON
DESIGNERS: PAMELA LEE, DAVE MASON
PHOTOGRAPHERS: JAMES LABOUNTY, VICTOR JOHN PENNER
WRITER: STEVE ZOUSMER
TYPEFACE: NEWS GOTHIC
PRINTER: H. MacDONALD PRINTING
PAPER: UTOPIA TWO BW MATTE 100 LB. TEXT, HAMMERMILL VIA NEUTRALS 80 LB. TEXT,
BECKETT CONCEPT 100 LB. COVER
CLIENT: SWISS ARMY BRANDS, INC.

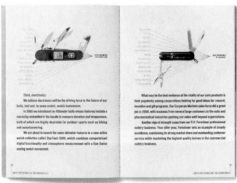

SWISS ARMY BRANDS, INC. 2000 ANNUAL REPORT

We were asked to communicate the Swiss Army Brands' position and possibilities to its stakeholders. We focused on the value of understanding the customer—who they are, what they want, how they live life—and how Swiss Army products meet their needs.

JURORS' COMMENTS

"A winner last year too, the design represents a consistent voice throughout turbulent times."

DESIGN FIRM: CAHAN & ASSOCIATES, SAN FRANCISCO

CREATIVE DIRECTOR: BILL CAHAN
DESIGNER: BOB DINETZ
PHOTOGRAPHERS: TARYN SIMON, A + C ANTHOLOGY; TONY ARRUZA, CORBIS; MARK LYON;
GRAHAM MACINDOE; JASON NOCITO; PAUL JASMIN, VISAGES
ILLUSTRATOR: BOB DINETZ
WRITER: KATHY COOPER PARKER
TYPEFACE: KAATSKILL
PRINTER: WOODS LITHOGRAPHICS
PAPER: POTLATCH MCCOY 80 LB. TEXT AND 80 LB. COVER
CLIENT: ASPECT COMMUNICATIONS

ASPECT COMMUNICATIONS 2000 ANNUAL REPORT

Aspect software allows a call center representative to recognize its
customers. It enables the user to treat each client individually by
knowing their names, purchasing customs and preferences. To convey the
power of what Aspect does in business affairs, the book shows what might
happen if Aspect could do the same for personal affairs.

JURORS' COMMENTS

"A really smart, very approachable book for a company that provides
relationship management software and services. And it makes its point
without using too many pages."

04

corporate communications design

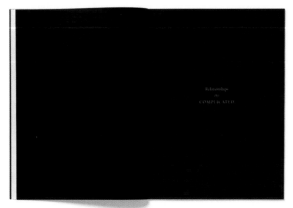

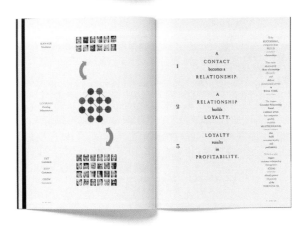

04

corporate communications design

DESIGN FIRM: HERMAN MILLER INC., ZEELAND, MICHIGAN; BBK STUDIO, GRAND RAPIDS, MICHIGAN

CREATIVE DIRECTOR: STEPHEN FRYKHOLM, HERMAN MILLER INC.
DESIGNER: YANG KIM, BBK STUDIO
ILLUSTRATORS: MICHELE CHARTIER, YANG KIM
WRITERS: BRUCE BUURSMA, CLARK MALCOLM
TYPEFACE: AVENIR
PRINTER: HENNEGAN
PAPER: BECKETT EXPRESSIONS 70 LB. TEXT, CTI GLAMA NATURAL 25 LB. TEXT AND 40 LB. COVER
CLIENT: HERMAN MILLER INC.

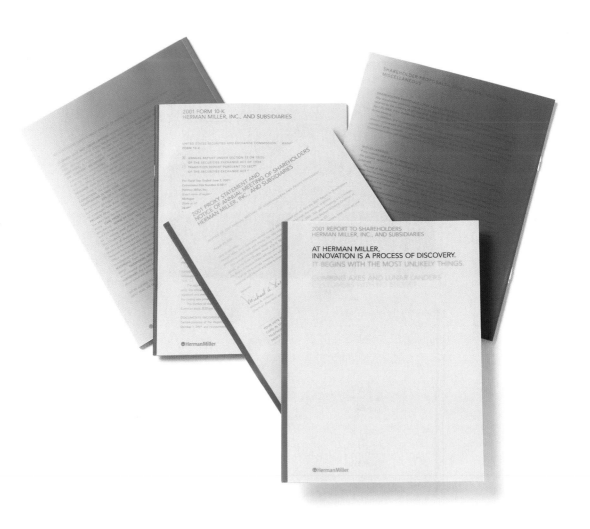

HERMAN MILLER 2001 ANNUAL REPORT

Herman Miller's main design criterion for this year's report was to express that we are an innovative company, with a history of innovation. It is a common theme among annual reports but nevertheless we strove toward this goal. We listed Herman Miller's product and business innovations, each on a single translucent sheet of paper. The result was a report that changes with every turn of a page, revealing facts about the company in an engaging way.

JURORS' COMMENTS

"The concept justifies the lavish production. We want to read it— and we can."

corporate communications design

DESIGN FIRM: SAMATAMASON, DUNDEE, ILLINOIS

CREATIVE DIRECTOR: GREG SAMATA
DESIGNER: STEVE KULL
PHOTOGRAPHER: SANDRO
WRITER: LAURENCE R. PEARSON
TYPEFACES: SWISS 722, TRADE GOTHIC
PRINTER: H. MacDONALD PRINTING
PAPER: CANSON SATIN 29 LB. TEXT, FRASER SYNERGY CITRUS GREEN SMOOTH 70 LB. TEXT,
UTOPIA ONE BW MATTE 100 LB. TEXT AND COVER
CLIENT: TUPPERWARE CORPORATION

TUPPERWARE CORPORATION 2000 ANNUAL REPORT

For the 2000 annual report, Tupperware not only wanted to showcase its products, but to focus on the fundamental strengths of the company: its brand, direct selling channels, expanding marketplaces and growing product lines. The result is a book that continues to support the Tupperware brand and its innovative products, while also placing emphasis on the consumer. In this case, we used bright colors and varnish techniques to show off images of a newer and younger audience that has evolved simultaneously with the design and style of today's Tupperware products.

JURORS' COMMENTS

"A great brand extension. Thoughtful and really well done."

DESIGN FIRM: RUTKA WEADOCK DESIGN, BALTIMORE

CREATIVE DIRECTOR: ANTHONY RUTKA
DESIGNER: ALLY WEINER
PHOTOGRAPHERS: JEFF BAKER, BOB KRIST, JERRY MILLEVOI, PETER MULLET, TONY RUTKA
WRITER: ODIE LeFEVER
TYPEFACES: FILOSOFIA, FRANKLIN GOTHIC
PRINTER: GRAPHTEC, INC.
PAPER: POTLATCH MCCOY VELVET 80 LB. TEXT, FRENCH FROSTONE TUNDRA 70 LB. TEXT,
MOHAWK OPAQUE 100 LB. COVER
CLIENT: GEORGE SCHOOL

GEORGE SCHOOL *VIEWBOOK*

George School is a coed Quaker boarding school for grades 9 to 12, in Newtown, Pennsylvania. *Viewbook*, the school's primary admission publication' is sent to prospective high school students and their parents.

We used candid images of students, activities, academics and the campus to convey both a sense of the physical environment and the tremendous energy of the George School community. We approached the images honestly and the result is a book that is appropriate to the Quaker values of the institution, compelling to its audience and budget-conscious. *Viewbook* was printed in a three-year quantity' the supplement text will be updated each year.

JURORS' COMMENTS

"Not overdone. You have to look at it a couple of times to get how great it is."

RESPECT FOR THE INDIVIDUAL Is a part of everything we do. You might have sensed that already as you flipped through the pages of this catalog and saw the photographs and quotes from students. We involved our students in writing this publication because we value their input. We try to involve students in just about everything that goes on here. We include them in our discussions about the dress code and other school regulations. We invite them to attend formal meetings in which students, faculty, administrators, and board members study issues of current concern. And we ask students to serve on major administrative committees. As you read through the following pages, you will meet some of the students who helped us prepare this catalog.

Ultimately, we want students to learn that education is a life-long process. We want them to be responsible, not just for themselves, but for others. We want them to learn that it is important to ask questions and equally important to listen to the answers. We want students to stand up for themselves and the things that they believe in. We want students to discover that their exposure to people from different backgrounds has taught them tolerance. And, most important, we want them TO VALUE INTEGRITY IN ALL THINGS.

DESIGN FIRM: VSA PARTNERS, CHICAGO

CREATIVE DIRECTORS: CURT SCHREIBER, JEFF WALKER, THOM WOLFE
DESIGNERS: MICHELLE PLATTS, ASHLEY WASEM
WRITERS: IBM, VSA
TYPEFACES: AKZIDENZ GROTESK, JANSON
PRINTER: ANDERSON LITHOGRAPH
PAPER: MOHAWK OPAQUE WHITE 60 LB. TEXT, MOHAWK OPTIONS TRUE WHITE 80 LB. TEXT AND COVER
CLIENT: IBM

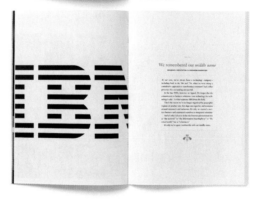

IBM 2001 ANNUAL REPORT

The year 2001 turned out to be a challenging year for the information
technology industry. With the IBM report we were charged with giving
shareholders and employees the confidence that the organization is
capable of making the tough decisions. The solution was to capture a
small selection of key decisions that IBM has made over the last nine
years that has transformed its performance, market position and operating
culture, while also delivering the direction of IBM and technology
in the coming years. The book is deliberately a simple formula for storytelling—nostalgic but future-focused, honest, strategic.

JURORS' COMMENTS

"A really good idea about how to communicate a complicated story.
Responsibly and masterfully done."

DESIGN FIRM: VSA PARTNERS, CHICAGO

DESIGNERS: JASON JONES, DAVE RITTER
PHOTOGRAPHER: CHARLIE SIMOKAITIS
WRITER: REID ARMBRUSTER
HISTORICAL CONSULTANT: HERBERT WAGNER
TYPEFACE: BEMBO
PRINTER: HENNEGAN
PAPER: FOX RIVER SUNDANCE ULTRAWHITE 80 LB. TEXT AND COVER
CLIENT: HARLEY-DAVIDSON MOTOR CO.

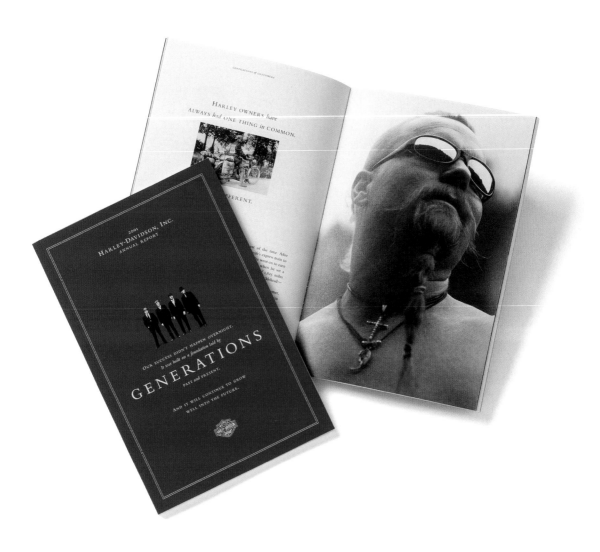

HARLEY-DAVIDSON 2001 ANNUAL REPORT

Generations is the first of three annual reports celebrating the enduring legacy of the Harley-Davidson Motor Company as it prepares for its 100th anniversary. Harley-Davidson is one of a select group of companies who can draw a line from the spirit exemplified by their founding fathers to current-day strategy, ethics and attitude. The 2001 annual report points to the people, passion and progress that have made the company everything it is today and creates the foundation for what it will become in the future.

JURORS' COMMENTS
"A very skillful, witty document."

04

corporate communications design

DESIGN FIRM: PENTAGRAM DESIGN INC., SAN FRANCISCO

CREATIVE DIRECTOR: KIT HINRICHS
DESIGNERS: BRIAN COX, BRIAN JACOBS, DOUGLAS McDONALD, HOLGER STRUPPEK
ANIMATORS: BRIAN COX, BRIAN JACOBS, DOUGLAS McDONALD, MATT ROGERS, HOLGER STRUPPEK
WRITER: DELPHINE HIRASUNA
TYPEFACE: NEWS GOTHIC
CLIENT: POTLATCH PAPER

Paper

Promotions

Potlatch

eMcCoyNorthwestVintage Tools&Tips McCoyN
ageMountieScoutMcCoyVintageMountieScou

POTLATCH PAPER WEBSITE

The Potlatch Paper website marries elegant interactivity with functionality. The site targets designers, printers, print producers and
corporations, providing them with interactive tools, resources, design
competitions, and informative and educational promotions. Orientated
toward the sensibilities of those who work in or around the graphic
design industry, the site makes use graphically of two of the industry's
core tools: type and paper. These elements are used in an innovative,
elegant and sometimes whimsical manner as a central part of the site
and the site navigation.

JURORS' COMMENTS

"A rare example of an interactive format that helps to deliver information."

04

corporate communications design

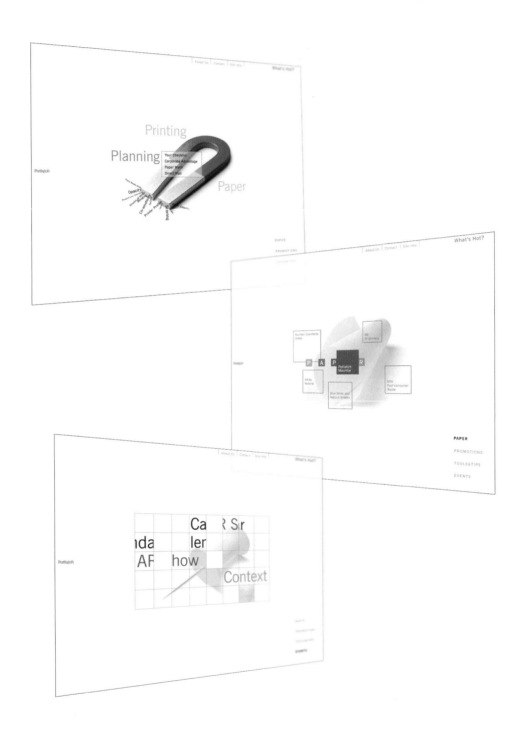

DESIGN FIRM: TOLLESON DESIGN, SAN FRANCISCO

ART DIRECTOR: STEVE TOLLESON
DESIGNERS: JOHN BARRETTO, STEVE TOLLESON
PHOTOGRAPHERS: THOMAS ARLEDGE, MORLEY BAER, CHIP FORELLI, ANTHONY GORDON,
SAL GRACEFFA, DAVID MARTINEZ, GLEN McCLURE, DAVID PETERSON, ROBERT SEBREE
STOCK: GRAPHISTOCK, IMAGEBANK, PHOTONICA
WRITER: JULIE CURTIS
TYPEFACES: BEMBO, SHISEIDO
PRINTER: WATERMARK
PAPER: LUCENCE STRATA PARCHMENT, POTLATCH KARMA 80 LB. TEXT, VELIN BFK RIVES COVER
CLIENT: SHISEIDO

SHISEIDO CONCEPT BOOK SERVICE BROCHURE

Shiseido approached Tolleson Design with the problem of designing a concept book that would serve as an invitation to experience Shiseido Studio—a store where nothing is for sale. Images of the human body and forms found in nature are juxtaposed with products to capture the spirit of this company, known for both its rich history and its sophisticated eye for design. Through words and images, guests to the Studio are faced with the question, "How do you experience beauty?" The small booklet should not only inspire answers to this question but should also provide a tactile beautiful experience in itself.

JURORS' COMMENTS

"A well-crafted object that you admire to the point of wanting to own it."

DESIGN FIRM: BROADSTREET, NEW YORK

DESIGNER: VANESSA BEAUGRAND
ANIMATOR: ERIC ACKLEY
PRODUCER: MICHELLE MASTRORIO
SOUND DESIGNER: RICH BROTMAN
CLIENT: APOLLO THEATER

APOLLO THEATER ANIMATION

To help the president of The Apollo Theater Foundation explain to the board of directors his plan to create a new performing arts center, we produced a compelling presentation featuring an opening animation chronicling the theater's rich history.

The design solution incorporated animated photos and music from the legendary entertainers who performed at the Apollo. These images, combined with architectural plans for the proposed center, were blended with a vertically ascending timeline to emphasize the venue's cultural impact over the past 70 years. To reflect the modernization of the theater, we selected a contemporary color palette and font, as well as elegant geometric shapes.

JURORS' COMMENTS

"It's all about the music. The audio is what a lot of other animated projects are missing."

john bielenberg

"POP! TECH CONFERENCE" STUFF BAG, 2001.

JOHN BIELENBERG, C2, BELFAST, MAINE

SINCE 1991, JOHN BIELENBERG HAS PRODUCED A SERIES OF PROJECTS UNDER THE PSEUDONYM
VIRTUAL TELEMETRIX, INC. THAT SATIRIZE THE PRACTICE OF GRAPHIC DESIGN AND CORPORATE
AMERICA. PROJECTS INCLUDE THE 1997 VIRTUAL TELEMETRIX ANNUAL REPORT
SEND-UP OF CORPORATE BRANDING, AND *CECI N'EST PAS UN CATALOG*, A BOOK WHICH PARODIES
DESIGNER PRODUCTS AND THE AMERICAN CONSUMER ECONOMY. SFMOMA HAS ACQUIRED
SIX OF THESE PROJECTS AND STAGED A VIRTUAL TELEMETRIX EXHIBITION AND MOCK IPO
(INITIAL PUBLIC OFFERING) THAT RAN FROM JULY TO OCTOBER 2000.
BIELENBERG RECENTLY CO-FOUNDED C2 (CREATIVE CAPITAL) A FIRM THAT SPECIALIZES
IN CORPORATE STORYTELLING. CLIENTS INCLUDE ACUMEN SCIENCES, DELOITTE CONSULTING,
INVESTMENT TECHNOLOGY GROUP, THE "POP! TECH CONFERENCE" AND VILLAGE SOUP.

lee green

THINKPAD I SERIES POSTER, IBM.

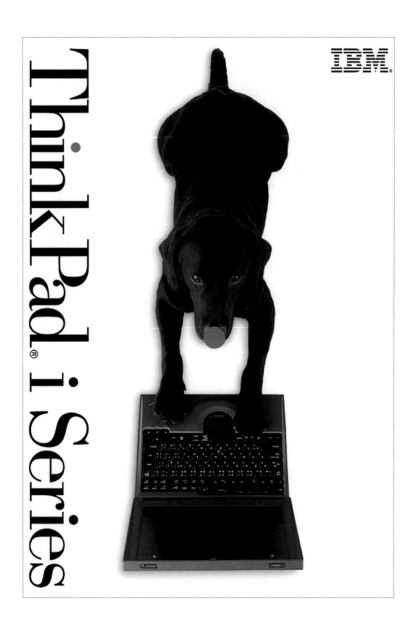

LEE GREEN, IBM, SOMERS, NEW YORK

LEE GREEN IS THE DIRECTOR OF CORPORATE IDENTITY AND DESIGN FOR IBM CORPORATION.
HE HAS RESPONSIBILITY FOR IBM'S WORLDWIDE PRODUCT DESIGN, INDUSTRIAL DESIGN,
IDENTITY PROGRAMS, GRAPHICS, PACKAGING AND INTERNET DESIGN. GREEN HAS
PLAYED A PIVOTAL ROLE IN RECENT BRANDING AND DESIGN INITIATIVES INCLUDING THE
LAUNCH OF IBM'S E-BUSINESS IDENTITY PROGRAM, THE NEW TECHNOLOGY BRANDING
PROGRAM AND THE REDESIGN OF IBM'S DESKTOP, MOBILE AND SERVER PRODUCTS. HE ALSO
LEADS THE CORPORATION'S EFFORTS IN THE AREA OF "ADVANCED CONCEPT DESIGN."
GREEN CURRENTLY SERVES ON THE BOARD OF DIRECTORS FOR THE DESIGN MANAGEMENT
INSTITUTE AND AS AN ADVISOR TO THE UNIVERSITY OF WESTMINSTER MBA PROGRAM.

lana rigsby

ANNUAL REPORT FOR WEYERHAEUSER COMPANY, 2001.

LANA RIGSBY, RIGSBY DESIGN, HOUSTON
LANA RIGSBY IS PRINCIPAL AND DESIGN DIRECTOR FOR RIGSBY DESIGN.
HER TEXAS-BASED FIRM IS KNOWN FOR CREATING ENGAGING, INTELLIGENT COMMUNICATIONS
FOR ORGANIZATIONS AS DIVERSE AS DELL COMPUTERS, WEYERHAEUSER,
AMERICAN ONCOLOGY RESOURCES AND STRATHMORE/INTERNATIONAL PAPERS.
RIGSBY TEACHES AND LECTURES FREQUENTLY, HAS SERVED AS A JUDGE FOR MANY
INTERNATIONAL DESIGN COMPETITIONS AND EXHIBITIONS, AND
HAS WRITTEN ABOUT DESIGN FOR *CRITIQUE* AND *GRAPHIS*.
RIGSBY IS A FOUNDING MEMBER OF AIGA'S TEXAS CHAPTER, AND HAS SERVED
ON THE BOARD OF NATIONAL DIRECTORS FOR AIGA.

05

information design

SELECTED WORKS EXHIBIT EXCELLENCE IN COMPLEX
QUANTITATIVE, STATISTICAL, SPATIAL OR EXPLANATORY INFORMATION.

JURORS
NIGEL HOLMES, WESTPORT, CONNECTICUT; ERIK SPIEKERMANN, BERLIN, LONDON, SAN FRANCISCO;
LISA STRAUSFELD, PENTAGRAM DESIGN INC., NEW YORK

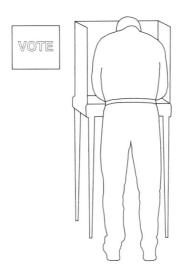

information design

WRITTEN BY JULIE LASKY

"When I called myself an information designer in the '70s, no one knew what it was," said juror Erik Spiekermann. "Now the term has made itself redundant." Spiekermann was helping to explain why so few maps, magazine graphics and annual reports turned up among the 101 entries to AIGA's information design competition. Because information design is now practiced so widely—by people who refer to themselves as everything from illustrators to information architects—many appropriate projects appear to have found their way to other AIGA competitions, such as editorial design or corporate communications design, if they were submitted at all.

The examples that did present themselves—from art catalogues to public policy manuals—had virtues, the jury agreed, but represented only a fraction of the discipline's breadth. "Designers think they should submit only big projects," lamented juror Nigel Holmes, who was surprised to find almost no newspaper graphics submitted and none of the excellent work currently produced by *The New York Times.* On the other hand, an odd subculture of entries was represented by three different pamphlets that present community-based environmental information for policymakers and voters. "They offer some of the best opportunities for information design," said juror Lisa Strausfeld of these pieces, "and are the most worthy of good design." The jurors ended up picking *Fight (or) Flight,*[1] a document produced by the Metropolitan Philadelphia Policy Center, from this trio.

PG 180

Digital entries were far from conspicuous. Of the eight finalists that were ultimately selected in this competition, seven were on paper. Only the University of Southern California's online career planner[2] was screen-based.

PG 176

Strausfeld sometimes wondered whether print designers, although they have the advantage of limited real estate, which helps them to impose elegance and economy on their designs, might take more cues from new technology. "Couldn't a retailer's offline catalog have sorted the inventory more imaginatively?" she asked at one point. And however well executed a bureaucratic form might be, "Do we need to fill out forms at all?" she mused. »

05

information design

Despite the seeming dispersal of information design to the winds of practice, however, a definite "look," has evolved for which the computer is at least partly responsible. "Information design can be a style, loaded with colored tables, vertical rules and other features that are handily built into software programs," Spiekermann insisted. "Designers tend to exploit the emotional power of these features to produce graphics that appear important without illuminating content," Spiekermann added. "There is no reason to have vertical lines in any chart. That's why God made white space."

Overall, the jury favored restrained projects and sprinkled them with reserved compliments. (In one instance, Spiekermann summoned up the word "adequate" to applaud a piece that ultimately didn't make the cut. "A lot of information design shouldn't push boundaries," he said in its defense.) They lavished some of their most stirring remarks on information-packed newsletters produced by the investment analyst Morningstar.[3] "This gets my 'Passion Award,'" said Holmes, noting gradient tints that shaded delicately from five percent to nothing and actually worked to set off information from its dense surroundings. "Someone obviously cared a lot and used an iron fist to do it his or her way." PG 175

While the jurors clearly felt the competition was deficient in examples of pure information design—from newspapers, magazines, annual reports and digital media—the selections that did make the cut were vigorously praised. The catalog *Van Gogh and Gauguin*,[4] a book companion to an exhibition mounted at the Art Institute of Chicago, won unanimous approval for detailed efforts to place the painters in historical, geographical and even meteorological contexts. A project to redesign forms for Art Center College of Design[5] in Pasadena, California, was lauded for its "brilliant premise" and "commendable effort." And extraordinary praise was heaped on "Design Your Future at USC," the[6] career-planning website. "Every screen is perfect," Spiekermann said. □ PG 177 PG 174 PG 176

DESIGN FIRM: SATELLITE DESIGN, SAN FRANCISCO

DESIGNER: AMY GUSTINCIC
PHOTOGRAPHERS: JIMMY CHIN, JERRY DODRILL, GREG VON DOERSTEN,
TOPHER DONAHUE, KRISTOFFER ERICKSON, CHRIS FIGENSHAU, JOHN KELLY, CAMERON
LAWSON, SCOTT MARKEWITZ, MELISSA McMANUS, CHRIS MURRAY, CARL SKOOG,
JAY SMITH, SCOTT SPIKER, MARK SYNNOTT, BETH WALD
ILLUSTRATOR: BETH KEPLER
TYPEFACE: ITC FRANKLIN GOTHIC
CLIENT: THE NORTH FACE

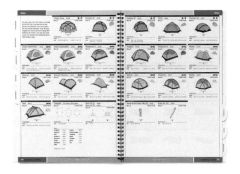

THE NORTH FACE FALL 2002 WORKBOOK

This trade catalogue is used primarily to accompany sales presentations to outdoor specialty store buyers. It also functions as a product reference for training store associates. Since The North Face products are evaluated based on extremely complicated product specifications, the challenge in designing this piece was to present all of the information in a clear and compelling way. Potential buyers must be able to compare multiple products and quickly understand differences between them. Both buyers and retail associates need to be educated as to the specific product fabrics and technologies.

JURORS' COMMENTS

"The use of drawings works well—better than photography." "This is classic information design, which there's not enough of."

CHAPTER THREE, "STUFF YOU NEED:"
DESIGN FIRM: AGNEW MOYER SMITH, PITTSBURGH

BOOK CREATIVE DIRECTOR: RICHARD SAUL WURMAN, TOP
INFORMATION ARCHITECTS: AGNEW MOYER SMITH, PITTSBURGH;
EXPLANATION GRAPICS, WESTPORT, CONNECTICUT;
KATZ DESIGN ASSOCIATES, PHILADELPHIA;
MEDICAL BROADCASTING COMPANY, PHILADELPHIA;
PENTAGRAM DESIGN INC., NEW YORK;
ONLY FOR CHAPTER THREE, "STUFF YOU NEED:"
SX2, CHICAGO; TOP, NEWPORT, RHODE ISLAND
CHAPTER THREE ART DIRECTORS: JOHN SOTIRAKIS, DON MOYER
DESIGNER: JOHN SOTIRAKIS
PHOTOGRAPHER: CAT ZACCARDI
ILLUSTRATORS: RICK HENKEL, KURT HESS
WRITER: AMY ORISS
TYPEFACES: FRANKLIN GOTHIC, MINION, ZAPF DINGBAT
CLIENTS: CIVITAS, TOP

UNDERSTANDING CHILDREN: THE GUIDEBOOK FOR CHILDREN 0 – 3

Understanding Children, a joint venture of TOP and CIVITAS, is a unique combination of leading-edge research and 21st-century design based on the principles of information architecture.

Our 5-spread chapter, about baby products, had to mesh with 13 other chapters in the book. Layout requirements included using the top two-thirds of the page to tell the story and the bottom one-third to state "action steps."

We began with a central, eye-catching illustration for each spread, supplemented with abundant facts and powerful visuals—baby photos, simple icons and vibrant colors.

JURORS' COMMENTS

"Heavily templated but not restrictive. Sometimes the template should be masked in the viewing experience, but in this case, it's a strength."

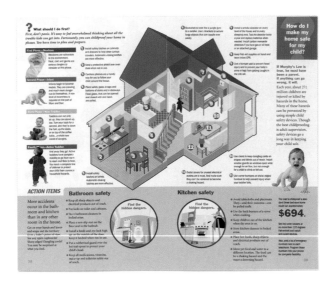

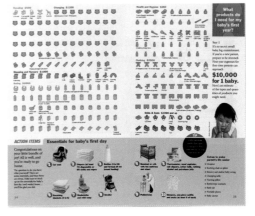

DESIGN FIRM: ART CENTER COLLEGE OF DESIGN, PASADENA, CALIFORNIA

DESIGNER: DANIELLE FRANSSEN
TYPEFACES: FUTURA, FUTURA BOOK, FUTURA CONDENSED
CLIENT: ART CENTER COLLEGE OF DESIGN

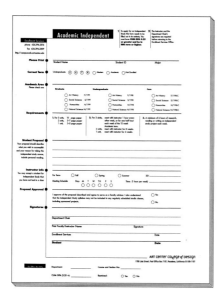

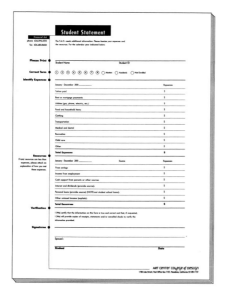

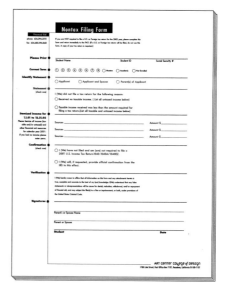

ART CENTER COLLEGE OF DESIGN FORM DEVELOPMENT PROJECT BOOKLET

The existing forms lacked cohesive nomenclature, visual hierarchy and user-friendliness. My only guidelines for their redesign were that the forms should be 8 1/2 by 11 inches, black and white, and reproducible by Xerox. I created a consistent and functional system that used design to inform, instruct and direct the intended user in universal applications.

JURORS' COMMENTS
"A brilliant premise and a commendable effort."

DESIGN FIRM: MORNINGSTAR INC., CHICAGO

DESIGNER: JASON ACKLEY
WRITER: MORNINGSTAR STAFF
TYPEFACES: ADOBE GARAMOND, LINOTYPE FUTURA, LINOTYPE UNIVERS CONDENSED,
MORNINGSTAR
PRINTER: R. R. DONNELLEY FINANCIAL
PAPER: HAMMERMILL ACCENT OPAQUE 60 LB. TEXT
CLIENT: MORNINGSTAR INC.

MORNINGSTAR FUNDINVESTOR AND *STOCKINVESTOR* NOVEMBER 2000 NEWSLETTERS

Morningstar FundInvestor and *StockInvestor* are monthly newsletters for individual investors with an intermediate to advanced level of investing knowledge. These publications seek to enable this audience to make better investing decisions and build better investment portfolios. The design of these newsletters seeks to bring clarity and vibrancy to the sometimes-complicated nature of such financial information. The use of color, texture and tints, together with a simple approach to the overall typographic structure, serves the needs of the information by celebrating the data and clarifying the editorial story being told.

JURORS' COMMENTS

"This gets my 'Passion Award.'" "Beautifully printed subject matter for people who are personally motivated to examine every detail."

DESIGN FIRM: PENTAGRAM DESIGN INC., SAN FRANCISCO

CREATIVE DIRECTOR: KIT HINRICHS
DESIGNERS: BRIAN COX, BRIAN JACOBS, DOUGLAS McDONALD
PHOTOGRAPHER: CHARLY FRANKLIN
ILLUSTRATORS: JEFF WEST, MICK WIGGINS
SOUND DESIGNER: BEN STOELTING
WRITER: DELPHINE HIRASUNA
TYPEFACES: FUTURA, TRADE GOTHIC
CLIENT: UNIVERSITY OF SOUTHERN CALIFORNIA

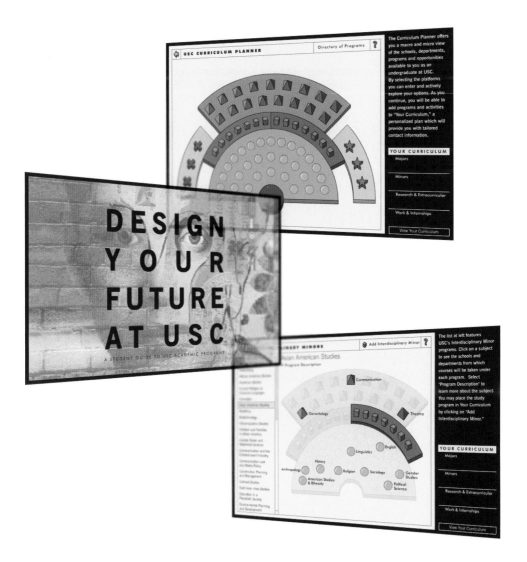

USC CURRICULUM PLANNER

As part of the University of Southern California's unique philosophy—
to "create Renaissance students for the 21st century"—students are
invited to design their own customized curriculum by combining elements
from the multitude of programs and activities on offer.

The challenge was to transform a large and complicated system
into a format that was approachable, easily understood and engaging.
Using a central interactive illustration depicting the various programs
as a simple conceptual diagram, the student can research, design and
print their desired curriculum.

JURORS' COMMENTS

"Every screen is perfect." "The right concept for the audience: it looks
good, functions well and adds something you couldn't have through
other technology."

DESIGN FIRM: STUDIO BLUE, CHICAGO

CREATIVE DIRECTORS: KATHY FREDRICKSON, CHERYL TOWLER WEESE
DESIGNERS: GARRETT NIKSCH, CHERYL TOWLER WEESE
ILLUSTRATOR: GARRETT NIKSCH
CARTOGRAPHER: TOM WILLCOCKSON, MAPCRAFT
TYPEFACES: BULLDOG, GARAGE GOTHIC, HIGHTOWER, WILMA
CLIENT: THE ART INSTITUTE OF CHICAGO

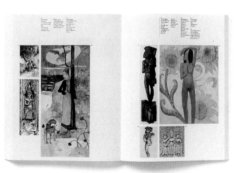

VAN GOGH AND GAUGUIN: THE STUDIO OF THE SOUTH CATALOGUE

This catalogue accompanied an exhibition that presented the relationship between Gauguin and Van Gogh—focusing on a ten-week period when they worked together—and the powerful influence that interaction had on their art.

Context was critical in the curators' story so we fleshed out the catalogue with detailed perspectival maps showing the locations and vantage points of the artists' paintings, and with daily calendars chronicling their work, correspondence, the weather and local events. The real trick here was presenting disparate, obscure information in a cohesive way—and we went through numerous revisions to get the final result.

JURORS' COMMENTS

"Every detail is considered, from the brilliantly designed heads to the nice maps. This is a catalogue with added value."

05
information design

DESIGN FIRM: POULIN + MORRIS, NEW YORK

ART DIRECTOR: L. RICHARD POULIN
DESIGNER: AMY KWON
WRITER: COOPER, ROBERTSON & PARTNERS
TYPEFACES: MINION, UNIVERS
CLIENTS: COOPER, ROBERTSON & PARTNERS, YALE UNIVERSITY

YALE UNIVERSITY: A FRAMEWORK FOR CAMPUS PLANNING BOOK

Yale University is undergoing an ambitious campus and building renovation program that seeks to improve individual physical facilities, create a stronger connection throughout the institution's various schools, departments and programs, and improve the University's physical and aesthetic relationship to the city of New Haven.

We were asked to establish a set of design guidelines that would respect the character and history of existing individual structures and still create this new cohesiveness.

The resulting 3-volume casebook set is comprised of a 244-page, full-color, bound volume containing design guidelines, implementation guidelines and in-depth analysis of the entire planning process.

JURORS' COMMENTS

"Someone's taken the trouble to put a large amount of data into an attractive format." "I've been in planning situations where I've wished I had a document like this."

05
information design

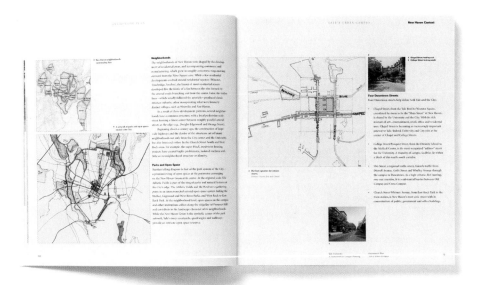

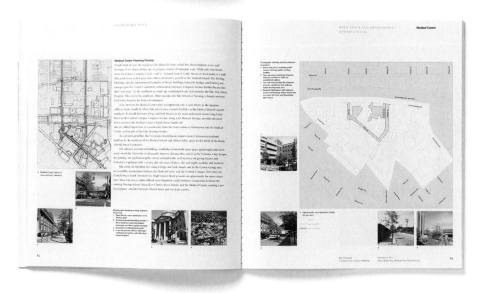

DESIGN FIRM: RUTKA WEADOCK DESIGN, BALTIMORE

CREATIVE DIRECTOR: ANTHONY RUTKA
DESIGNER: ALLY WEINER
MAP/CHART DESIGNER: JEN LIAO
WRITER: MARGARET PUGH O'MARA
TYPEFACES: MRS. EAVES, TRADE GOTHIC
PRINTER: PEAKE PRINTERS, INC.
CLIENT: METROPOLITAN PHILADELPHIA POLICY CENTER

FLIGHT (OR) FIGHT? REPORT

This report, produced by the Metropolitan Philadelphia Policy Center, covers issues such as urban blight, suburban sprawl, employment, education and taxation that affect the Philadelphia region. The challenge was to take a lot of weighty—and sometimes very negative—information and put it into a format that would make it accessible to a wide audience of corporate heads, legislators and policy makers.

The perfect-bound book begins with a 32-page, 4-color section that carries the positive messages. We used conceptual illustrations and typography to play up key words so readers could get the messages without reading the entire book. We redesigned charts and maps to make them easy to understand.

JURORS' COMMENTS

"Lively copy, lively spreads. The graphics are clear. Just charts. No more than you need."

information design

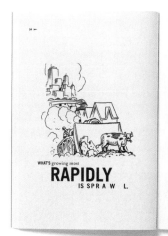

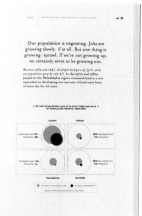

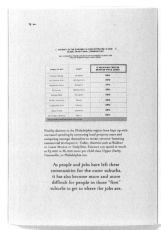

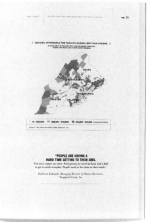

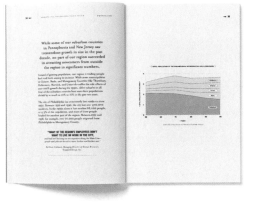

nigel holmes

MAP OF MANHATTAN/WORLD TRADE CENTER,
ROLLING STONE, SEPTEMBER 11 MEMORIAL ISSUE, 2001. ART DIRECTED BY GAIL ANDERSON.

NIGEL HOLMES, WESTPORT, CONNECTICUT

NIGEL HOLMES SPENT 16 YEARS AS *TIME* MAGAZINE'S GRAPHICS DIRECTOR, BEFORE SETTING UP
A COMPANY COMMITTED TO USING THE POWER OF PICTURES TO HELP READERS UNDERSTAND OTHERWISE
ABSTRACT NUMBERS AND DIFFICULT SCIENTIFIC CONCEPTS. HIS CLIENTS HAVE INCLUDED
APPLE, GM, HOLIDAY INN, MCI, NIKE, SONY, UNITED HEALTHCARE, US AIRWAYS
AND VISA, AND HE CONTINUES TO DO EXPLANATORY GRAPHICS FOR PUBLICATIONS SUCH
AS *BUSINESS 2.0*, *FORBES ASAP*, *HARPER'S*, THE *NEW YORKER* AND *THE NEW YORK TIMES*.
NIGEL HOLMES HAS WRITTEN SIX BOOKS ON ASPECTS OF INFORMATION DESIGN AND
IS CURRENTLY WORKING ON A VISUAL EXPLANATION OF HOW THE U.S. GOVERNMENT WORKS
(WITH *THE NEW YORK TIMES*). TOGETHER WITH HIS SON, HE PRODUCES SHORT ANIMATED FILMS
ABOUT STATISTICS; THE LATEST ONES WERE FOR *FORTUNE*'S CONFERENCE DIVISION.

05

information design

juror

erik spiekermann

AUDI DESIGN MANUALS, AUDI, 1994.

ERIK SPIEKERMANN, BERLIN, LONDON, SAN FRANCISCO
ERIK SPIEKERMANN IS AN INFORMATION ARCHITECT AND A TYPE DESIGNER.
IN 1979, ERIK SPIEKERMANN FOUNDED METADESIGN, GERMANY'S LARGEST DESIGN FIRM, WHOSE
PROJECTS INCLUDED CORPORATE DESIGN PROGRAMS FOR AUDI, SKODA, VOLKSWAGEN, LEXUS,
HEIDELBERG PRINTING, BERLIN TRANSIT AND DUESSELDORF AIRPORT. HE HOLDS A PROFESSOR-
SHIP AT THE ACADEMY OF ARTS IN BREMEN, IS VICE PRESIDENT OF THE GERMAN DESIGN
COUNCIL AND PRESIDENT OF THE INTERNATIONAL INSTITUTE OF INFORMATION DESIGN.
SPIEKERMANN, HAVING WITHDRAWN FROM THE MANAGEMENT OF METADESIGN BERLIN, NOW
LIVES AND WORKS AS A FREELANCE DESIGN CONSULTANT IN BERLIN, LONDON AND SAN
FRANCISCO. IN 2001, HE REDESIGNED *THE ECONOMIST* MAGAZINE IN LONDON, AND IS CURRENTLY
WORKING ON ALL PRINTED INFORMATION FOR GERMANY'S STATE RAILWAYS, DEUTSCHE BAHN.

05
information design
juror

lisa strausfeld

1

MEDIA WALL FOR RENOVATION OF PENN STATION, 2001.

2

MILLENNIUM PROJECT IMMERSIVE HISTORICAL INFORMATION SPACE, 1995.

1

2

LISA STRAUSFELD, PENTAGRAM DESIGN INC., NEW YORK
IN 2002, LISA STRAUSFELD JOINED PENTAGRAM DESIGN INC. AS A PARTNER IN
THE FIRM'S NEW YORK OFFICE. HER TEAM SPECIALIZES IN DIGITAL INFORMATION DESIGN
PROJECTS THAT RANGE FROM SOFTWARE PROTOTYPES AND WEBSITES TO
LARGE-SCALE MEDIA INSTALLATIONS. PROJECTS HAVE INCLUDED THE DESIGN OF A
200-FOOT LONG MEDIA WALL FOR THE RENOVATION OF PENN STATION AT MANHATTAN'S
FARLEY POST OFFICE BUILDING AND THE DESIGN OF INTERPRETIVE DISPLAYS
AT THE NEW YORK BOTANICAL GARDENS VISITORS CENTER. PRIOR TO THIS, STRAUSFELD CO-
FOUNDED PERSPECTA, AN INFORMATION ARCHITECTURE SOFTWARE COMPANY,
WHERE SHE LED THE DEVELOPMENT OF CUSTOMIZED SOFTWARE
FOR CLIENTS THAT INCLUDED *ENCYCLOPEDIA BRITANNICA*, *FORTUNE* MAGAZINE
AND MERRILL LYNCH. SHE ALSO WORKED FOR THE DIGITAL SPORTS ENTERTAINMENT
COMPANY QUOKKA SPORTS WHERE SHE LED THE DEVELOPMENT OF INTERFACES
FOR "IMMERSIVE SPORTS EXPERIENCES."

06

environmental graphic design

SELECTED WORKS REPRESENT THE YEAR'S BEST DESIGNS
FOR BUILT AND NATURAL ENVIRONMENTS.

JURORS
AYSE BIRSEL, OLIVE 1:1 INC., NEW YORK; STEFF GEISSBUHLER, CHERMAYEFF & GEISMAR INC., NEW YORK;
EMANUELA FRATTINI MAGNUSSON, EFM DESIGN, NEW YORK

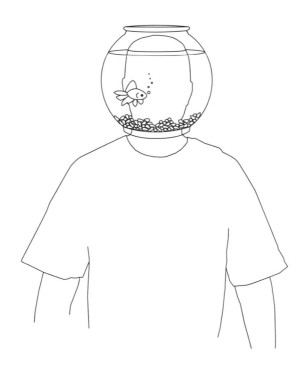

06
environmental graphic design
WRITTEN BY JULIE LASKY

The hybrid animal that is environmental graphic design posed challenges for jurors Ayse Birsel, Emanuela Frattini Magnusson and Steff Geissbuhler. Among the 121 submissions to AIGA's environmental graphic design competition were many projects that highlighted interior design or architecture without a strong graphic component. An elegant showroom for the contract furniture company Teknion, for instance, failed to push its graphic contribution much beyond the use of color and artwork, and thus missed a chance to forge a memorable identity.

Much was redeemed, however, by the 14 finalists, including one that knocked the jury's socks off— Imaginary Forces' video projections on the façade of Morgan Stanley's building[1] near Times Square in New York. PG 197 Said Birsel,"This really answers the question of how you move from two dimensions to three. You have three bands of windows that are totally transparent, and then three bands of structure splashed with moving images. When people are working in there and the windows are lit, you can't tell if you're looking at the graphics or the real thing." And unlike some of its video-enhanced neighbors, Frattini Magnusson remarked, the Morgan Stanley building "is not being used as a billboard; the images are specific to it; they tell a story."

Another Times Square façade that won high marks was the Toys 'R' Us storefront[2]—an ingenious rigging of louvered PG 193 panels displaying rotating graphics. "The different images radically change the face of the building," Birsel noted with approval.

The third architectural finalist, a retail environment for the online bank ING Direct,[3] carried a seamless and PG 198 playful connection between graphic and dimensional design into the building, much to the jury's satisfaction. "At first it looked like supergraphics on the inside and a little dated," Geissbuhler said. "But on second look, it is much more integrated than just paint." »

Toying with viewers' spatial perception was key to all of these projects' success. But nowhere were such efforts more appropriate than in Sussman Prejza's retail and theater signage for the Hollywood and Highland mall[4] in Los Angeles. Here, the idea of illusionary projection—the confusion of real and applied shadows—was played out in every detail, even on the restroom doors.

PG 204, 206

Along with these architectural projects, seven of the finalists fell into the more modest subcategory of exhibition design. Two showcased the design talents of Durfee, Regn, Sandhaus working for the California Institute of the Arts on the diverse subjects of panoramic photographs of the American West[5] and treasures of the great libraries of Los Angeles.[6] And while the jury took some issue with the photo show's typography, they were enthusiastic about the book show's vitrines, which were sandblasted with images that helped to position and enhance the works displayed within. "This is beautifully done, and it's not easy to interpret books in a new way," Geissbuhler said. He should know. His firm's innovative design for the "AIGA 50 Books/50 Covers 2001" exhibition won praise from the other jurors for making all aspects of the books visible.

PG 196
PG 200

Two exhibitions had the challenge of designer subjects: one devoted to Czech modernist Karel Teige at the Wolfsonian-FIU museum[7] in Miami, and one to Swiss modernist Le Corbusier at Princeton University.[8] Both triumphed for their appropriate and sensitive environments and furnishings.

PG 208
PG 205

The remaining two finalists were the purest evocations of information design in three dimensions. The jury declared xSITE's timeline tracing the history of the furniture company Knoll[9] more than effective. And a construction barrier created by Chermayeff and Geismar for a new Manhattan building[10] stylishly provided the history of the entire block. "It's so encouraging that a developer hired a designer, instead of putting up those advertising posters," Birsel said. □

PG 209
PG 207

06
environmental graphic design

DESIGN FIRM: GENSLER, NEW YORK

DESIGN DIRECTOR: JOHN BRICKER
DESIGNERS: JEAN KOEPPEL, PETER LAUDERMILCH, BETH NOVITSKY
ARCHITECTS: CARLOS ESPINOSA, TOM KOWALSKI
GRAPHICS PROJECT MANAGER: JILL WITTNEBEL
FABRICATORS: DIAZIT, FOCUS LIGHTING, SHOW AND TELL, INC., VOMELA HARVARD GRAPHICS
CLIENT: TOYS 'R' US

TOYS 'R' US TIMES SQUARE STOREFRONT

The intention of this project was to design and build a storefront for the international flagship store of Toys 'R' Us in the heart of New York's Times Square. The world's largest toy store needed to be positioned as a premiere destination for tourists, customers and passersby. To help the building stand out within a media-dense area, we developed an innovative billboard that would generate its own advertising revenue.

The "building board" consists of 165 individual modules. Each is controlled by a scrolling mechanism, allowing up to seven separate scenes to be displayed, creating a continuously changing choreographed show. An eighth panel, which is clear, reveals the interior of the store.

JURORS' COMMENTS

"A very successful use of the grid. Playful and appropriate."

06

environmental graphic design

DESIGN FIRM: AMERICAN MUSEUM OF NATURAL HISTORY, NEW YORK

CREATIVE DIRECTOR: DAVID HARVEY
ART DIRECTOR: TIM NISSEN
GRAPHIC DESIGNER: STEPHANIE REYER
SENIOR MEDIA PRODUCER: GERALYN ABINADER
FABRICATORS: AMERICAN MUSEUM OF NATURAL HISTORY, SHOWMAN FABRICATORS INC.
CLIENT: AMERICAN MUSEUM OF NATURAL HISTORY

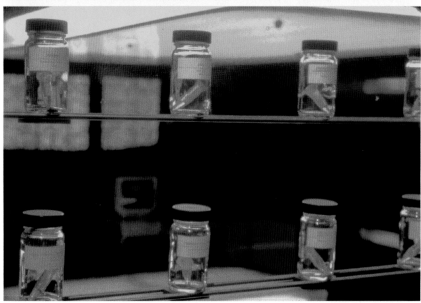

"THE GENOMIC REVOLUTION" EXHIBITION

Keeping pace with one of the greatest scientific achievements of modern times, the American Museum of Natural History created the first comprehensive exhibition on the field of genomics. "The Genomic Revolution" enabled visitors to grasp the relevance and ramifications of deciphering the code of life.

Mounted in a 7,500-square-foot gallery, the exhibition featured a range of techniques—models, hands-on and computer interactives, animations, soundscapes and video projections—that engaged visitors of all ages. Controversial topics, from cloning and gene therapy to genetically modified foods, captured the attention of visitors, who could then voice their opinions at computer polling stations.

06

environmental graphic design

DESIGN FIRM: DURFEE REGN SANDHAUS, LOS ANGELES

DESIGNERS: TIM DURFEE, IRIS REGN, LOUISE SANDHAUS
FABRICATOR: GARY MURPHY
GRAPHICS: SKYE GRAPHICS
PROJECT TEAM: TIM DURFEE, GEOFF KORF, KATHERINE LALLY, JEN McKNIGHT, PETRA MICHEL,
CHRISTOPHER MUELLER, IRIS REGN, LOUISE SANDHAUS, TRICIA SANEDRIN
TYPEFACES: SQUARE 621, TT SMILE
CLIENTS: CLAUDIA BOHN-SPECTOR, THE HUNTINGTON LIBRARY AND BOTANICAL GARDENS,
JENNIFER WATTS

"THE GREAT WIDE OPEN: PANORAMIC PHOTOGRAPHS OF THE AMERICAN WEST" EXHIBITION

For this exhibition, we sought to create an environment that appeared open and boundless—referring to the panoramic western landscapes that inspired the featured photographers.

At the entrance, wide-angle viewfinders allowed visitors to see the gallery through the type of lens used to create the work in the show. Looking through the lens, a small title for each thematic section appeared superimposed over its corresponding location in the space.

The platform-like surfaces—their shapes derived from the paths of circulation through the exhibit—abstractly referenced landscape features and allowed works to be seen from an ideal viewing distance.

The white walls contributed to the effect of openness while the low, orange surfaces complemented the predominantly sky-blue color of the landscape photographs.

JURORS' COMMENTS
"Wise use of the space."

06

environmental graphic design

DESIGN FIRM: IMAGINARYFORCES, NEW YORK

CREATIVE DIRECTOR: MIKON van GASTEL
ART DIRECTOR: SARA MARANDI
DESIGNERS: MATT CHECKOWSKI, MIKON van GASTEL, CHUN-CHIEN LIEN, SARA MARANDI,
EDDIE OPARA, FABIAN TEJADA, EMILY WILSON
PHOTOGRAPHER: GILES DUNNING
ARCHITECT: KOHN PEDERSEN FOX
TYPEFACES: MSTriad, NEWS GOTHIC
CLIENT: MORGAN STANLEY

745 SEVENTH AVENUE BUILDING FAÇADE PROJECTIONS

We developed content for the Morgan Stanley building façade signage to provide a counterpoint to the fast-paced, hyper-commercial nature of its Times Square environment. In collaboration with the architect, we created a sign that doesn't stick out from, or cover up, the building; it is the building. Thirty minutes of non-linear branding content acts like a kinetic sculpture on an otherwise static building. Slow-moving images and subtle messages weave the client's name, personality and brand attributes into the fabric of the message. All content was specifically designed and programmed for this particular screen configuration and is activated by the architectural building grid.

JURORS' COMMENTS

"Our favorite above and beyond everything else. Beautifully done."

06
environmental graphic design

DESIGN FIRM: GENSLER, NEW YORK

DESIGN DIRECTOR: JOHN BRICKER
DESIGNERS: JAMIE BRIZZOLARA, BETH NOVITSKY, TRACY SILVERSTEIN
ARCHITECTS/INTERIOR DESIGNERS: LAURENT LISIMACHIO, GREG OKSHTEYN, PETER WANG
GRAPHICS PROJECT MANAGER: JILL WITTNEBEL
FABRICATORS: ASI SIGN SYSTEMS, COLOR-X
TYPEFACES: EUROSTILE, NEESKENS
CLIENT: ING DIRECT

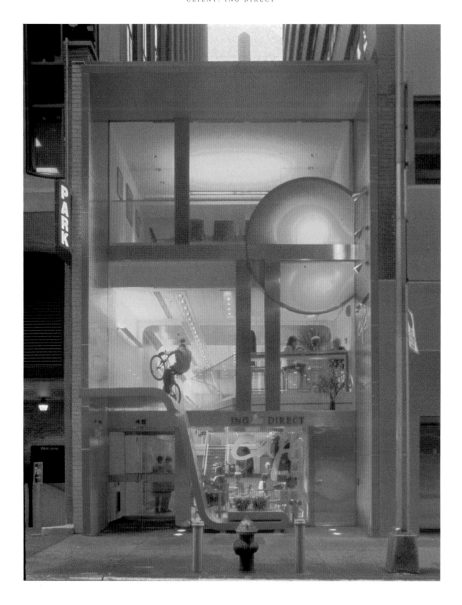

ING DIRECT RETAIL ENVIRONMENT

ING Direct, an internet savings and loan bank, wanted the brand recognition, street presence and emotional reassurance that a "three-dimensional" bank creates. The result was ING Direct Café, an upbeat environment where current and potential customers can learn about financial products and access account information online.

The design solution translates the graphic language of the ING Direct website into an environment that integrates architecture, graphic design, retail design and digital media. The bright orange color palette directly reflects the bank's corporate colors and the large translucent panels add graphic character and convey brand messages.

JURORS' COMMENTS

"It pays attention to three dimensions at every level. The right balance of environmental and graphic design."

06

environmental graphic design

06

environmental graphic design

DESIGN FIRM: DURFEE REGN SANDHAUS, LOS ANGELES

DESIGNERS: TIM DURFEE, IRIS REGN, LOUISE SANDHAUS
STRUCTURAL DESIGNER: PATRICK HUFF
FABRICATOR: RALPH HUDSON, IRONWOOD
GRAPHICS: PLATON GRAPHICS, SKYE GRAPHICS, VINYL ART
PROJECT TEAM: TIM DURFEE, BARBARA ELLIS, KATHERINE LALLY, PETRA MICHEL,
CHRISTOPHER MUELLER, IRIS REGN, LOUISE SANDHAUS
LIGHTING CONSULTATION: GEOFF KORF
TYPEFACES: CHOLLA, SQUARE 721
CLIENT: UCLA HAMMER MUSEUM

"THE WORLD FROM HERE: TREASURES OF THE GREAT LIBRARIES OF LOS ANGELES" EXHIBITION

The design strategy for this exhibit of books was to turn the gallery inside out—to invest all visual activity in the insides of the display cases, at the scale of the book. We chose to exploit the two main restrictive factors in the display of rare books. The low light levels took the emphasis away from the ambient brightness of the gallery and allowed the glow of the vitrines and the reading room to illuminate the gallery. The restricted access for inspection of the objects was overcome by creating special stations that allowed closer scrutiny of the books, through facsimile, video views into the book or audio readings.

JURORS' COMMENTS

"Informative and engaging. The books are interpreted in a new way, and that's not easy to do."

DESIGN FIRM: PENTAGRAM DESIGN INC., NEW YORK

ART DIRECTOR: PAULA SCHER
DESIGNERS: RION BYRD, TINA CHANG, DOK CHON, PAULA SCHER
ARCHITECT: POLSHEK PARTNERSHIP ARCHITECTS
FABRICATOR: SEROTA SIGNS BROADWAY MAINTENANCE
TYPEFACES: EAGLE, NOBLE
CLIENT: SYMPHONY SPACE

SYMPHONY SPACE ENVIRONMENT

The 2002 renovation of Symphony Space designed by James Stewart Polshek in collaboration with Paula Scher marries architecture and graphics to give the community-based arts organization a physical presence to match the quality of its cultural activity. The signage program incorporates the identity and typography designed by Scher. The interior renovation preserves the existing auditorium but expands the facility into a two-theater performing arts space by uniting it with the adjacent Thalia Theater, a repertory movie house. Outside, a new marquee awning connects Symphony Space to the Thalia, extending its reach out over the corner of 95th Street and Broadway and using the building's architecture and graphics to talk to the street.

JURORS' COMMENTS

"Looks formal—almost severe—because of the use of metal, but it really holds together."

DESIGN FIRM: SUSSMAN/PREJZA & CO., INC., CULVER CITY, CALIFORNIA

CREATIVE DIRECTORS: ERIC LEVINE, PAUL PREJZA, DEBORAH SUSSMAN
DESIGNERS: TAD HARA, JOHN JOHNSTON, PAUL NAGAKURA, HSIN HSIEN TSAI
ILLUSTRATOR: JEEUN KIM
STRUCTURAL DESIGNERS: JULIUS BHANG, RANDY WALKER
FABRICATOR: VOMAR PRODUCTS
TYPEFACE: SCALA SANS
CLIENT: TRIZECHAHN DEVELOPMENT CORPORATION

HOLLYWOOD & HIGHLAND RETAIL ENVIRONMENT SIGNAGE

Conceptually, the project-related graphics for the Hollywood & Highland retail environment are inspired by the cinematic interplay between light and shadow on a flat surface. The system uses only black and white to brand and identify this part of Hollywood as a place formed originally by the art of moving pictures. Classic film icons such as searchlights, extreme perspective and cropped images—attributes made "real" by the eye of the camera—inspired the identity.

JURORS' COMMENTS

"Though these are two projects (page 206), they relate together because of their play of shadow and light. Really imaginative and appropriate."

06
environmental graphic design

DESIGN FIRM: PLUS DESIGN INC., BOSTON

DESIGN DIRECTORS: ANITA MEYER, GRAPHIC DESIGN; JESSE A. REISER, ARCHITECTURE
DESIGNERS: VIVIAN LAW, ANITA MEYER, GRAPHIC DESIGN; JESSE A. REISER, NONA YEHIA, ARCHITECTURE
CURATOR: SUSAN TAYLOR
FABRICATORS: ARTISTIC METALWORKS, FRANKLIN GLASS INC., EUROPEAN WOODWORKING INC.
TYPEFACES: BLOCK GOTHIC, GARAMOND
CLIENT: PRINCETON UNIVERSITY ART MUSEUM

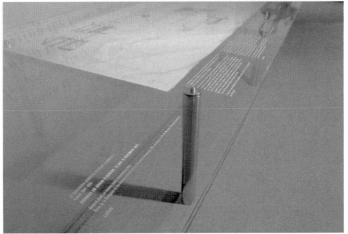

"LE CORBUSIER AT PRINCETON: 14–16 NOVEMBER 1935" EXHIBITION

The intention of this exhibition was to capture the spirit of Le Corbusier's philosophy of mass production and his five points of architecture. The project gave us the opportunity to collaborate with an architectural firm, bringing together our different visions and expertise to create a unique exhibition design. In addition, the architects worked with Princeton University students to create the illuminated models. Le Corbusier's drawings and his use of cement columns inspired the gray drawing tubes we used for the invitation design as well as the unconventional museum exhibition entrance signage and the exhibition table legs.

JURORS' COMMENTS

"Really smacks of Le Corbusier, but it's not warmed-over modernism. The use of materials is sparse but bright."

06
environmental graphic design

DESIGN FIRM: SUSSMAN/PREJZA & CO., INC., CULVER CITY, CALIFORNIA

CREATIVE DIRECTOR: HOLLY HAMPTON
DESIGNERS: SHARON BLAIR, HOLLY HAMPTON, ANA LLORENTE-THURIK
STRUCTURAL DESIGNER: RANDY WALKER
MANUFACTURER: VOMAR PRODUCTS
TYPEFACES: SAVOYE, SCALA SANS
CLIENT: TRIZECHAHN DEVELOPMENT CORPORATION

HOLLYWOOD & HIGHLAND KODAK THEATRE SIGNAGE

The Kodak Theatre is the new home for Hollywood's most glamorous event, the Academy Awards. Our environmental design took its lead from the core concept of light and shadow as seen through the eye of a camera. Working within the confines of an extremely lean fabrication budget, our restraint in the use of color allowed us to use special materials in key locations. The elegance of the Academy Awards event inspired the use of internally illuminated glass with a graduated reverse sandblast, creating the cast shadow of the Opera Box identification signs, while Austrian crystal punctuates the "W" and "M" of the restroom signs.

06
environmental graphic design

DESIGN FIRM: CHERMAYEFF & GEISMAR INC., NEW YORK

CREATIVE DIRECTOR: JONATHAN ALGER
DESIGNERS: BILL CARRIG, ADRIAN NIVOLA, LINDA POST, CHRIS ROVER
FABRICATORS: SPRING SCAFFOLDING, WALTER SIGN
TYPEFACE: NEWS GOTHIC
CLIENTS: INSIGNIA/ESG REALTY, JRT REALTY, TIAA-CREF REALTY DIVISION

"HISTORY IN THE MAKING" CONSTRUCTION FENCE

"History in the Making" was a public history exhibition in the form of a construction barricade. Our client wanted to disguise some necessary building work and encourage lease renewals. We proposed to do both by unearthing the distinctive history of the building's little-known Turtle Bay neighborhood. The result was a collision of the practical and the literary—the only construction fence we know of with a bibliography. The audience was comprised of tenants, passersby, cab-passengers, drivers, neighbors and the public in general. The exhibition was free and open to public view 24 hours a day for about 6 months.

JURORS' COMMENTS

"This takes a structure most people never look at and really does something with it. Sets a great example for other developers and neighborhoods."

06
environmental graphic design

DESIGN FIRM: THE WOLFSONIAN-FLORIDA INTERNATIONAL UNIVERSITY, MIAMI BEACH

DESIGNER: RICHARD MILTNER
STRUCTURAL DESIGNERS: STEVE FORERO-PAZ, JOHN NOONAN, KEVIN VELLAKE
TYPEFACE: EUROSLAVIC SANS
CLIENT: THE WOLFSONIAN-FLORIDA INTERNATIONAL UNIVERSITY

"DREAMS AND DISILLUSION: KAREL TEIGE AND THE CZECH AVANT-GARDE" EXHIBITION

"Dreams and Disillusion: Karel Teige and the Czech Avant-Garde" was the first U.S. exhibition on Karel Teige, the most important Czech proponent of the European avant-garde. A graphic designer and architectural theorist, Teige was an innovator in many artistic areas including book design, stage sets and collage. The exhibition design needed to be sympathetic to Teige's design work. Gallery graphics were inspired by Teige's book cover designs. The circle motif was used in two- and three-dimensional formats in the exhibit design. A full-scale model of a theoretical architectural environment was created as a gallery space using Sintra and vinyl mesh flooring.

JURORS' COMMENTS
"Distinctive at every scale."

06
environmental graphic design

DESIGN FIRM: XSITE, NEW YORK

CREATIVE DIRECTORS: INGEBORG BLOEM, KLAUS KEMPENAARS
DESIGNER: MARK CREMER
FABRICATOR: BIG APPLE VISUAL
TYPEFACE: HELVETICA NEUE
CLIENT: KNOLL

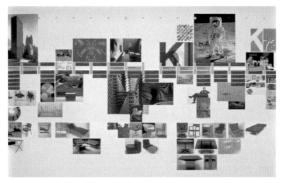

KNOLL TIMELINE

Knoll asked us to make an 80-foot-long company timeline for their newly renovated museum in Greenville, Pennsylvania. We created an intense image-oriented timeline in two layers. As a base we used historic imagery complimented in the second layer by text boxes, grouped by world events, corporate information and Knoll products.

By using the 3M process color vinyl print technology, we had no limitation in color or photography. Applied in pieces of 4 by 9 feet, as adhesive wallpaper, the vinyl is durable and color proof for a minimum of 10 years. It is a relatively easy procedure to add new information to the existing timeline.

JURORS' COMMENTS

"Lively and well-organized. Why does a timeline need to be more than this?"

06
environmental graphic design
juror

ayse birsel

1

OSCAR, NUOVA MERATI SRL, 2001.

2

RESOLVE WORKSYSTEM, HERMAN MILLER INC., 1999.

1

2

AYSE BIRSEL, OLIVE 1:1 INC., NEW YORK

AYSE BIRSEL IS THE PRINCIPAL OF OLIVE 1:1 INC., A NEW YORK CITY-BASED DESIGN STUDIO
SPECIALIZING IN INNOVATIVE PRODUCT DESIGN. SHE WAS BORN IN IZMIR, TURKEY,
A 2,000-YEAR-OLD CITY ON THE AEGEAN SEA. DRIVEN BY HER INTEREST IN DESIGN, BIRSEL
MOVED TO NEW YORK, WHERE SHE ATTENDED PRATT INSTITUTE AS A FULBRIGHT SCHOLAR.
HER MASTER'S THESIS, *THE WATER ROOM*, LAID THE GROUNDWORK FOR HER CONTINUED
WORK IN PARADIGM-BREAKING SOLUTIONS THAT SERVE AND DELIGHT THE USER.
BIRSEL HAS WORKED ON A WIDE RANGE OF PRODUCTS—FROM RESOLVE, A MODULAR OFFICE
SYSTEM FOR HERMAN MILLER INC., TO ZOE, A PERSONAL WASHLET TOILET FOR
TOTO JAPAN. HER USER-CENTERED PHILOSOPHY, MIXED WITH INSTINCT AND ALCHEMY,
ENSURES A SOLUTION THAT IS BOTH VITAL AND HUMAN.

06
environmental graphic design
juror

steff geissbuhler

NEW VICTORY THEATRE, NEW YORK, 1996.

STEFF GEISSBUHLER, CHERMAYEFF & GEISMAR INC., NEW YORK
STEFF GEISSBUHLER IS A LEADING DESIGNER OF CORPORATE IDENTITY GRAPHICS
AND PROGRAMS. AMONG THE MANY HE HAS CREATED, IN MORE THAN 26 YEARS AS PARTNER
AND PRINCIPAL AT CHERMAYEFF & GEISMAR, ARE THOSE FOR CARE INTERNATIONAL,
MERCK, TIME WARNER, NBC, NATIONAL PUBLIC RADIO, TELEMUNDO, UNION PACIFIC
CORPORATION AND THE U.S. ENVIRONMENTAL PROTECTION AGENCY. HE ESTABLISHES CLOSE
WORKING RELATIONSHIPS WITH HIS CLIENTS; MANY, INCLUDING CRANE BUSINESS PAPERS
AND THE MAY DEPARTMENT STORES COMPANY, RELY ON HIM FOR ONGOING ADVICE
AND CONSULTATION. GEISSBUHLER IS ALSO KNOWN FOR HIS ILLUSTRATIONS AND GRAPHICS
THAT EXPRESS THE CHARACTER OF LARGE ORGANIZATIONS AND MEET THEIR SPECIAL
NEEDS, SUCH AS THE ARCHITECTURAL GRAPHICS FOR THE IBM BUILDING IN NEW YORK
CITY AND A COMPLETE SIGN SYSTEM FOR THE UNIVERSITY OF PENNSYLVANIA.

06
environmental graphic design
juror

emanuela frattini magnusson

AIGA NATIONAL DESIGN CENTER, NEW YORK, 1999.

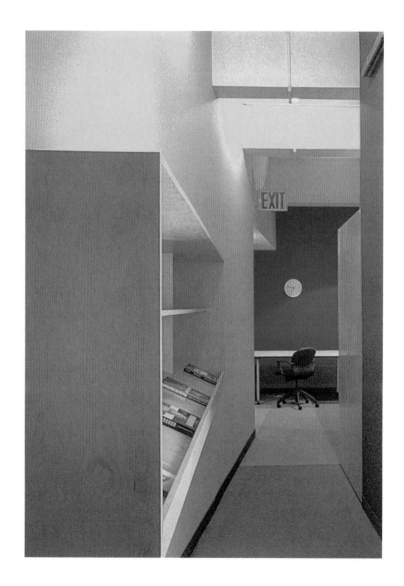

EMANUELA FRATTINI MAGNUSSON, EFM, NEW YORK

EMANUELA FRATTINI MAGNUSSON, BORN AND TRAINED AS AN ARCHITECT IN MILAN,
HAS PRACTICED ARCHITECTURE IN SEVERAL EUROPEAN COUNTRIES, AUSTRALIA
AND THE U.S. SHE HAS HAD HER OWN ARCHITECTURE AND DESIGN FIRM IN NEW YORK CITY
SINCE 1990. SHE PRODUCED AND MARKETED HER PRODUCT DESIGNS UNDER THE NAME
OF EFM PRIOR TO THEIR BEING DISTRIBUTED BY MoMA. FRATTINI MAGNUSSON'S WORK—
OR THE VARIETY OF CLIENTS INCLUDING AIGA, KNOLL, RUSSELL ATHLETIC, SPINNEYBECK
AND STEUBEN GLASS—RANGES IN SCALE FROM ARCHITECTURE, INTERIOR AND
EXHIBIT DESIGN TO FURNITURE, INDUSTRIAL DESIGN, GRAPHICS AND WEBSITES.
HER WORK WAS SELECTED TO APPEAR IN "BIENNALE DONNA," PADIGLIONE DI ARTE
CONTEMPORANEA, FERRARA IN 2002 AND IN "WOMEN DESIGNERS IN THE U.S.A.,"
BARD INSTITUTE, NEW YORK IN 2001.

07

design for film and television

SELECTED WORKS REPRESENT THE YEAR'S BEST-DESIGNED
WORK FOR FILM AND TELEVISION.

JURORS
KEIRA ALEXANDRA, BROOKLYN, NEW YORK; HILLMAN CURTIS, HILLMANCURTIS INC., NEW YORK;
MIKON VAN GASTEL, IMAGINARY FORCES, NEW YORK

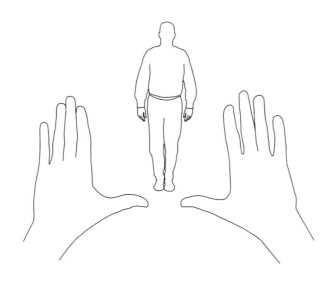

07

design for film and television

WRITTEN BY PETER HALL

The year 2001 saw a degree of retrenchment in the world of design for film and television, as creative cautiousness followed the economic downturn. Television, in particular, was caught in a me-too game with the web. Jurors Keira Alexandra, Hillman Curtis and Mikon van Gastel grew increasingly impatient with the televisual attempts to ape the vector graphics and Flash animations of the internet that have proliferated in the last year. "There was a huge amount of this sort of Flash-esque animation, and we all responded negatively to that because it's so overdone," said Curtis. Flash was developed for the low-bandwidth limitations of the web, but on high-bandwidth television, the jurors noted, it became mannerist—a surface treatment. "What television took from the web, sadly, was an aesthetic," said van Gastel. "It didn't take behavioral qualities of typography or imagery or any thinking about variables."

As if to remonstrate style for style's sake, the jurors of AIGA's design for film and television competition picked work with a low-tech, bare-bones, low-budget feel, which seemed more likely to accompany idea-driven rather than style-driven design. All but two of the finalists were unslick, or handmade in some way, and, in some cases, came with a deadpan, jaded sense of humor. A spot for Burton Snowboards,[1] for example, showed a jump being performed—to a hillbilly banjo soundtrack—by a snowboarder completely obscured by a giant Burton logo: it was as if sports sponsorship had been taken to its illogical extreme. An opening sequence and bumpers by Open for the MTV show "So Five Minutes Ago,"[2] meanwhile, seemed to sum up the ephemeral nature of a hip idea in the world of motion graphics. With hokey PowerPoint-style bar charts, pie charts and graphs illustrating phenomena like "retro, neo-retro and meta-retro," the openers and bumpers blazed through the pseudoscience of trend analysis with a gleeful sense of parody. By the time a pie chart had illustrated how "bad" and "good" sometimes produce "so bad it's good," the jurors began to feel that the designers of the work had nailed the main issue of the day: faddishness. "They touched on all the things we talked about," said van Gastel. "And there's more content here than in many music videos."

A more joyful counterpoint to MTV-style nihilism was provided by the "Freeform Summer Poems" for Noggin,[3] which featured selected poems and observations by children »

PG 224 [1]
PG 225 [2]
PG 227 [3]

217

aged 6 to 11, read over a delightfully mish-mashed sequence of images. Home video footage of frogs and ponds was interspersed with crude, pixellated graphics and animations. "I think they properly identified the theme, which is innocence," said Curtis. Innocence is fragile, however, and vanishes with repetition. The jurors singled out only one of the three poetry collections entered—"Summer"—for an award, arguing that, as van Gastel put it, "in executing the theme three times their innocence was lost."

Space was reserved on the podium, however, for slicker work that demonstrated masterfully choreographed and executed moves, as was the case in the Target spots[4]— which featured Olympic-style pictograms interacting with Target's beaming male and female models—and Imaginary Forces' dazzling computer-generated animations for The One.[5] Yet despite their technical virtuosity, both sequences demonstrated a formal simplicity and limited color palette in keeping with the rest of the jurors' picks.

PG 222 [4]

PG 229 [5]

The thrill of design for film and television is when sound and vision come together in fresh alliances—but, rather than innovation, simplicity was clearly the prevailing theme of the day for the jurors. The One opening was predominantly monochrome, and the high-concept teasers for a Yoko Ono exhibition[6] and television movie The Killing Yard[7] were presented entirely in black and white. The perennial popularity of black and white in film, photography and advertising has been duly noted elsewhere; monochrome has journalistic, documentary connotations, as well as its implications of nostalgia, honesty and truth. It hardly needs to be observed that as television drifts into visual representations of information and color saturation overload, our awards jury found itself increasingly drawn to work that conveys simplicity, truthfulness and strong ideas.

PG 228 [6]

PG 221 [7]

If that sounds like a retro-Modernist mantra, so be it. As Curtis pointed out, evidence of a certain amount of retrenchment in a batch of competition entries is not always a bad thing. "I'm not really blown away by it, which wasn't the case a couple of years ago. But I see that as a positive thing; we're butting our heads against another step, and there's going to be some real innovation and great work in the next couple of years." □

DESIGN FIRM: MOTION THEORY, VENICE, CALIFORNIA

CREATIVE DIRECTORS: MATHEW CULLEN, MOTION THEORY; PAULA MERMELSTEIN, SHOWTIME
ART DIRECTOR: CHRISTINA BLACK, SHOWTIME
DESIGNER: MATHEW CULLEN
ANIMATOR: MATHEW CULLEN
DIRECTORS OF PHOTOGRAPHY: DAN KOHNE, BILLY ROBINSON
EDITOR: MARK HOFFMAN
SOUND DESIGNER: PETE KNESER
WRITER: LIZA BERNSTEIN
TYPEFACE: AKZIDENZ GROTESK CONDENSED
CLIENT: SHOWTIME NETWORKS

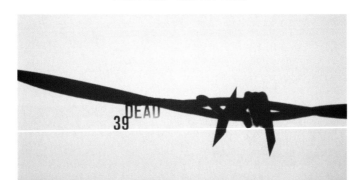

THE KILLING YARD TEASER

After producing *The Killing Yard*, a true-life story of the Attica riots, Showtime Networks wanted a teaser that referenced not just the film's courtroom aspects, but also the historical importance and deeper values inherent in the story.

The stark contrast between a single strand of barbed wire and a gently drifting feather forms the basis of the visuals, while the sound bed begins with an ominous wind rising and falling.

JURORS' COMMENTS

"I love the transition where the barbed wire turns into a feather. It's a nice juxtaposition and an unexpected twist. The timing was right. I give it an 'A' for the transition and 'A' for the fact that it is a teaser that's not using footage of the film and therefore doesn't give the film away."

DESIGN FIRM: FUEL, SANTA MONICA, CALIFORNIA

CREATIVE DIRECTOR: JUSTIN LEIBOW
DESIGNERS: ELAINE ALDERNETTE, JUSTIN LEIBOW, JUAN MONASTERIO
ANIMATORS: JUSTIN LEIBOW, JENS MEBES, JUAN MONASTERIO
DIRECTOR OF PHOTOGRAPHY: KARSTEN "CRASH" GOPINATH
EDITOR: JUSTIN LEIBOW
WRITERS: JANET ARLOTTA, JUSTIN LEIBOW
CLIENT: PETERSON MILLA HOOKS, FOR TARGET; A BAND APART, FOR TARGET

TARGET "SYMBOLS" TELEVISION ADS

Our client approached us to extend Target's new print campaign, using three crucial elements: the color red, universal male and female symbols, and models in sporty outfits. These ingredients were intended to further establish the pop vitality of the Target brand. We designed props, outfits and hairstyles for the symbols. We wrote and storyboarded scenes with live models interacting with the graphics.

JURORS' COMMENTS

"Initially I responded to the cleverness of the sequence and the smooth transitions between product shots. After repeated viewings, I started to respond negatively to the folks and their PhotoDisc world. But that's what Target is. It's free-for-all consumerism." "It's a loud, bright, happy, 30-second pleasure moment. You can hate the happy or appreciate it for happy's sake."

DESIGN FIRM: JAGER DI PAOLA KEMP DESIGN, BURLINGTON, VERMONT

CREATIVE DIRECTOR: MICHAEL JAGER
DESIGNERS: INGA FISK, RUBY LEE, JOE PEILA, MEGHAN PRUITT
ANIMATOR: WILL ATKIN
DIRECTOR: LANCE VIOLETTE
EDITOR: JOE PEILA
SOUND DESIGNERS: ERIC THIBODEAU, VANESSA WYLIE
CLIENT: BURTON SNOWBOARDS

BURTON "CRACKER" ANIMATED BRAND IDENTITY TAG

Burton wanted us to design an animated brand identity tag for web, video tour and e-mail purposes. It had to be small enough in file size that it could be e-mailed or shown on the web, but conceptually strong enough to convey a sense of the Burton brand in 14 seconds. We were throwing out ideas for the animation. Michael Jager was eating some stoned wheat crackers during the meeting and someone suggested that it would be funny to see the logo actually do some tricks itself, rather than just showing some more action footage. So he started moving the cracker around like a rider. And that was how we came up with the name "Cracker."

JUROR'S COMMENTS

"Because dumb is in. But it will soon be so five minutes ago."

07
design for film and television

DESIGN FIRM: OPEN, NEW YORK

DESIGNER: SCOTT STOWELL
ANIMATOR: BRYAN KEELING
MUSIC: AMALGAMATED SUPERSTAR
WRITER: SCOTT STOWELL
TYPEFACE: AVENIR
CLIENT: MTV NEWS + DOCS

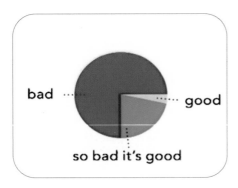

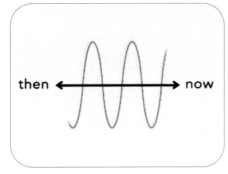

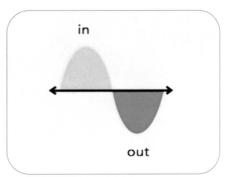

MTV "SO FIVE MINUTES AGO" SHOW PACKAGING

"So Five Minutes Ago" is an MTV series about things that just went out of style, created by filmmaker/producer Christopher Wilcha. Since the show makes fun of things that are no longer "cool," we had to figure out a way for the show itself to not become "un-cool"—at least not right away.

  We created a family of charts and graphs that plot the subjective criteria of trendiness in seemingly un-trendy ways. As both the schedule and budget were extremely limited, this conceptual approach worked well since it relies on ideas and words, not production values.

JURORS' COMMENTS

"As a spoof of PowerPoint graphics, it's funny." "It has some good writing in it. It's a smart set-up." "It's our gentle nod toward putting some content into design projects."

DESIGN FIRM: JAGER DI PAOLA KEMP DESIGN, BURLINGTON, VERMONT

CREATIVE DIRECTOR: MICHAEL JAGER
DESIGNER: MALCOLM BUICK
ANIMATORS: JON BOYER, MALCOLM BUICK
DIRECTOR: JON BOYER
EDITOR: JON BOYER
SOUND DESIGNERS: JON BOYER, MALCOLM BUICK
CLIENT: BURTON SNOWBOARDS

BURTON "ONE HIT" PROMOTIONAL SPOT

The purpose of the "One Hit" spot was to capture a pure moment in snowboarding, the kind that seems to be getting lost in the mix of "extreme" events and broadcast portrayal of youth indy sports. Burton Snowboards is a premier brand and a dedicated veteran in protecting the true soul of snowboarding. We wanted to keep it simple and true. The largest obstacles were the weather, timing and budgetary limitations. We were in our first days of production and the budget needed to be cut in half to reallocate funds elsewhere. We took a deep breath and dropped in anyway.

JURORS' COMMENTS

"I liked the mountain spot. I love the beautiful lockup and the fact that the spot was silent for a long time."

DESIGN FIRM: MTV NETWORKS, NEW YORK

CREATIVE DIRECTOR: BRENDA SCHAIT
DESIGNER: MATTHEW DUNTEMANN
ANIMATOR: MATTHEW DUNTEMANN
WRITERS: ADAM IDELSON, CHILDREN AGES 6-11
TYPEFACES: MITERRA, OCRA, PIONEER, PRAXIS
CLIENT: NOGGIN

"FREEFORM SUMMER POEMS" SPOTS

The "Freeform Summer Poems" enhances Noggin's image as a place where kids go to express themselves, to explore their creativity and to connect with other kids. The poems were designed to reach kids ages 6 to 11 and inspire them to express themselves freely and creatively through the convergence of television and the accompanying website.

JURORS' COMMENTS

"It's all over the map, but that's how kids are. I liked the irreverent use of different kinds of imagery—the pixel stuff, the strange typography, the home movie footage—which spoke of children and poetry." "It's beautifully confused. Fucked-up in a good way." "I think they appropriately represented the theme, which is innocence."

DESIGN FIRM: PLANET PROPAGANDA, MADISON, WISCONSIN

CREATIVE DIRECTOR: KEVIN WADE
DESIGNERS: BEN HIRBY, DAN IBARRA
ANIMATORS: BEN HIRBY, DAN IBARRA
WRITER: YOKO ONO
TYPEFACE: FRANKLIN GOTHIC
CLIENT: WALKER ARTS CENTER

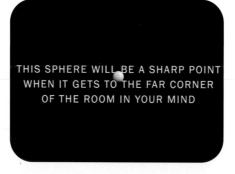

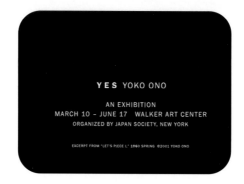

YOKO ONO "YES" TELEVISION ADS

Our goal with this campaign for The Walker Art Center was to announce Yoko Ono's upcoming show in a provocative manner.

We wanted to keep the television spots minimal and elegant, so the type and image are sparse and slow to reveal. We also chose written works that did not necessitate any spoken dialogue and created a soundtrack that was only the recorded sound of snow falling, a reference to one of Yoko's poems.

JURORS' COMMENTS

"Maybe the execution isn't stunning, but nonetheless, it makes me want to see the exhibition." "It raises the question of how do you advertise art. Do you interfere or do you remain neutral?"

07

design for film and television

DESIGN FIRM: IMAGINARY FORCES, LOS ANGELES

CREATIVE DIRECTOR: KYLE COOPER
ART DIRECTOR: AHMET AHMET
DESIGNER: AHMET AHMET
ANIMATORS: RICHARD BAILY, ASA HAMMOND, CHARLES KHOURY, BEN LOPEZ
EDITORS: CARSTEN BECKER, DANIELLE WHITE
TYPEFACE: TIC
CLIENT: COLUMBIA PICTURES

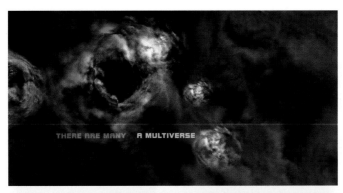

THE ONE OPENING SEQUENCE

The One opening sequence is a prologue that sets up the plot of the film. The various elements of this backstory involve concept of time, space and parallel universes. To visually interpret such ideas, we created a mood of heightened drama and expectation while exploring the context in which all of these concepts come into play.

JURORS' COMMENTS

"It's ridiculously beautiful eye candy that I can't resist. It's communicating a story through beautiful animations, where the cell splits apart, like a Bill Viola piece that becomes spiky." "The animation wasn't decorative, it was actually storytelling." "The typography, I felt, took away from the purity."

keira alexandra
MTV SPRING BREAK PACKAGING, 2000.

KEIRA ALEXANDRA, BROOKLYN, NEW YORK
KEIRA ALEXANDRA IS A DESIGNER IN NEW YORK CITY. BEFORE WORKING INDEPENDENTLY,
SHE WAS A DESIGNER AT MTV ON-AIR DESIGN, NUMBER SEVENTEEN, BUREAU AND M&CO.
HER WORK HAS RECEIVED AWARDS FROM AIGA AND THE AMERICAN CENTER FOR DESIGN AND
WAS INCLUDED IN THE ART DIRECTORS CLUB'S FIRST TWO "YOUNG GUNS" EXHIBITIONS.
SHE LIVES IN AN OLD FACTORY BUILDING IN BROOKLYN WITH 35 CORDED TELEPHONES
(ALL CONNECTED), HUNDREDS OF SMALL ITEMS PLACED IN 2 BY 2 INCH ZIPLOC BAGS, AND
NUMEROUS INCARNATIONS OF ARTIFICIAL NATURE—WITH A FOCUS ON DEER AND LOGS.
HER APARTMENT AND ITS CONTENTS HAVE BEEN FEATURED IN THE MAGAZINES *METROPOLIS* AND *BUST*.

hillman curtis

ADOBE STUDIO IDENTITY DESIGN, ADOBE SYSTEMS INC., 2001.

HILLMAN CURTIS, HILLMANCURTIS.COM INC., NEW YORK

HILLMAN CURTIS IS THE PRINCIPAL AND CHIEF CREATIVE OFFICER OF HILLMANCURTIS.COM, INC., A DIGITAL DESIGN FIRM IN NEW YORK CITY. HILLMAN'S FIRST BOOK, *FLASH WEB DESIGN* (NEW RIDERS, 2000) HAS SOLD MORE THAN 100,000 COPIES AND HAS BEEN TRANSLATED INTO 12 LANGUAGES. HIS LATEST BOOK IS *MTIV, PROCESS, INSPIRATION AND PRACTICE FOR THE NEW MEDIA DESIGNER* (NEW RIDERS, 2002). CURTIS IS CURRENTLY WORKING ON TWO SHORT DVD FILM PROJECTS.

mikon van gastel

SPHERE OPENING TITLE SEQUENCE, WARNER BROS., 1998.

MIKON VAN GASTEL, IMAGINARY FORCES, NEW YORK
MIKON VAN GASTEL IS CREATIVE DIRECTOR AND PARTNER AT IMAGINARY FORCES,
AN INTERNATIONALLY RECOGNIZED FILM AND DESIGN STUDIO BASED IN LOS ANGELES.
VAN GASTEL JOINED IMAGINARY FORCES IN 1997 AND RECENTLY OPENED ITS
NEW YORK OFFICE, WHERE HE CONTINUES TO WORK ON A WIDE RANGE OF PROJECTS,
INCLUDING FILM TITLES, TRAILERS, TELEVISION COMMERCIALS AND ENVIRONMENTAL
MEDIA. SOME OF HIS MORE RECENT WORKS INCLUDE THE DESIGN OF NON-LINEAR
CONTENT FOR A MULTIMEDIA SCREEN ON THE FAÇADE OF A SKYSCRAPER IN NEW YORK'S
TIMES SQUARE, A MULTI-SCREEN VIDEO INSTALLATION FOR THE WEXNER CENTER IN
COLUMBUS, OHIO, DEVELOPED IN COLLABORATION WITH GREG LYNN AND JEFFREY KIPNIS,
AND NIKE'S LATEST AIR JORDAN CAMPAIGN WITH DIRECTOR SPIKE LEE.

08

experience design

SELECTED WORKS DOCUMENT THE BEST IN
DIGITAL MEDIA AND LIVE EXPERIENCES DESIGNED TO INTERACTIVELY
INFORM, EDUCATE OR ENTERTAIN.

JURORS
RED BURNS, NYU TISCH SCHOOL FOR THE ARTS INTERACTIVE TELECOMMUNICATIONS PROGRAM, NEW YORK;
NATHAN SHEDROFF, SAN FRANCISCO; GONG SZETO, FORM+CONTENT, NEW YORK

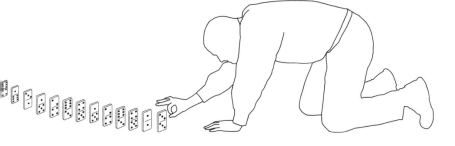

08

experience design

WRITTEN BY DAVID WOMACK

"Everything has a website," Red Burns sighed, leaning back in her chair and looking over stacks of printouts of sites for business schools, facial products, supermarket chains, golfing tours and asphalt manufacturers submitted to AIGA's experience design competition. The other jurors nodded, staring into their coffee cups. In 2001, new media became old news, which isn't necessarily bad news.

"We've seen a very rapid catch-up over the past year," Nathan Shedroff remarked, "very little here was poorly considered. Nearly every site was well executed." The flipside of the increase in the overall level of competence was that few designers or businesses were taking big risks. Gone were those spectacular failures—the dotcoms—and with them most attempts to push the boundaries of the web.

Even as the internet economy was in free fall and many web companies were facing cutbacks or closing, the standards for what constitutes a compelling experience continued to rise. "I'm looking for something that engages me emotionally, not just visually," Burns explained. Shedroff pointed to the continuing lack of integration between design skills and programming knowledge as a reason why most sites were still functioning primarily as brochures. Gong Szeto remained optimistic about the web's potential: "The interface can be a window into vast sets of data that the designer can make accessible in new and exciting ways."

Of the dozens of interfaces that the jurors considered only Morphosis.net[1] succeeded as both a data portal and a compelling experience. This site mimics a relational database, allowing users to browse details of the architecture firm's many projects while using visual elements to engage them. The jurors also selected Climbmeru.com,[2] a site based on a climbing expedition in the Himalayas. The site uses a linear narrative to orient the user while providing a rich array of supplemental maps, videos and audio clips that help users engage intellectually and emotionally with the expedition and the team.

The "Talking Tools" game,[3] a board game designed to help dysfunctional children discuss difficult issues, demonstrated that an effective experience need not be digital. One advantage of digital projects, however, is that they can be easier to judge. Scient's "Innovation Acceleration Lab: Workshop One,"[4] a workshop designed to »

PG 242
PG 246
PG 244
PG 245

promote communication and encourage creativity, forced the question of how effectively experiences could be judged in the confines of a competition. "We didn't go through the workshop!" Burns exclaimed. The other jurors pointed to the strength of the collateral, which includes manuals, a t-shirt and a pocket reminder of the *Fun*damentals [sic] of creativity. In both "Talking Tools" and the Scient workshop, it was not the experience itself that was evaluated, but the materials that structured and guided the experience.

The projects that seemed to best exemplify the sometimes-slippery category were those that combined digital and traditional media to make a personal connection with the user. The Evolutionary Continuity Interactive Project[5] by the American Museum of Natural History brings the human genome to a human scale using large interactive models. By manipulating the models, museum visitors can explore their own genetic makeup as well as their connection to all other life.

5
PG 241

It was Edwin Schlossberg Inc.'s project for the American Family Immigration History Center,[6] however, that showed how experiences could be extended across media and across generations. Based in the Ellis Island Immigration Museum, the Center includes interactive installations that explore the immigrant experience. Workstations on site provide multimedia tools and allow access to more than 3½ million pages of ships' logs listing people who passed through the island. The real genius of the project is that it allows each visitor to contribute personal recollections, stories and photographs to the database thereby enriching the experience for all visitors. The records and mementos are accessible through the website. "They can take something away that they can continue to develop. This is a perfect example of the potential of the web to enhance an experience," said Shedroff.

6
PG 248

In 2001, experience design was defined by creative applications of existing technology—from board games to databases—rather than by the rapid technological advances of the previous years. As one crash followed another, designers focused, either by choice or necessity, on doing smaller projects better. This didn't yield the kind of exploratory, big-budget projects that tend to do well in competitions, but it did yield a wealth of projects that were consistent and sustainable. Szeto summed up the ethos of 2001 saying, "It was a time to be safe." □

DESIGN FIRM: AMERICAN MUSEUM OF NATURAL HISTORY, NEW YORK

SENIOR MEDIA PRODUCER: GERALYN ABINADER
MEDIA MANAGER: FRANK RASOR
PRODUCER/ELECTRONIC INTERACTION DESIGNER: JOSEPH STEIN
GRAPHIC INTERFACE DESIGNERS: PATRICK BELL, RICHARD GUY
INSTALLATION DESIGNER: PHILLIP POND
PROGRAMMING: DIERDRE DIXON
FABRICATORS: KARL MATSUDA, SHOWMAN FABRICATORS INC.
CLIENT: AMERICAN MUSEUM OF NATURAL HISTORY

"EVOLUTIONARY CONTINUITY" INTERACTIVE STATION

Within the context of the exhibition "The Genomic Revolution," the American Museum of Natural History wished to show museum visitors the surprisingly large number of genes they share with other organisms.

At the interactive station "Evolutionary Continuity," the visitor selects one of ten backlit images of different organisms. This image is shown on a large plasma screen together with live video of the visitor. A display then shows that, to take one example, humans and mice share 90 percent of their genes.

The game format of this interactive encourages visitors to participate and understand their involvement in this controversial field.

JURORS' COMMENTS

"A valiant effort to address a complex subject. This project brings the human genome to a human scale."

08

experience design

DESIGN FIRM: GARDEN DIGITAL, LOS ANGELES

DESIGNERS: PETER BLESZYNSKI, ROBYN SAMBO
TYPEFACES: ÉMIGRÉ LO-RES 12, MINIML HOOGE 05_54, MINIML KROEGER 05_53, MINIML
KROEGER 05_55, MINIML STANDARD 07_54
CLIENT: MORPHOSIS ARCHITECTS

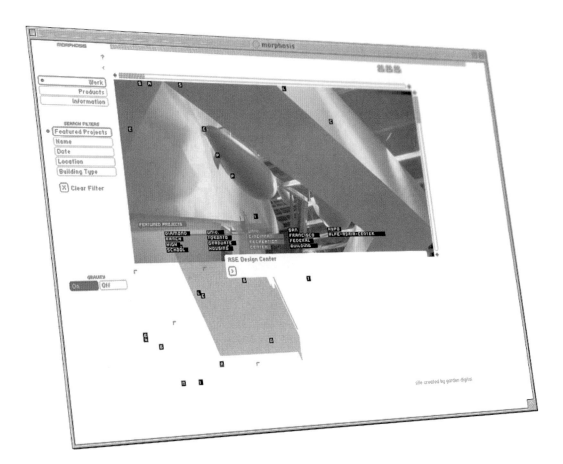

MORPHOSIS WEBSITE

Morphosis.net is an online database of buildings and projects by
Morphosis Architects. An infinite number of compositions is generated
by the layering of everyday website elements with a life-like
simulation of the database. Each project is represented by a particle
that operates as a discrete personality within this dynamic ecology.
A vector path traces the user's browsing history, mapping the mechanics
of their interactions. The reductive and elementary appearance of the
interface is reminiscent of an earlier aesthetic, reassuring the user as
they navigate the unfamiliar.

JURORS' COMMENTS

"This site has all the right ideas—it explores navigation, database
principles and automation in new and interesting ways."

08
experience design

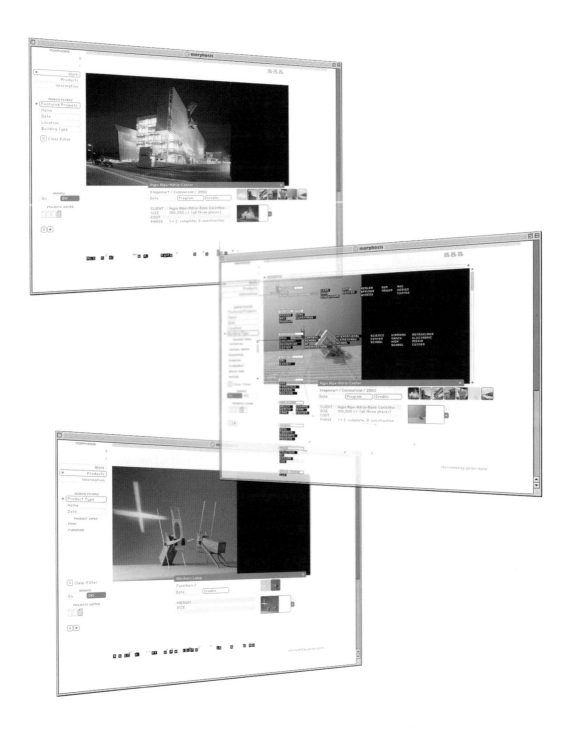

08

experience design

DESIGN FIRM: SPUNK STUDIO, MINNEAPOLIS

CREATIVE DIRECTOR: JEFF JOHNSON
DESIGNERS: JIM ANDERSON, ANGEE HAGEN, JEFF JOHNSON, JASON WALZER
ILLUSTRATORS: JIM ANDERSON, JEFF JOHNSON
WRITERS: JIM ANDERSON, JEFF JOHNSON
TYPEFACE: VAG ROUNDED
CLIENT: CHILDSWORK/CHILDSPLAY

"TALKING TOOLS" GAME

We created, illustrated, tested, funded, re-tested and delivered this product ourselves. It was made with the common studio goal of creating a cost-effective book of therapeutic board games for caregivers to play with "at-risk" kids.

Partnering with certified school psychologist, Jim Anderson, we identified hard issues, such as divorce, death, self-image and conflict-resolution, that had to be presented in a safe, role-playing environment. The solution had to be inexpensive to produce to bring the cost per unit down to a teacher-friendly level. Careful testing, critique and directed redesign from industry experts and kids brought "Talking Tools" to a higher level.

JURORS' COMMENTS

"I admire the fact that this game addresses a very difficult audience—dysfunctional children—and encourages communication. It is also engaging, portable and inexpensive."

DESIGN FIRM: UNDERSTANDING LAB, NEW YORK

DESIGNERS: ELIZABETH PASTOR, GK VANPATTER
FACILITATORS: DR. MIN BASADUR, TONY FROSS, LISA NOBLE, ELIZABETH PASTOR,
GK VANPATTER, CHARLES WARREN
WRITERS: DR. MIN BASADUR, ELIZABETH PASTOR, GK VANPATTER
TYPEFACE: SS THESIS SANS
CLIENT: SCIENT CORPORATION

SCIENT'S "INNOVATION ACCELERATION LAB: WORKSHOPONE"

WorkshopONE was a one-day innovation skill-building workshop delivered to more than 2,000 Scient employees and diverse client teams in the firm's Innovation Acceleration Labs located in New York and San Francisco. It was intended to help build an inclusive culture of innovation across the organization.

JURORS' COMMENTS

"The Lab teaches the principles of interaction and creativity, which is always valuable." "It brings up issues about nature of experience, which can be used either to inspire or manipulate, or both."

08

experience design

DESIGN FIRM: TEXTURE MEDIA, DENVER

CREATIVE DIRECTORS: ANDREW DAVISON, BRENDAN KIERNAN
DESIGNERS: KAMERON KERGER, MATT LUDWIG
ANIMATOR: MAX CHADWICK
PRODUCERS: JEN NORTHWAY, FRANK PICKELL
SOUND DESIGNER: FRANK PICKELL
WRITERS: BRENDAN KIERNAN, PETE TAKEDA
TYPEFACE: ARIAL
CLIENTS: MARMOT MOUNTAIN LTD., W.L. GORE & ASSOCIATES, *CLIMBING* MAGAZINE

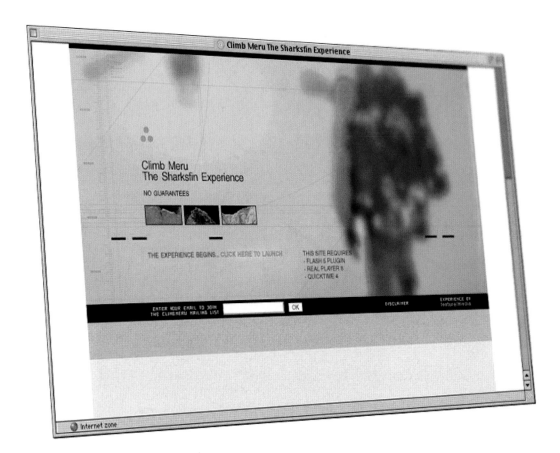

CLIMB MERU: AN INTEGRATED BRAND EXPERIENCE WEBSITE

The client's goal was to communicate the authenticity of their brand
to a core group of influencers. When designing and producing this
website, we needed to consider several factors: an episodic timeline,
the remote location of the event and the requirement to design for the
needs of multiple platforms. Our solution was the timed release of
various media artifacts such as CD-ROMs, interactive kiosks, stickers,
print ads, feature articles, a documentary film, tradeshow booth imagery
and multimedia presentations.

JURORS' COMMENTS

"I like the narrative, which provides for continuity and orients
the user. The experience is really enhanced by the maps and supplements,
which the user can explore without getting lost."

08

experience design

DESIGN FIRM: ESI DESIGN, NEW YORK

PRINCIPAL DESIGNER: EDWIN SCHLOSSBERG
DESIGNERS: JOHN BRANIGAN, MATTHEW MOORE, EDWIN SCHLOSSBERG
INTERACTIVE DESIGNERS: GIDEON D'ARCANGELO, ANGELA GREENE
PRODUCTION MANAGERS: MARK CORRAL, DEAN MARKOSIAN
PROJECT MANAGERS: JAN BURDICK, STACEY LISHERON
WRITER/RESEARCHER: CLAY GISH
TYPEFACE: NEW CENTURY SCHOOLBOOK (CUSTOMIZED)

AMERICAN FAMILY IMMIGRATION HISTORY CENTER COMPUTER-BASED ACTIVITIES

This series of computer-based activities allows visitors to the American Family Immigration History Center to learn about their family history and the history of American immigration. In 2 key activities, visitors can search over 20 million records to find information about family members who immigrated through Ellis Island and create multimedia Family History Scrapbooks that are then added to the Ellis Island Archives. Our primary challenge for this project was creating activities that can be easily accessed and navigated both online and at the center.

JURORS' COMMENTS

"This project is truly exceptional. It engages its audience on a physical and emotional level. It allows people to contribute something valuable and then take the experience with them and continue to develop it."

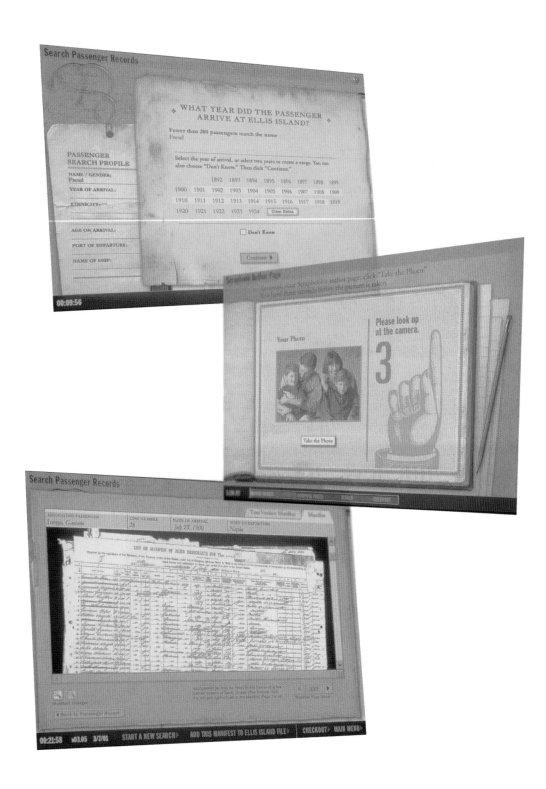

08
experience design
juror

red burns

"CHAOS: A FANTASY ADVENTURE GAME," HARPERCOLLINS PUBLISHERS, 1995.

RED BURNS, NYU TISCH SCHOOL FOR THE ARTS INTERACTIVE TELECOMMUNICATIONS PROGRAM, NEW YORK
RED BURNS IS CHAIR OF THE INTERACTIVE TELECOMMUNICATIONS PROGRAM AT THE
TISCH SCHOOL OF THE ARTS, AT NEW YORK UNIVERSITY. DURING THE 1970s AND 1980s,
SHE DESIGNED AND DIRECTED A SERIES OF TELECOMMUNICATIONS PROJECTS,
INCLUDING TWO-WAY TELEVISION FOR AND BY SENIOR CITIZENS, TELECOMMUNICATIONS
APPLICATIONS TO SERVE THE DEVELOPMENTALLY DISABLED AND ONE OF
THE FIRST FIELD TRIALS OF TELETEXT CORRECT AT WETA IN THE UNITED STATES.
THIS INNOVATIVE RESEARCH LED TO THE CREATION OF THE INTERACTIVE
TELECOMMUNICATIONS PROGRAM AT NYU IN 1979. HER OTHER PROJECTS INCLUDE A
CD-ROM ON CHAOS THEORY FOR HARPERCOLLINS, AND "THE ELECTRONIC NEIGHBORHOOD,"
AN INTERACTIVE CABLE/TELEPHONE EXPERIMENT FUNDED BY NYNEX AND VIACOM.
BURNS IS THE PRINCIPAL INVESTIGATOR OF THREE ON-GOING RESEARCH PROGRAMS FUNDED
BY GRANTS FROM INTERVAL, INTEL AND MICROSOFT.

08
experience design
juror

nathan shedroff

1

HERMAN MILLER RED WEBSITE, HERMAN MILLER, 2001.
FURNITURE MATRIX FOR THE HERMAN MILLER RED WEBSITE INFORMATION DESIGN, 2001.

2

NATHAN SHEDROFF'S WORLD WEBSITE, NATHAN SHEDROFF, 2001–PRESENT.

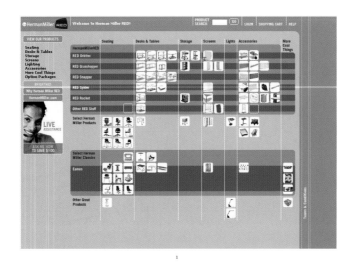

1

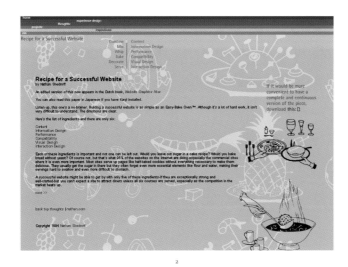

2

NATHAN SHEDROFF, SAN FRANCISCO

NATHAN SHEDROFF HAS BEEN AN EXPERIENCE DESIGNER FOR 13 YEARS. HE DEVELOPS
EXPERIENCE AND BRAND STRATEGIES FOR COMPANIES INCLUDING HERMAN MILLER RED,
AZURE NUTRITCUETICALS, NIKE AND BANK OF AMERICA AND WORKS IN VARIOUS MEDIA,
INCLUDING PRINT, DIGITAL, ONLINE AND PRODUCT DESIGN. HE CO-FOUNDED
VIVID STUDIOS—A DECADE-OLD COMPANY, ONE OF THE PIONEERS OF INTERACTIVE MEDIA—
AND WORKED WITH RICHARD SAUL WURMAN AT UNDERSTANDING BUSINESS.
HE IS ON THE STEERING COMMITTEE FOR AIGA EXPERIENCE DESIGN AND IS A PROGRAM
CONSULTANT FOR AIGA MIAMI'S "INTERACTION ONLY CONFERENCE." HIS BOOK
EXPERIENCE DESIGN (NEW RIDERS, 2001) EXPLORES COMMON CHARACTERISTICS IN ALL
MEDIA THAT MAKE EXPERIENCES SUCCESSFUL, AND HIS WEBSITE, WWW.NATHAN.COM/ED,
PROVIDES RESOURCES ON EXPERIENCE DESIGN.

gong szeto

U.S. PATENT 6,282,713: METHOD AND APPARATUS FOR PROVIDING
ON-DEMAND ELECTRONIC ADVERTISING, 2001.

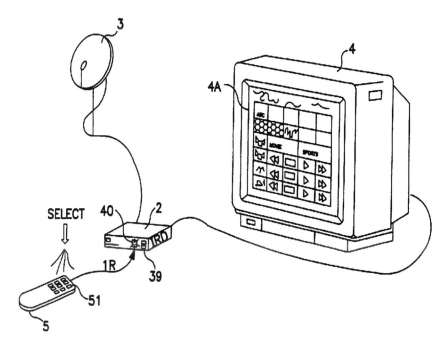

U.S. Patent   Aug. 28, 2001   Sheet 2 of 11   **US 6,282,713 B1**

FIG. 2

GONG SZETO, FORM+CONTENT, NEW YORK

GONG SZETO IS AN AWARD-WINNING DESIGN PRACTITIONER AND STRATEGIST BASED IN
NEW YORK CITY. HE HAS STUDIED ARCHITECTURE AND COMPUTER SCIENCE AT THE
UNIVERSITY OF TEXAS AT AUSTIN AND MIT, AND HAS OWNED AND WORKED FOR BOTH SMALL
AND LARGE DESIGN FIRMS IN HIS 12-YEAR DESIGN CAREER. SZETO IS CURRENTLY
THE EDITOR OF *GAIN: AIGA JOURNAL OF DESIGN FOR THE NEXT ECONOMY*, AIGA'S NEW ONLINE
PUBLICATION ON BUSINESS AND DESIGN, AND SERVES ON THE BOARD OF DIRECTORS
FOR AIGA AND THE VAN ALEN INSTITUTE FOR PUBLIC ARCHITECTURE. HE IS A PARTNER OF
SZETO PARTNERS VENTURES, A NEW PRODUCT DEVELOPER AND INCUBATOR,
FOUNDED WITH HIS BROTHER NAM, AND WAS RECENTLY AWARDED HIS FIRST U.S. PATENT
IN INTERACTIVE TELEVISION, WORK HE DID WITH SONY CORPORATION.

09

promotional design and advertising

SELECTIONS DEMONSTRATE EXCELLENCE IN WORK DESIGNED
TO INTRODUCE, SELL OR PROMOTE PRODUCTS, IDEAS OR EVENTS.

JURORS
JOHN BIELENBERG, C2, BELFAST, MAINE;
JOHN WATERS, WATERSDESIGN, NEW YORK; ALLISON MUENCH WILLIAMS, DESIGN: M/W, NEW YORK

09
promotional design and advertising
WRITTEN BY ANDREA CODRINGTON

Call it the year of the little book. Everywhere jurors
looked in AIGA's promotional design and advertising
competition, there was another smartly conceived and
tightly executed miniature publication. Whether a thick
paperback prospectus for a Midwestern design school,[1]
a *McSweeney's*-inspired Thanksgiving party invitation[2] or a
covetable gift book from a photographer, promotional design
seems to have taken a distinctly literary turn in 2001.

PG 270

PG 263

"Designers have really stepped up to the plate in making
nice things in a very economically reductive time,"
commended Allison Muench Williams of this year's selections.
None of last year's national crises appears to have
diminished the ability of designers to create smart,
effective communications for promotional purposes. Unlike
in years past, there was no dominant aesthetic that
emerged in the entries, rather an attitude of economy
and, in most cases, extremely clever writing.

The catalogue for an exhibition called "Fact Show,"[3] for
instance, is comprised almost entirely of text laid out
in blocky expanses. Created with the intention of showing
"artists around the globe grappling with 21st-century
insecurity," the catalogue's text is a continuous list of
odd facts. ("In Chile, the favorite topping for pizza is
mussels and clams.") "The multiple levels of the project
are really good," said Williams. "It's more than just a
record of the show." An emphasis on words continues in a
small red booklet called *Typathology*,[4] which was created
as a promotion for a small company that specializes in
editorial proofreading. An alphabetical listing of the
most amusing spelling mistakes the company has encountered
(beginning with "advange"), the book is beautifully
typeset on French-folded cream paper and uses blown-up
proofreading marks as recurring decorative elements.

PG 276[3]

PG 269[4]

Clever text and lists of words also made an appearance in
the registration brochure for AIGA's "Voice" conference,[5]
which turned out to be postponed because of travel issues
associated with the events of September 11. "People had
strong opinions about this in my studio," remembered John
Waters of the publication, which features page after page of
Andreas Gursky-reminiscent photographs of shopping aisles. »

PG 278[5]

57

promotional design and advertising

"It's a really refreshing take on the theme of voice," said Williams, who believed that the visual and verbal rhetoric of design activism has grown tired and hackneyed in recent years. Accompanying the images are facts about first-world consumption; flanking the contents in the front and back of the brochure are lists of products. The jurors admitted to being a little queasy about the overwhelmingly pink toy aisle—which was replicated in a series of all-pink pages that listed conference speakers and sponsors—and the general tenor of consumer hysteria. "It documents the visual environment we live in," said Bielenberg, "which is always a perverse attraction."

Even though the cerebral approach may have been a recurrent theme this year, there was plenty of visceral pleasure as well. The most lust-inducing project of the day was Rigsby Design's small promotion for the Texas-based photographer Terry Vine,[6] a boxed and tissue-papered book made of letter-pressed white flock cover and 25 exquisite black-and-white portraits of Mexican people of all walks of life. "It is just obsessively crafted," admired Bielenberg of the book. "It's a design fetish object, but in the best way. The typography is beautiful and there's an innovative use of materials." The jurors couldn't help responding sensually to such a project, and each spent time going through the book in an expressly physical manner: petting the cover, going over the letter-pressed type with fingertips, delicately separating tissue paper from the top-stitched book.

There was one exception to the bookishness of this year's selections: a series of commercials created for the design-conscious budget chain Target.[7] Closer in spirit to independent film shorts than previous commercials that feature the store's red bull's-eye logotype, this series continues to expand the chain's mastery of visual branding. "They've re-defined the use of graphics on television," noted Bielenberg on the spots, which follow the exploits of a young guitarist's innovative use of toilet paper and an aging lounge act called Marty and Elayne. "I can't think of another instance where graphic design is so obvious, even in live-action stuff." □

6
PG 266

7
PG 264

—

DESIGN FIRM: DOYLE PARTNERS, NEW YORK

DESIGNER: STEPHEN DOYLE
PHOTOGRAPHER: VICTOR SCHRAGER
TYPEFACE: SABON
PRINTER: HERITAGE PRESS
PAPER: MOHAWK SUPERFINE ULTRAWHITE 80 LB. TEXT
CLIENT: ART DIRECTORS CLUB

ADC PAPER EXPO 2001 POSTER

This poster was conceived to announce a paper expo at the Art Directors Club. In these days of "virtuality," this poster celebrates the tactile qualities of paper. Featuring a photograph of a sheet of paper folded into eighths, the poster itself is folded into ninths. The resulting object is an ever-changing study of the interaction of light and paper, and paper's remarkable ability to carry a fold—both real and reproduced.

DESIGN FIRM: NESNADNY + SCHWARTZ, CLEVELAND

CREATIVE DIRECTORS: MICHELLE MOEHLER, JOYCE NESNADNY, MARK SCHWARTZ
DESIGNERS: JENNIFER CRAWFORD, MICHELLE MOEHLER, JOYCE NESNADNY
PHOTOGRAPHER: ROBERT A. MULLER
WRITERS: JULIE FOGEL, STACY SIMS
TYPEFACES: CENTURY SCHOOLBOOK, TRADE GOTHIC
PRINTER: FORTRAN PRINTING
PAPER: SMART CARNIVAL, SMART KROMEKOTE, SMART KNIGHTKOTE
CLIENT: CLEVELAND INSTITUTE OF ART

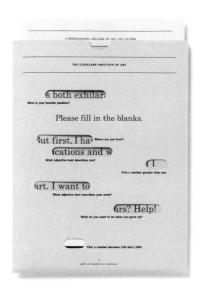

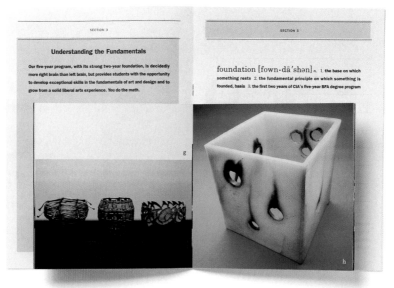

CLEVELAND INSTITUTE OF ART 2001 DIRECT MAIL

The direct mail piece is the cornerstone of the Cleveland Institute of Art's recruiting efforts. The Institute wanted the package to challenge the audience of high school students and set a new standard for college recruiting materials. The result is a whimsical parody of a standardized test—something that all students can identify with. The piece has word problems set in large type and commonly used symbols to guide the reader. The request to "fill in the blanks" on the outside sleeve encourages students to personalize their own copies. The piece has been extremely popular at college fairs.

JURORS' COMMENTS

"It's almost childlike." "It's really clever. I feel like they slotted the content in. It's pretty smart without being in your face."

DESIGN FIRM: RESERVOIR, SAN FRANCISCO

DESIGNER: DAVID SALANITRO
STOCK: GETTY ONE
WRITER: DAVID SALANITRO
TYPEFACE: MINION
PRINTER: OSCAR PRINTING
PAPER: MEAD SIGNATURE DULL
CLIENT: DAVID SALANITRO

HOLIDAY PARTY™ INVITATION

Reservoir conceived, wrote and designed this invitation for its sixth annual Holiday Party™. It should be noted that in keeping with SEC requirements, no detail is left unreported or unchecked. Every detail is carefully considered, from explicit instructions for proxy voting to information on the whereabouts of absent (and fictitious) shareholder, Eric Estrada. Dialing Mr. Estrada's last-known phone number will put you in touch with a friendly receptionist at the Holiday Inn in Torrance, California (where Mr. Estrada purportedly once lived).

JURORS' COMMENTS

"It's so simple. It's a *McSweeney's* kind of thing." "It gets my copywriting award."

DESIGN FIRM: PETERSON MILLA HOOKS, MINNEAPOLIS

CREATIVE DIRECTOR: DAVE PETERSON
ART DIRECTOR: DAVID RICHARDSON
COPYWRITER: NATE MORLEY
AGENCY PRODUCER: GARY TASSONE
ACCOUNT SUPERVISOR: LISA NELSON
DIRECTOR: GREGORY MAYA, THE ARTISTS COMPANY
DIRECTOR OF PHOTOGRAPHY: TIM IVES
PRODUCTION COMPANY: THE ARTISTS COMPANY
EDITOR: BRETT ASTOR, FISCHER EDIT
MUSIC: MARTY & ELAYNE, COVERING "I WILL SURVIVE"
MUSIC PRODUCTION: WOW AND FLUTTER
CLIENT: TARGET STORES

"MARTY & ELAYNE" TELEVISION ADVERTISEMENT

In order to help Target highlight its sponsorship of the hit series "Survivor," we created a spot starring Marty and Elayne, the legendary lounge duo that has drawn hipsters to LA's Dresden Room for 20 years. Set on a campy red background, the spot features Marty and Elayne singing their unique version of the classic song, "I Will Survive." A title card saying "You Don't Need A Million Dollars to Survive" was used to make the Target/"Survivor" connection.

JURORS' COMMENTS

"I think it's about how this series works together in a certain sense." "They've done a masterful job of hooking content, product and coolness to their Target logo."

09
promotional design and advertising

DESIGN FIRM: KIRSHENBAUM, BOND AND PARTNERS, MINNEAPOLIS

EXECUTIVE CREATIVE DIRECTOR: ROB FEAKINS
CREATIVE DIRECTORS: UCEF HANJANI, KIRSHENBAUM, BOND AND PARTNERS;
ERIC ERICKSON, TARGET
ART DIRECTORS: AARON ALDEN, KIRSHENBAUM, BOND AND PARTNERS;
JOHN MAYHEW, TARGET
DIRECTOR: DOUG NICHOL
DIRECTOR OF PHOTOGRAPHY: JOE ZIZZO
EDITOR: ANDRE BETZ, BUG
SOUND DESIGNERS: ASCHE & SPENCER, SOUND LOUNGE, TOMANDANDY
COPYEDITOR: DAVID BLACK
AGENCY PRODUCER: BETSY SCHOENFELD
PRODUCTION COMPANY: PARTIZAN
POST EFFECTS: NICE SHOES
EFFECTS: SPONTANEOUS COMBUSTION
TARGET ART BUYER: DENISE WEBER
CLIENT: TARGET STORES

"GUITAR KID" TELEVISION ADVERTISEMENT

The Target brand promise is "Expect More. Pay Less." We wanted to create a campaign that emphasized the "pay less" side of this promise in an upscale, sophisticated way. The solution was to team with vendor partners to create scenarios featuring huge quantities of product being used in an unusual, madcap way. In this spot, we needed to show a lot of product and prominently feature the Charmin logo. In addition, we developed a simple set that worked well with Charmin colors and packaging. The result was a spot that was quirky, entertaining and stimulated an increase in sales of the featured product.

JURORS' COMMENTS

"They've redefined the use of graphics on television."

265

promotional design and advertising

DESIGN FIRM: RIGSBY DESIGN, HOUSTON

CREATIVE DIRECTOR: LANA RIGSBY
DESIGNERS: LANA RIGSBY, PAMELA ZUCCKER
PHOTOGRAPHER: TERRY VINE
TRANSLATIONS: RAUL PAVÓN
WRITER: LANA RIGSBY
TYPEFACES: CLARENDON, SCALA, TRADE GOTHIC
PRINTER: H. MACDONALD PRINTING | BLANCHETTE PRESS
PAPER: FOX RIVER STARWHITE VICKSBURG ARCHIVA 80 LB. TEXT
TRIM SIZE: 7 3/4 X 6 BOOK IN 8 1/8 X 6 3/8 BOX
PAGES: 56; SIDE-SEWN BOOK WITH DEBOSSED TISSUE COVER;
INSERTED INTO CUSTOM CLAMSHELL BOX
CLIENT: TERRY VINE PHOTOGRAPHY

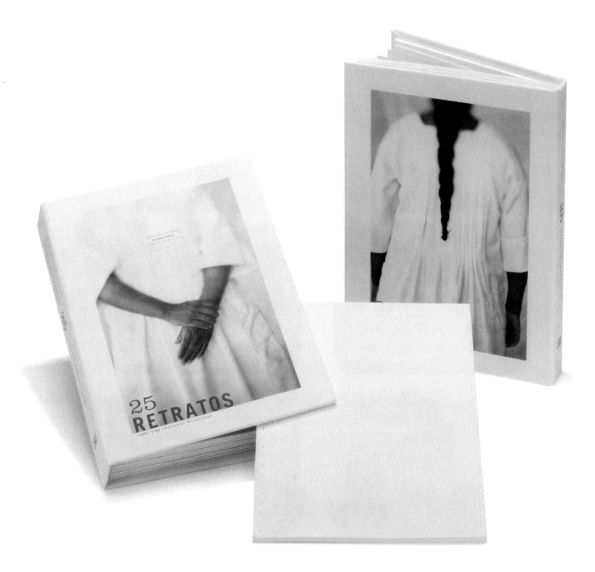

25 RETRATOS: TERRY VINE IMÁGENES MEXICANAS BOOK

This book is photographer Terry Vine's portrait of the central-Mexican village of San Miguel de Allende. The intimate images offer a peek at Mexican festivals, holy days and "diversiones" seldom seen by outsiders—from cockfights to quinciñaeras to crucifixions.

JURORS' COMMENTS

"It's obsessively well-crafted." "It's a design fetish object, but in a good way. The typography is beautiful. For all the bells and whistles it has, it's not over the top. There's innovative material. It's an elegant reflection of the culture."

09
promotional design and advertising

09
promotional design and advertising

DESIGN FIRM: MINNEAPOLIS COLLEGE OF ART AND DESIGN, MINNEAPOLIS

CREATIVE DIRECTOR: PAMELA ARNOLD
DESIGNER: CHAD KLOEPFER
PHOTOGRAPHERS: RHONDA ANDERSON, STEPHANIE KAYS, DANIEL MILLER,
MICHELLE OTT, MATT REZAK, SARAH WERT
ILLUSTRATOR: PETER LOCHNER
WRITERS: PAMELA ARNOLD, ARLENE BIRT, GWEN LUNSKI, JULYNA WEBB, SARAH WERT
TYPEFACES: AACHEN, BLACK FOREST, HELVETICA, HELVETICA NEUE, PIONEER,
Y.A.H. BY CHAD KLOEPFER
PRINTER: COOPERATIVE PRINTING
PAPER: DOMTAR WINDSOR OFFSET TEXT, DOMTAR CORNWALL LEATHER COVER
CLIENT: MINNEAPOLIS COLLEGE OF ART AND DESIGN

YOU ARE HERE BOOKLET

You Are Here is a recruiting tool for the Minneapolis College of Art and Design. The target audience is students already admitted to MCAD who are considering transferring to another competing art and design college because the location—Minneapolis—is either too urban or too bucolic. The solution appeals to art and design students' narcissism by presenting them as hip, intelligent and worldly. The photography is both aloof and captivating; juxtaposing images convey expected stereotypes with unexpected truths about this Midwestern city.

The book was designed and produced entirely by students at MCAD. Under the direction of Pam Arnold, director of MCAD's in-house studio program, MCAD DesignWorks, the book and DVD were a commissioned project of the provost, Andrea Nasset.

DESIGN FIRM: MIRES, SAN DIEGO

CREATIVE DIRECTOR: JOHN BALL
DESIGNER: JOY CATHEY PRICE
ILLUSTRATOR: JOY CATHEY PRICE
WRITER: ERIC LA BRECQUE
TYPEFACE: ITC GOLDEN COCKEREL
PRINTER: BORDEAUX PRINTERS
PAPER: CLASSIC CREST NATURAL WHITE 70 LB. TEXT, PEGASUS BLACK 100 LB. COVER
CLIENT: ERIC LA BRECQUE

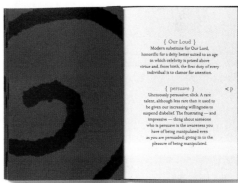

TYPATHOLOGY BOOKLET

Writer Eric La Brecque asked us to design a promotion celebrating the process—and sometimes-humorous consequences—of working with type and words. He had compiled a list of common typographic errors and wrote interpretive definitions for the resulting newly formed words. This content suggested the format of a dictionary and the use of typographers' marks as illustrative elements. Given that the book would be sent to clients and colleagues as a holiday greeting, Eric requested that the piece be small, precious and gift-like. We delivered a final product that had a tactile quality and allowed the subtle humor of the content to shine.

DESIGN FIRM: STUDIO D DESIGN, MINNEAPOLIS

DESIGNER: LAURIE DeMARTINO
PHOTOGRAPHERS: GENE PITTMAN, RIK SFERRA, DEAN WILSON
WRITER: ANASTASIA FAUNCE
TYPEFACES: CLARENDON, NEWS GOTHIC
PRINTER: RIPON PRINTING
PAPER: OFFSET 70 LB. TEXT, NEWSPRINT 5PT. AND 18 PT.
CLIENT: MINNEAPOLIS COLLEGE OF ART AND DESIGN

MINNEAPOLIS COLLEGE OF ART AND DESIGN RECRUITMENT CATALOGUE

When the recruitment catalogue for the Minneapolis College of Art and Design was designed, the goal was to make it hip enough to spark the interest of its student audience, yet structured and easily navigable enough to gain credibility in the eyes of their parents.

By creating a catalogue that doubles as a sketchbook—with dual front covers—we hoped to encourage potential recruits to keep the catalogue and use it to project their own work onto its pages.

The overall size, printing process and utilitarian design approach were significantly influenced by the production budget. Printed open web offset—a cost-effective, industrial printing method—on two different stocks, the catalogue was then drilled top and bottom for placement of a rubber band closure to use as bookmark.

09

promotional design and advertising

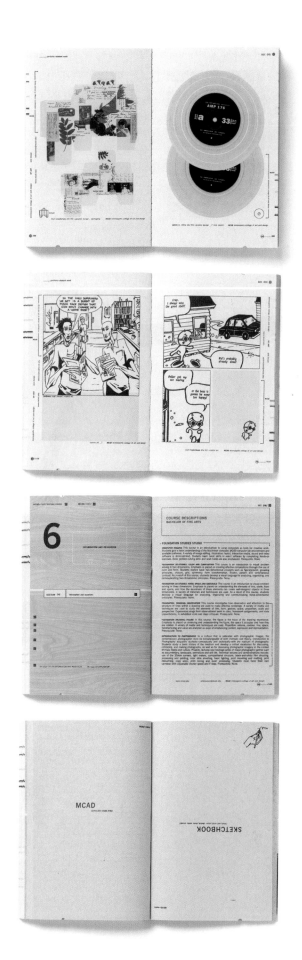

DESIGN FIRM: SAGMEISTER, INC., NEW YORK

CREATIVE DIRECTOR: STEFAN SAGMEISTER
DESIGNER: MATTHIAS ERNSTBERGER
ILLUSTRATOR: MATTHIAS ERNSTBERGER
TYPEFACE: ERNSTBERGER
PRINTER: MATTHIAS ERNSTBERGER
PAPER: VINTAGE ALBUM COVERS
CLIENT: CLASS OF '81, BORG SCHOREN, AUSTRIA

When asked to design the invitation for my "Class of '81" high school reunion, we decided to overprint different vintage record albums, all published in 1981. It took our intern a good while to find enough albums from that year in vintage record stores and it took our designer Matthias some time to silk-screen them all.

JURORS' COMMENTS

"It's a smart idea. And music was so evocative of my time in college. The idea of it being a record from that time is smart. And the graphics works really well as a screen over many different albums."

09
promotional design and advertising

DESIGN FIRM: VSA PARTNERS, CHICAGO

CREATIVE DIRECTOR: DANA ARNETT
DESIGNER: HANS SEEGER
PHOTOGRAPHER: FRANCOIS ROBERT
TYPEFACE: HELVETICA NEUE
PRINTER: WILLIAMSON PRINTING
PAPER: FOX RIVER STARWHITE 80 LB. TEXT
CLIENTS: AIGA, DFW

FRONT

BACK

SOME CLEARLY FOCUSED THOUGHTS AND FILMS BY DANA ARNETT POSTER

The purpose of this communication was to promote a Dana Arnett lecture at AIGA's Dallas chapter. We wanted to reveal some of the comedy hidden in our work and our profession. As the poster was entirely blurred, the viewer had to get really close to the piece to read it. We also had to convince the printers not to focus the artwork as they were naturally afraid of delivering a flawed job.

JURORS' COMMENTS

"I like how it functions at a poster level and at a microscopic level. There's an ephemerality that seems so delicate." "There's a clear idea as a poster and the timing is right. It's also very Dana." "There's an absolute intrigue that accompanies the blurred image."

DESIGN FIRM: VSA PARTNERS, CHICAGO

CREATIVE DIRECTOR: JAMIE KOVAL
DESIGNERS: NICHOLE DILLON, JAMIE KOVAL, PRINT; TIM GUY, DAVE RITTER, WEB
PHOTOGRAPHERS: HOWARD BJORNSON, PAUL ELLEDGE, KIPLING SWEHLA
ILLUSTRATOR: VSA PARTNERS, INC.
WRITER: ANDY BLANKENBURG
TYPEFACE: HELVETICA
PRINTER: BRUCE OFFSET, A WALLACE COMPANY
PAPER: MEAD SIGNATURE DULL TEXT AND COVER
CLIENT: MEAD COATED PAPERS

"MEAD SHOW" 2001 COLLATERAL (PRINT AND WEBSITE)

Legacy Mead Paper—now MeadWestvaco Papers Group—asked VSA Partners
to provide the concept for both the printed and online materials for
the 45th annual "Mead Show." Our challenge was twofold: communicate
the fact that the show had evolved—with the addition of a new
corporate brochure category—as well as create a program that
positions Mead top of mind with their target audience (designers,
corporations, printers and merchants). We added additional content,
imagery and humor to the program.

JURORS' COMMENTS

"That tongue-in-cheek dead-white-male thing works. It's very whimsical.
I almost like the website more, but it's complementary with the print."

09

promotional design and advertising

DESIGN FIRM: WALL-TO-WALL STUDIOS, INC., PITTSBURGH, PENNSYLVANIA

CREATIVE DIRECTORS: JAMES NESBITT, BERNARD UY
DESIGNER: BRETT YASKO
WRITERS: VICKY CLARK, DAVID MADDEN, BRETT YASKO
TYPEFACE: HELVETICA
PRINTER: SCHIFF PRINTING
PAPER: WEYERHAEUSER COUGAR OPAQUE 100 LB. TEXT
CLIENT: VICKY CLARK, PITTSBURGH CENTER FOR THE ARTS

"THE FACT SHOW" CATALOGUE

We took facts from every source imaginable including the internet, books, newspapers and my grandmother.

We worked with the printer to make the format as big and with as many pages as possible within the tight budget. We used the cheapest paper we could find and printed half of it on a 4-color press and half on a 2-color press. The best part of the whole project was having various people come up to me weeks later and dispute different facts throughout the book. I still can't believe I wasn't the only one who read them all.

JURORS' COMMENTS

"The multi-level nature of the project is really good. It's more than a record of the show—it gives me more information and background."

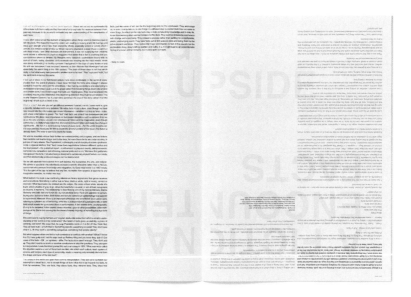

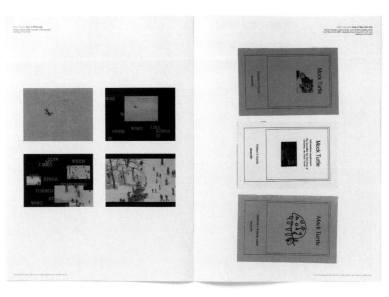

DESIGN FIRM: RESERVOIR, SAN FRANCISCO

CREATIVE DIRECTOR: DAVID SALANITRO
DESIGNERS: TED BLUEY, DAVID SALANITRO
PHOTOGRAPHER: LENNY GONZALES
WRITERS: ANDREA CODRINGTON, DAVID SALANITRO,
LAUREL SAVILLE, ALICE TWEMLOW
TYPEFACE: FRANKLIN GOTHIC
PRINTER: HENNEGAN
PAPER: MOHAWK SUPERFINE ULTRAWHITE 100 LB. TEXT AND COVER
CLIENT: AIGA

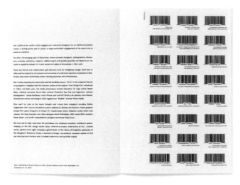

"VOICE: AIGA NATIONAL DESIGN CONFERENCE" REGISTRATION BROCHURE

When we were asked by "Voice" creative director Sean Adams to design
the registration brochure for AIGA's National Design Conference, we took
the premise that "design pervades every aspect of our society, our
culture and our individual lives." We came up with a list of 1,952
objects and concepts that suggest the scope of design's reach and wrote
statistical captions about a further 50 of them to accompany Lenny
Gonzalez's deadpan photographs of supermarket aisles.

JURORS' COMMENTS

"I remember getting it, and spent a lot of time with it. It talked about
'Voice' in a timeless fashion." "It documents the visual environment we
live in, which is always a perverse attraction."

09
promotional design and advertising

DESIGN FIRM: CONCRETE DESIGN COMMUNICATIONS INC., TORONTO

CREATIVE DIRECTORS: DITI KATONA, JOHN PYLYPCZAK
DESIGNER: MELISSA AGOSTINO
WRITER: JOHN PYLYPCZAK
TYPEFACE: TRADE GOTHIC
PRINTER: BOWNE
PAPER: MONADNOCK DULCET 80 LB. TEXT, UV/ULTRA 11 RADIANT WHITE 28 LB.,
ESKA BOARD 80 PT.
CLIENT: UNISOURCE

"FPO 21ST ANNUAL UNISOURCE LITHO AWARDS" CALL FOR ENTRIES

This is a call for entries directed at both printers and designers. We used pixilated images of predictable, dull, contrived corporate stock photography with the well-known accompanying disclaimer: "This image is for position only and is not intended for final use. The situations depicted are purely fictional and any similarities to actual persons, places, events and/or submitted contest materials are purely coincidental." The unique format of the pad provides entrants a convenient way to pull out and use several entry forms.

JURORS' COMMENTS

"This just kills me. I love the functionality, because you can take the whole front off. The detailing is really nice."

john bielenberg

VIRTUAL TELEMETRIX 1997 ANNUAL REPORT, VIRTUAL TELEMETRIX, INC. 1998.

JOHN BIELENBERG, C2, BELFAST, MAINE

SINCE 1991, JOHN BIELENBERG HAS PRODUCED A SERIES OF PROJECTS UNDER THE PSEUDONYM
VIRTUAL TELEMETRIX, INC. THAT SATIRIZE THE PRACTICE OF GRAPHIC DESIGN AND CORPORATE
AMERICA. PROJECTS INCLUDE THE *QUANTITATIVE SUMMARY OF INTEGRATED GLOBAL
BRANDSTRATEGY* BOOKLET AND VIDEO, PRODUCED FOR AIGA'S "BRANDESIGN" CONFERENCE.
SFMOMA HAS ACQUIRED SIX OF THESE PROJECTS AND STAGED A VIRTUAL TELEMETRIX EXHIBITION
AND MOCK IPO (INITIAL PUBLIC OFFERING) THAT RAN FROM JULY TO OCTOBER 2000.
BIELENBERG, WHO IS A MEMBER OF AIGA'S NATIONAL BOARD OF DIRECTORS, IS CURRENTLY
WORKING TO CREATE THE THE BIELENBERG INSTITUTE FOR DESIGN AND CULTURE ON THE COAST OF
MAINE. A SUMMER WORKSHOP FOR GRADUATING DESIGN STUDENTS WILL BE LAUNCHED IN JULY 2003.

09

promotional design and advertising
juror

john waters

INTERACTIVE GREETING, AOC, INC., 2001.

JOHN WATERS, WATERSDESIGN, NEW YORK

JOHN WATERS, PRESIDENT AND CEO OF WATERSDESIGN, IS RESPONSIBLE FOR THE OVERALL STRUCTURE, STRATEGY AND VALUES OF THE FIRM. SINCE FORMING THE COMPANY IN 1977, WATERS HAS MAINTAINED THE STRENGTHS THAT SET WATERSDESIGN APART—THE HIGHEST STANDARDS OF CREATIVE EXCELLENCE, COMMUNICATION VALUE, TECHNICAL EXPERTISE AND CLIENT SERVICE. UNDER HIS LEADERSHIP, THE FIRM PIONEERED THE USE OF DIGITAL TECHNOLOGIES IN 1985, GIVING IT A SOLID LEAD IN THE INTERACTIVE MEDIA REVOLUTION. WATERS HAS DEVELOPED CORPORATE IDENTITY PROGRAMS, DESIGNED ANNUAL REPORTS AND PRODUCED INTEGRATED COMMUNICATIONS PROGRAMS FOR MANY OF THE WORLD'S MOST RESPECTED COMPANIES. HE IS A FORMER PRESIDENT OF THE INTERNATIONAL DESIGN BY ELECTRONICS ASSOCIATION AND A FORMER BOARD MEMBER OF AIGA'S NEW YORK CHAPTER.

09
promotional design and advertising
juror

allison muench williams

WILSONWENZL.COM, WILSON/WENZEL INC., 2001.

ALLISON MUENCH WILLIAMS, DESIGN: M/W, NEW YORK

ALLISON MUENCH WILLIAMS, ALONG WITH HER PARTNER, J. PHILLIPS WILLIAMS, FOUNDED THE NEW
YORK CITY-BASED STUDIO DESIGN: M/W IN 1993. THE COMPANY SPECIALIZES IN ESTABLISHING THE
IMAGES OF CLIENTS THROUGH COLLATERAL, PACKAGING AND INTERACTIVE WORK. RECENT PROJECTS
INCLUDE BRAND IDENTITY, PRINT COLLATERAL, ADVERTISING AND AN E-COMMERCE WEBSITE FOR
WEST ELM, A NEW MODERN HOME FURNISHINGS BRAND FOR THE WILLIAMS-SONOMA GROUP.
AT DESIGN: M/W, WILLIAMS HAS DONE EXTENSIVE WORK FOR TAKASHIMAYA NEW YORK
INCLUDING SEVERAL DIRECT MAIL CATALOGS, ADVERTISING AND PACKAGING PROGRAMS.
DESIGN: M/W HAS RECEIVED NUMEROUS AWARDS FOR ITS DESIGN WORK, INCLUDING A GOLD
CLIO AWARD, BEST OF CATEGORY: DESIGN AND BEST OF CATEGORY: PACKAGING, FROM
I.D. MAGAZINE, AND A RED DOT "BEST OF THE BEST" AWARD.

10
package design

SELECTED WORKS REPRESENT THE YEAR'S BEST-DESIGNED
CONSUMER PACKAGING, LABELS, SHOPPING BAGS AND GIFT OR SPECIALTY PRODUCTS.

JURORS
ANDY DREYFUS, APPLE COMPUTER, CUPERTINO, CALIFORNIA;
DEBBIE MILLMAN, STERLING GROUP, NEW YORK; ALLISON MUENCH WILLIAMS, DESIGN: M/W, NEW YORK

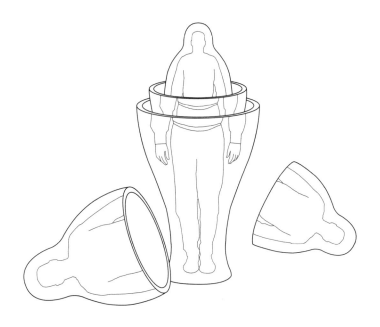

10

package design

WRITTEN BY ANDREA CODRINGTON

In the world of package design, 2001 bore both good news and bad news. "I don't think that people need to feel like shit to shop anymore," pronounced Allison Muench Williams, herald of the good news. Williams and her fellow jurors, Andy Dreyfus and Debbie Millman, were discussing the year's most hyped design product, Rem Koolhaas's Prada store in downtown New York, and its tendency to make shoppers and gawkers alike feel woefully sub-par. It used to be, the jurors agreed, that striking some hipper-than-thou pose was a sure way of winning brand cachet in the marketplace. But a bad economy and uncertain political climate have changed things. Prada's individual cosmetics "monodoses" may have a certain cool factor, but the Dentyne Ice blister pack "is one of the breakthroughs in terms of functionality for gum," as Dreyfus pointed out. "Too bad the graphics are so bad."

Modesty and originality trumped flash in AIGA's package design competition but the bad news is that potato chips packages still look stupid. "I'm totally depressed," said Millman, who, unlike the other jurors specializes in, branding the products that line supermarket shelves. Indeed, the jurors concurred that the language of fast-moving consumer goods is nothing less than hackneyed—the domain of "sweaty" cans and bottles (sports drinks) and outsized logotypes in screaming colors like red, yellow and orange (snack foods). "The words 'package design' are almost oxymoronic," Millman continued. "What makes a good package isn't necessarily going to be aesthetically pleasing."

Millman's perspective engendered an often-heated discussion about the very nature of package design. Was the essential purpose of a package to *hold* or to *sell*? The most mass-market product of the winning selections—the GapColor Cosmetic Line packaging[1]—did both, the jurors agreed, with an alluring but sensible design approach. "From a cost perspective it's a brilliant idea," said Williams of the neo-minimal generic-look packages that are produced en masse and then categorized with different-hued stick-on strips indicating product color. Even more impressive were the sophisticated matte black containers that, according to Dreyfus, "take the cosmetics out of the Maybelline category."

On the opposite end of the consumer spectrum was the architecturally compelling shopping bag created for the upscale design store Troy.[2] "This is a cultural badge," »

PG 294

PG 298

remarked Millman of the handsome origami-reminiscent bag that is so understated that the store's name is barely visible, peeking demurely from a side fold. (Assumedly customers who think nothing of spending a few thousand dollars on a small design bibelot don't need their egos bolstered by a blaring brand name.) Although the bag does nothing to actually sell the product that fits within its handsome confines, the jurors declared it an effective piece of portable branding that will join the ranks of Tiffany, Hermes and other recognizable bags that make the kitchen recycling cut.

Indeed, packages for niche markets generally feature more interesting designs than mainstream products. The boxes for Callaway's Hx Blue and Hx Red golf balls,[3] for instance, sport crisp information graphics that show drag and lift coefficients—as well as the balls' hallmark hexagonal dimpling—on its highly illustrated sides. Although it could be argued that the packages are almost too hip for the golf world, Dreyfus contends that the information and its tongue-in-cheek presentation offer real purchase-point advantages. "The packaging is solving a lot of interesting problems well," agreed Williams.

PG 296

Interestingly enough, the day's hands-down covetable turned out to be a duo of vinyl LPs[4] that feature close-up photographs of indy rock-looking guys on the spacious front cover and a colorful, abstract pattern on the back taken from music software graphics. The fetishization of the LPs' materiality is taken that much farther with a deliciously pale seafoam-green translucent disc that slides into a plain white sleeve. "This is really authentic," said Williams, who was a DJ during college and has handled her own share of indy vinyl. A clever design paean to both analog and digital music—with graphical representations of both—the packaging is entirely suited to the obsessive, audiophilic audience that is its target.

PG 291

Although at the end of the day the jury was largely satisfied with their selection, there was a sense of disappointment that there weren't more mainstream consumer packages to consider. Where were the Tazo Teas and Fresh Samanthas of 2001, those grassroots products that hit the big time, partially because of their quirky design appeal? "McDonald's should never look like Jil Sander," concluded Dreyfus, "but there's got to be something in between." □

10
package design

DESIGN FIRM: VSA PARTNERS, CHICAGO

DESIGNER: HANS SEEGER
PHOTOGRAPHER: RICHARD BURBRIDGE
TYPEFACE: HELVETICA NEUE
CLIENT: AESTHETICS

1 OF 2 IN 1000, 2 OF 2 IN 1000 ALBUM PACKAGING

1 of 2 in 1000, 2 of 2 in 1000 is a limited edition, vinyl-only release by pulseprogramming on the Chicago-based Aesthetics label. With the packaging, our intent was to create something precious and fleeting and, at the same time, infuse a little warmth and humanity into the electronic music genre. The iconic imagery juxtaposed against the portraits features the music itself. The sleeves are printed four-color offset on cardstock, with a matte varnish.

JURORS' COMMENTS

"This is really authentic. The photography is nice."

10
package design

DESIGN FIRM: RED INK, LOS ANGELES

DESIGNER: JORDAN CRANE
ILLUSTRATORS: JORDAN CRANE (COVER, INDEX); NICK BERTOZZI, BRIAN BIGGS,
MAT BRINKMAN, BRIAN CHIPPENDALE, DAVID CHOE, GREG COOK, JORDAN CRANE, TOM DEVLIN,
JASON, ULF K., DAVE KIERSH, MEGAN KELSO, JAMES KOCHALKA, PAUL LYONS, PAUL POPE,
PSHAW, BRIAN RALPH, RON REGE JR., STEVEN WEISSMAN, KURT WOLFGANG
STRUCTURAL DESIGNER: JORDAN CRANE
PRINTER: QUEBECOR
TYPEFACE: HAND-DRAWN BY JORDAN CRANE
CLIENT: RED INK

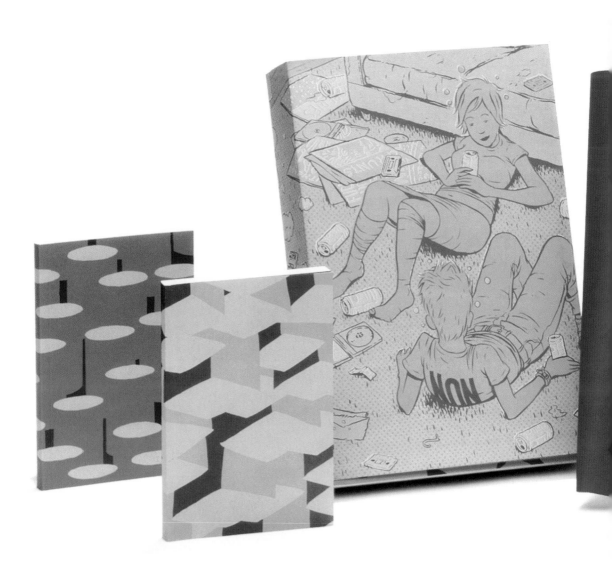

NON NO. 5

Because of the diversity of art and storytelling used by the comics in this collection, the primary challenge was to unify without taking away from the individual voice of each story. Two stories were too long for the main book, and were printed in books of their own, and the same unified versus individual identity problem was presented. I used a two-color patterned cover—based on a single shape that is derived from the book's content—with the same colors being used again on the inside, the darker color as line art. The books, while maintaining their individuality, appear to be a set when presented together.

10
package design

DESIGN FIRM: GAP INC., SAN FRANCISCO

DESIGN DIRECTOR: JENNIFER DURRANT
DESIGNER: MATTHEW FADNESS
PRODUCTION ARTISTS: MATTHEW FADNESS, KEITH TELEKI
STRUCTURAL DESIGNER: TED WANG
PRINTER: PACKAGING SPECTRUM
MANUFACTURER: HCT
TYPEFACE: AKZIDENZ GROTESK
CLIENT: GAP INC.

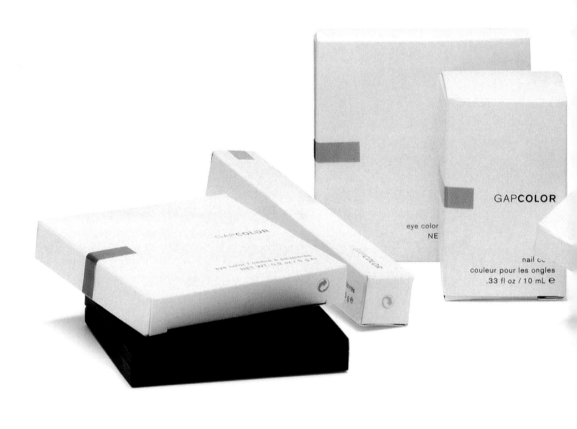

GAPCOLOR COSMETIC LINE PACKAGING

Our aim for the new Gap cosmetics collection was to create a design that represents the clean, modern essence of the brand. The fresh white packaging sets off colored labels that indicate product color at a glance. We organized the information carefully to minimize the visual impact of all legally required type.

JURORS' COMMENTS

"It makes the product seem more expensive than it is. It's very clear with color. It compares well with other cosmetics." "This feels more Gap to me than the flowery stuff the company was doing for a while. From a cost perspective, it's a brilliant idea. The sticker is a good way of communicating the metallic nature of the product. For this price point, it's amazing. I'd be really happy to take this out of my purse."

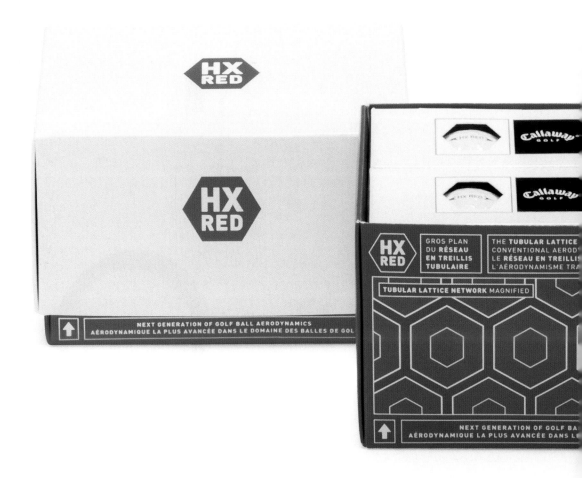

CALLAWAY HX RED, HX BLUE GOLF BALL PACKAGING

With the packaging of its new HX lines, Callaway wanted to highlight innovations in the design of its golf ball. To accommodate this need and still keep the outside of the box graphically clean, we put the technical information on the covered sides of the box. The lid is short and exposes a peek of the information underneath, sliding up to reveal diagrams on ball aerodynamics and structure. The boxes have been embossed, debossed and treated with matte and gloss varnishes to give them a tactile quality that relates to the ball surface.

JURORS' COMMENTS

"The packaging is solving a lot of interesting problems."

DESIGN FIRM: PENTAGRAM DESIGN INC., NEW YORK

ART DIRECTOR: WOODY PIRTLE
DESIGNERS: DAISUKE ENDO, CHARISSE GIBILISCO, HSIN-YING WU
PRINTER: IVY HILL GRAPHICS
CLIENT: CALLAWAY GOLF COMPANY

DESIGN FIRM: RADIS JENSETHAWAT, BROOKLYN, NEW YORK

DESIGNER: RADIS JENSETHAWAT
STRUCTURAL DESIGNER: RADIS JENSETHAWAT
PRINTER: RTR PACKAGING CORPORATION
CLIENT: TROY SOHO

TROY SHOPPING BAG

The problem was the need to design new packaging for Troy products that would identify those products with the contemporary furniture store. The shopping bag was designed to hold the box packaging that was already in use. Because furniture has dimension, we gave the letter "T" dimension through its positioning on the bag.

JURORS' COMMENTS

"This is reductivist. It's iconographic. Think of a bag more than as just a bag. Somebody thought of the space of the bag. This is right for the store. It's a great proportion, since half the clientele is probably male. It's masculine; it's hard to make a male bag." "This is a cultural badge."

10
package design

DESIGN FIRM: WERNER DESIGN WERKS, INC., MINNEAPOLIS

CREATIVE DIRECTOR: MINDA GRALNEK, TARGET STORES
ART DIRECTOR: RON ANDERSON, TARGET STORES
DESIGNERS: SARAH NELSON, SHARON WERNER, WERNER DESIGN WERKS, INC.
ILLUSTRATORS: SARAH NELSON, SHARON WERNER, WERNER DESIGN WERKS, INC.
PRINTER: RAVERY DENNISON
TYPEFACE: HANDWRITTEN
CLIENT: TARGET CORPORATION

HALLOWEEN 2001 PROMOTIONAL PACKAGING

Werner Design Werks worked with Target to determine the look of Halloween 2001 at Target stores, and these hangtags were part of a comprehensive system. Miss Witch was just one of a much larger cast of friendly, ghoulish characters who appeared throughout the store on everything from signage, T-shirts and pajama bottoms to paper towels and candy packaging.

JURORS' COMMENTS
"I think it's very sweet." "It's very approachable and well considered."

10
packaging design
juror

andy dreyfus

1
iMAC PACKAGING, APPLE COMPUTER, 1999.

2
iPOD PACKAGING, APPLE COMPUTER, 2001.

1

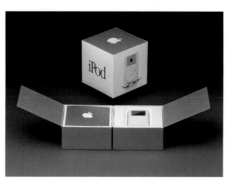

2

ANDY DREYFUS, APPLE COMPUTER, CUPERTINO, CALIFORNIA:
ANDY DREYFUS WAS PART OF THE TEAM PUT TOGETHER BY STEVE JOBS IN 1997 TO RESUSCITATE APPLE
COMPUTER. HE AND HIS GRAPHIC DESIGN TEAM WERE RESPONSIBLE FOR THE NEW CORPORATE IDENTITY,
PRODUCT LAUNCHES, PACKAGING, WEBSITE, MERCHANDISING, TRADESHOWS AND APPLE STORES.
IN HIS PACKAGE DESIGN FOR APPLE—FROM THE ORIGINAL iMAC TO THE iPOD—DREYFUS FOCUSED
ON THE OWNER'S EXPERIENCE OF OPENING A BOX AS AN UNFOLDING AND REVELATORY PROCESS.
REMARKS DREYFUS, "NOTHING IS GRATUITOUS, BUT WE WANT PEOPLE TO THINK THAT APPLE
THOUGHT OF EVERY LAST DETAIL." AMONG HIS OTHER PROJECTS, DREYFUS DESIGNED THE IDENTITY
FOR THE BAY AREA ANIMATION STUDIO PIXAR.

10

packaging design
juror

debbie millman

1
STAR WARS EPISODE II: ATTACK OF THE CLONES BRAND IDENTITY AND PACKAGING,
LUCAS LICENSING, TROY ALDERS, KUMARS MOGHTADER, 2002.

2
BURGER KING GLOBAL BRANDING, IDENTITY AND PACKAGING, BURGER KING, 2001.

1

2

DEBBIE MILLMAN, STERLING GROUP, NEW YORK

DEBBIE MILLMAN IS A MANAGING PARTNER AT STERLING GROUP, ONE OF THE COUNTRY'S
LEADING MARKETING CONSULTANCIES AND BRAND IDENTITY FIRMS. SHE DIRECTS ALL
CLIENT SERVICES, SALES AND MARKETING FOR THE FIRM, AND OVERSEES BRAND
DESIGN FOR CLIENTS SUCH AS GILLETTE, BURGER KING, KRAFT, COLGATE-PALMOLIVE,
PEPSI-COLA, CAMPBELLS AND UNILEVER. CURRENTLY, MILLMAN IS ALSO THE
OFF-STAFF CREATIVE DIRECTOR FOR EMMIS BROADCASTING'S HOT 97 WHERE, SINCE 1992,
SHE HAS HELPED TRANSFORM THE IMAGE OF THE RADIO STATION FROM A DANCE MUSIC
FORMAT TO A VIBRANT HIP-HOP STATION, THE NUMBER ONE STATION IN ITS DEMOGRAPHIC.
PRIOR TO WORKING AT STERLING GROUP, MILLMAN WAS A SENIOR VICE PRESIDENT
AT INTERBRAND, A BRAND CONSULTANCY; SHE WAS ALSO THE DIRECTOR OF MARKETING AT
FRANKFURT BALKIND, AN ENTERTAINMENT COMMUNICATIONS AND ADVERTISING AGENCY.

10
packaging design
juror

allison muench williams

VOLUME NINE, TAKASHIMAYA NEW YORK, 2001.

ALLISON MUENCH WILLIAMS, DESIGN: M/W, NEW YORK

ALLISON MUENCH WILLIAMS, ALONG WITH HER PARTNER, J. PHILLIPS WILLIAMS, FOUNDED THE
NEW YORK CITY-BASED STUDIO DESIGN: M/W IN 1993. THE COMPANY SPECIALIZES IN ESTAB-
LISHING THE IMAGES OF CLIENTS THROUGH COLLATERAL, PACKAGING AND INTERACTIVE WORK.
AMONG THEIR RECENT PACKAGE DESIGN PROJECTS ARE THE TEA BOX FOR TAKASHIMAYA, WHICH
WON *I.D.* MAGAZINE'S BEST OF CATEGORY AWARD, AND A PACKAGE DESIGN PROGRAM FOR
BANANA REPUBLIC. THEY ARE CURRENTLY WORKING ON THE PACKAGING FOR SAKS FIFTH AVENUE'S
PRIVATE LABEL "BATH AND BODY" LINE AND THEIR GOURMET FOOD DEPARTMENT. AT DESIGN: M/W,
PRINT WORK IS INFLUENCED BY THE MATERIALITY AND EXPERIENTIAL NATURE OF PACKAGING.

11

brand and identity systems design

SELECTED WORKS REPRESENT THE YEAR'S BEST-DESIGNED GRAPHIC IDENTITIES
FOR CORPORATIONS, ORGANIZATIONS, INSTITUTIONS AND INDIVIDUALS.

JURORS
ANDY DREYFUS, APPLE COMPUTER, CUPPERTINO, CALIFORNIA;
MARC GOBÉ, DESGRIPPES GOBÉ GROUP, NEW YORK;
ANN WILLOUGHBY, WILLOUGHBY DESIGN GROUP, KANSAS CITY

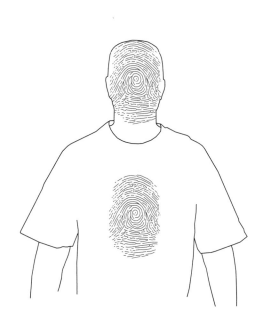

11

brand and identity systems design

WRITTEN BY JULIE LASKY

A slender 6 out of 695 entries were selected as finalists in AIGA's competition for brand and identity systems design. "Something really has to step up to get in," explained juror Ann Willoughby midway through the judging. "And we have to find that place where it happens."

Eventually, she and the other jurors, Marc Gobé and Andy Dreyfus, agreed on the precise point of elevation, and they returned again and again to the same word to describe it: humanity. Competent—even excellent—designs dropped out of the running if they seemed prim, mechanical, overly crowd-pleasing or produced by a committee. And though good craft was a prerequisite for any serious consideration by the panel, warmth, wit and bold approaches of the sort that would make most clients tremble put the winning entries over the top.

Dreyfus articulated the jury's standards across the board in speaking about the redesign of Citibank's identity—an elaborate project involving four different firms that was ultimately not selected: "It should be able to say, 'This is who we are. These are our values. If you want to join us, welcome. If you don't, thank you anyway.'" Mourning the passing of a realistic umbrella that used to appear in the bank's logo, Dreyfus noted that too many corporate clients have the opposite attitude: "They believe, 'If we make the design bland, everyone will join us.' And yet it's impossible not to offend someone."

There are certainly exceptions to the cold-and-bland rule among major corporations, the jurors insisted, naming Apple and BP as models at large. But almost no exemplary work from big business made its way to the competition. In the end, the finalists included five stationery systems for modest concerns and one graphics and packaging program for a heavy hitter, Pottery Barn.

The identity system for Pottery Barn Kids,[1] in fact, PG 312 topped the jury's hit parade. "It's not over your head; it's funny," commented Dreyfus. "It gets the human, but it satisfies all the things a good logo should do: be able to scale, print in one color." Willoughby applauded the program's effortless-seeming sensitivity to its market: "It's very difficult to find a palette and feel that works for boys and girls and is gender-neutral," she pointed out. »

11

brand and identity systems design

The panel showered equal praise on a stationery system for the St. Louis Art Museum[2]—particularly on the logo, PG 314[2] which presented the museum's name without word spacing and yet was astonishingly legible. "It's a risk. Can you imagine selling this thing to a client?" Gobé wondered. "What I like about it is that an art museum doesn't feel the need to compete with its art by being colorful and bold," Dreyfus said.

Just as the humanity of the museum's identity lies in its extraordinary refinement—no committee or machine could have made such subtle choices—a set of business cards for a Wisconsin seamstress[3] revealed a human touch in a PG 315[3] tactile use of materials. The cards feature snippets from antique clothing patterns and letterpress type, and were stitched with an actual sewing machine. And though the jurors found the logo too inconspicuous and the embedded threads a bit clichéd, they were struck by the cards' emotional power. (As it turned out, they were designed by the client's daughter.) "The stitching's been done before, but it reminds people that it's okay to use your hands," Gobé remarked, adding that he found the project "very sincere and direct."

No less direct was a stationery system for the Bronx Defenders Office[4] in New York City—its very mission statement PG 316[4] was incorporated in the design. "I love it when work for not-for-profits is well done," Willoughby said. "Just the way they used the photography is really nice."

The panel was also taken with the print and digital applications of the identity for Harmonic,[5] a company PG 311[5] that produces online advertising. Dreyfus especially admired the typography, and Willoughby singled out the website's animation for praise.

And they applauded the honesty of a stationery system for Norman Design,[6] a project Gobé deemed "very consistent and PG 317[6] imaginative." Dreyfus called it a "nice example of good, old graphic design, done very well, with perfect typography and a great color palette."

"If I were to say anything about all of the finalists, including the animation," Willoughby concluded, "it's that there's a real sense that a human hand touched every one. There was real thoughtfulness." □

DESIGN FIRM: ELSEWHERE CREATIVE LLC, SAN FRANCISCO

CREATIVE DIRECTOR: MARIE KACMAREK
DESIGNER: BRENNA RAMIREZ
ILLUSTRATOR: FLINCH
TYPEFACES: BELIZIO, PROFORMA
PRINTER: WATERMARK PRESS
PAPER: GILBERT NEUTECH
CLIENT: HARMONIC

HARMONIC IDENTITY SYSTEM

Harmonic launched as a marketing firm offering advertising services and a software platform to automate the distribution of digital communications. Digital technologies require the collaboration of engineers, analysts and managers—three groups that have problems communicating with each other. The target audience—senior marketing management—was feeling these tensions acutely. Our solution was to focus on "harmony," a high-level concept desirable in all team environments. The logo demonstrates that all the letters in the word are of equal value and works with the humorous, illustrated caricatures, the strong red color, the elegant paper stock and the classic, balanced type treatment, altogether creating a substantial presence.

JURORS' COMMENTS
"Fresh, but not overdone. The typography is really good."

pottery barn kids

GIFT REGISTRY

DESIGN FIRM: CHARACTER, SAN FRANCISCO

DESIGNERS: PATRICIA EVANGELISTA, BENJAMIN PHAM, RISHI SHOURIE
PHOTOGRAPHER: MICHAEL MUNDY
ILLUSTRATOR: AARON GERBICH
WRITERS: HEATHER BOURDAUX, CHARACTER, KIM ROTH
TYPEFACES: AGARAMOND, FUTURA
PRINTER: COLORGRAPHICS
PAPER: MEAD
CLIENT: POTTERY BARN KIDS

POTTERY BARN KIDS RETAIL SYSTEM

Pottery Barn Kids, the brand extension for Pottery Barn, provides casual furnishings and textiles that emphasize fine materials, sophisticated color palettes and an eclectic, well-designed aesthetic. In capturing the essence of the Pottery Barn Kids line of products, we designed a branding system that was sophisticated yet whimsical. We created original icons illustrating children interacting with Pottery Barn products in a playful way. The icons were inspired by Norman Rockwell's spirit of celebrating childhood and graced all product packaging and collateral, including boxes, shopping bags, labels, tags and brochures.

JURORS' COMMENTS

"When I saw this, I said, 'I wish I had done it.' It gets the human into the design, while satisfying all the things a good logo should do."

11

brand and identity systems design

DESIGN FIRM: KUHLMANN LEAVITT, INC., ST. LOUIS

CREATIVE DIRECTOR: DEANNA KUHLMANN-LEAVITT
DESIGNER: MICHAEL B. THEDE
TYPEFACES: UNIVERS 45 LIGHT, UNIVERS 55
PRINTER: REPROX
PAPER: MONADNOCK ASTROLITE
CLIENT: FORUM FOR CONTEMPORARY ART

CONTEMPORARY ART MUSEUM OF ST. LOUIS IDENTITY SYSTEM

The Forum for Contemporary Art asked us to design the identity for their new museum—the Contemporary Art Museum of St. Louis. Our idea was to combine these words into a single piece of art. The viewer can find sub words like "tempt" and "muse" that comment on the many ways art speaks to us. Much like the works of art that will inhabit the spaces in the museum, the mark challenges the viewers and demands their attention. A clean two-color design and international sizing reinforce the aspirations of this institution to be a world-class museum.

JURORS' COMMENTS

"If I showed this to my mother, she would say, 'What's the big deal?' but the typography is brilliantly handled; it's amazing that you can read it so easily."

11

brand and identity systems design

DESIGN FIRM: JENNIFER KATCHA, JERSEY CITY, NEW JERSEY

DESIGNER: JENNIFER KATCHA
TYPEFACES: FILOSOFIA, FOUND TYPE
PRINTER: MIKE SHEAHEN, FIRECAST LETTERPRESS
PAPER: ASSORTED SAMPLE CARDSTOCK
CLIENT: PATTI KATCHA

PATTI KATCHA BUSINESS CARD

Patti Katcha, my mother, had retired and decided to work part-time as a seamstress out of her home. Her client base would be friends, family and a small amount of word-of-mouth business. Patti wanted a special business card that clients would keep. She did not want to spend a lot of money on the project.

Four hundred cards were letter-pressed dark brown onto various pieces of colored sample cardstock. I hand-glued vintage sewing patterns onto the backs and the cards were diecut, giving each back a unique design. As a final detail, each card was sewn across the middle with a simple zig-zag stitch.

JURORS' COMMENTS

"There's a certain integrity, honesty and sincerity in the message. You get it visually and emotionally."

DESIGN FIRM: PAMELA HOVLAND DESIGN, WILTON, CONNECTICUT

DESIGNER: PAMELA HOVLAND
PHOTOGRAPHER: JOANNE DUGAN
WRITER: ROBIN STEINBERG
TYPEFACES: THESANS, THESERIF
PRINTER: SUCCESS PRINTING
PAPER: STRATHMORE WRITING SOFT WHITE
CLIENT: THE BRONX DEFENDERS

THE BRONX DEFENDERS IDENTITY SYSTEM

The assignment was to create an appropriate and distinctive visual identity for a group of public defense lawyers, social workers and investigators committed to changing the criminal justice system in the Bronx. The audience for these materials includes the public defense community, the criminal court system, government leaders, and the organization's clients, financial supporters and potential employees.

The end product is a unique system that avoids the typical tone and manner of most non-profit materials yet conveys the complexity of the community it represents. An array of photographic images captures aspects of life in the Bronx through the juxtaposition of people, urban details, infrastructure, community and architecture.

JURORS' COMMENTS
"An honest use of photography. Really thoughtful."

brand and identity systems design

DESIGN FIRM: NORMAN DESIGN, CHICAGO

DESIGNER: ARMIN VIT
TYPEFACES: BAUHAUS (CUSTOMIZED), FILOSOFIA
PRINTERS: LADENDORF BROTHERS, ROHNER LETTERPRESS
PAPER: FRENCH PAPER SMARTWHITE
CLIENT: NORMAN DESIGN

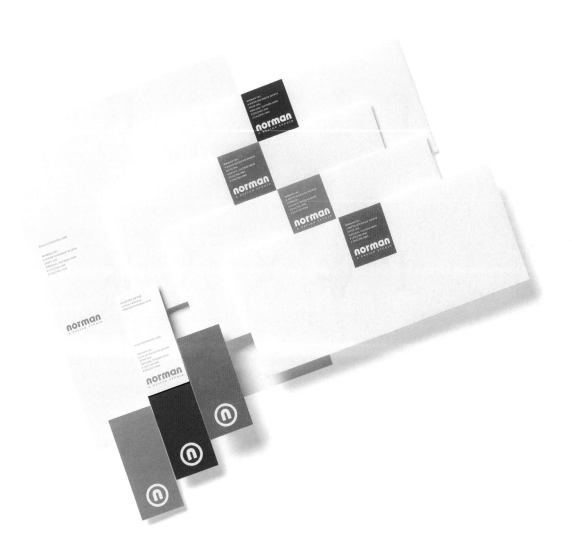

NORMAN DESIGN IDENTITY

We at Norman Design wanted to revitalize our brand to better define who we are and what we do. The system is distributed to both clients and prospects. We emphasized our name, Norman, and added a tagline—A Design Studio—which is more descriptive and boutique-like in nature. We also developed an icon that can stand alone and created a complementary typographic treatment. The four-ink palette enables the mixing and matching of components. The business cards stand out with their irregular shape, vertical orientation and two-sided printing. Letterpress provides a tactile experience.

JURORS' COMMENTS
"Very consistent and imaginative. Expertly done."

andy dreyfus

PIXAR LOGO, 1995.

ANDY DREYFUS, APPLE COMPUTER, CUPERTINO, CALIFORNIA

ANDY DREYFUS HAS WORKED IN THE BAY AREA FOR THE PAST 17 YEARS—BESIDES APPLE HE WORKED FOR CKS AND LANDOR. HIS CLIENTS INCLUDE PIXAR ANIMATION STUDIOS, UNITED AIRLINES, NORWEGIAN CRUISE LINES, NIKE, SONY, SATURN AND MERCEDES BENZ. DREYFUS WAS PART OF THE TEAM PUT TOGETHER BY STEVE JOBS IN 1997 TO RESUSCITATE APPLE COMPUTER. HE AND HIS GRAPHIC DESIGN TEAM WERE RESPONSIBLE FOR THE NEW CORPORATE IDENTITY, PRODUCT LAUNCHES, PACKAGING, WEBSITE, MERCHANDISING, TRADESHOWS AND APPLE STORES. DREYFUS IS A GRADUATE OF THE ART CENTER COLLEGE OF DESIGN. HE HOLDS DEGREES IN BOTH ENVIRONMENTAL AND GRAPHIC DESIGN.

11
brand and identity systems design
juror

marc gobé

BOTTLES AND PACKAGING, VICTORIA'S SECRET, 2001.

MARC GOBÉ, DESGRIPPES GOBÉ GROUP, NEW YORK

MARC GOBÉ IS PRESIDENT, CHIEF EXECUTIVE OFFICER AND EXECUTIVE CREATIVE DIRECTOR OF THE DESGRIPPES GOBÉ GROUP NEW YORK, ONE OF THE WORLD'S TOP TEN BRAND IMAGE CREATION FIRMS. HE IS THE AUTHOR OF *EMOTIONAL BRANDING* (ALLWORTH PRESS, 2001), A MARKETING AND BUSINESS BESTSELLER, AND *CITIZEN BRAND* (ALLWORTH PRESS, 2002). GOBÉ'S INTEGRATED APPROACH TO BRAND BUILDING AND HIS BROAD EXPERIENCE IN PACKAGING, STRUCTURAL DESIGN AND ARCHITECTURE HAS ATTRACTED A MULTIFACETED MIX OF APPAREL, BEAUTY AND CONSUMER BRAND CORPORATIONS, INCLUDING ANN TAYLOR, VICTORIA'S SECRET, GILLETTE, THE LIMITED INC., BROOKS BROTHERS, REEBOK, GATORADE, GODIVA, COCA-COLA, STARBUCKS, IBM AND AIR FRANCE.

ann willoughby

IDENTITY, ENVIRONMENT AND MERCHANDISE DESIGN, THREE DOG BAKERY, 1998.

ANN WILLOUGHBY, WILLOUGHBY DESIGN GROUP, KANSAS CITY

AS A MEMBER OF AIGA BRAND EXPERIENCE LEADERSHIP BOARD, ANN WILLOUGHBY IS WORKING ON INITIATIVES TO EXPOSE MEMBERS TO FRESH PERSPECTIVES ON PROMOTING AND BUILDING EFFECTIVE BRANDS. WILLOUGHBY IS THE FOUNDING PARTNER AND CREATIVE DIRECTOR OF KANSAS CITY-BASED WILLOUGHBY DESIGN GROUP AND HER ONGOING CLIENTS INCLUDE LEE COMPANY, HALLMARK AND INTERSTATE BRANDS CORPORATION. WILLOUGHBY'S HOLISTIC APPROACH TO DESIGN AND BUSINESS IS REFLECTED IN THE UNIQUE STUDIO ENVIRONMENT SHE HAS CREATED, DESIGNED TO FUNCTION AS A COLLABORATIVE SPACE WHERE DESIGNERS WORK ALONGSIDE ENTREPRENEURS AND CEOS TO VISUALIZE NEW BUSINESS MODELS AND RETAIL CONCEPTS. THE OFFICE, COMPLETE WITH A MEDITATION ROOM AND AN OFFSITE DESIGN-BARN RETREAT, HELPS ATTRACT AND RETAIN TOP CREATIVE TALENT AND BRINGS BLUE CHIP CLIENTS TO KANSAS CITY.

12
comprehensive brand strategies

SELECTED WORKS DEMONSTRATE EXCELLENCE IN THE STRATEGIC THINKING
BEHIND BRAND DESIGN FOCUSING PRIMARILY ON COMPREHENSIVE STRATEGIC SOLUTIONS
FOR POSITIONING (OR REPOSITIONING) BRANDS.

JURORS
LEE GREEN, IBM, NEW YORK; NATHAN SHEDROFF, SAN FRANCISCO;
ANN WILLOUGHBY, WILLOUGHBY DESIGN GROUP, KANSAS CITY

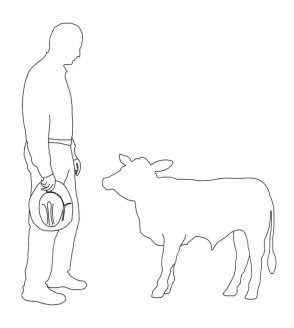

42
comprehensive brand strategies
WRITTEN BY JULIE LASKY

Speaking of the 43 branding strategies submitted to AIGA's comprehensive brand strategies competition, juror Nathan Shedroff said, "This category is almost a bellwether for the state of design as a strategic discipline. A lot of designers are only now, for the first time, approaching strategy. I'm sure a lot of them say they do it, and try to do it, and believe they do it, but too often their understanding of strategy is simply the concept behind a design."

Shedroff and his fellow jurors, Ann Willoughby and Lee Green, agreed that the entries as a whole showed the stirrings of a more comprehensive approach, combining long-term objectives for brand development with graceful and appropriate designs. But only one—a strategy for Aerus' (formerly the floor-cleaning- PG 329[1] products company Electrolux)—presented a nearly flawless model. Comprised of meticulously researched information about competing manufacturers, a studious timetable of brand evolution that includes plans for new products and a corporate identity that rigorously and beautifully adheres to the concept of cleanliness, the Aerus program towered over the other submissions. The jurors furthermore applauded the easy-to-follow presentation, which, unlike many entries, respected their intelligence and didn't try their patience with business-school jargon. "The only problem is that the project's in development, so there isn't a lot of application," Shedroff said. "But what's here is well done, and the strategy itself is so impressive."

What inspiration lay behind such a triumph? "I'd like to point out that it was a collaboration between three firms: a strategy firm, an industrial design firm and a graphic design firm." Willoughby said.

The sad fact, the jurors suggested, is that rarely do designers acquire the business acumen required for deeply considered branding strategies that anchor their visual talents; such expertise is not taught in art school and is most easily picked up in practice at a large firm, a professional course that many designers eschew. By the same token, it's the unusual client that assembles a truly collaborative team of marketing and design professionals, as Aerus did.

As a result, the rest of the entries showed a lopsided tilt toward either conceptual strategy or design execution, ranging from treatises on brand methodology »

comprehensive brand strategies

(and even a textbook) at the former extreme, to graphic displays with no real explanation of how or why they were conceived at the latter.

Even the other four finalists showed strengths in one or the other direction, though they ultimately possessed merits that the jurors couldn't ignore. An elaborate environmental graphics program for the music retailer Sam Goody[2] offered an inventive and well-articulated program for luring customers to the stores and helping them sample the merchandise. The panel, however, was less enthusiastic about the design of the program's many elements, which they believed lacked consistency and could have been better integrated.

PG 2 336

An in-store branding system for Michael Graves' Target products,[3] on the other hand, featured stunning graphics but almost no talk of strategy. The jurors had to infer most of the branding intentions from the display itself, and deemed it to be a masterly example of a "store within a store" that transmitted distinct yet complementary identities of the architect and his corporate patron. "We think the strategy was set by Target and Michael Graves before the project reached the designer," Willoughby said, "so it was embedded in the execution."

PG 3 330

Also light on strategy was the rebranding campaign for Strathmore's Elements line,[4] which wittily connects the periodic table with cultural elements, such as fashion and fads. But given the project's narrow mission and highly targeted audience, the panel was forgiving. "It's a relaunch of a paper marketed to designers," Willoughby explained. "Basically they were using it for one- or two-color jobs and the company wanted to reposition it for four-color design applications and multiple formats. It's pretty subtle." Added Shedroff, "It's not a corporate-level brand strategy; it's a product strategy, and does a really good job of it."

PG 4 332

Finally, the jury found much to commend in a branding strategy for Idea Exchange,[5] a website that rates and sells information related to everything from training a house pet to outsmarting a used-car salesman. "It's not just a new website, not a brand, but a whole new category they had to position," Shedroff said. "How they went about doing that was portrayed as consistently human, in the verbal language, the visual language—every application." □

PG 5 334

12
comprehensive brand strategies

DESIGN FIRM: ADDIS, BERKELEY, CALIFORNIA

CREATIVE DIRECTOR: JOHN CRESON
DESIGNER: MONICA SCHLAUG
TYPEFACE: FRANKLIN GOTHIC
CLIENT: AERUS

fulfillment

ELECTROLUX

AERUS BRAND STRATEGY

A three-way collaboration repositioned and launched a renewed brand: Aerus. Cheskin oversaw consumer research; Lunar Design handled product design; Addis was charged with brand positioning, naming, brand architecture, corporate identity and consumer communication.

Our work centers on the essence of fulfillment to pave the way for significant product expansion and to shift the focus from solely functional benefits to a more emotional appeal.

JURORS' COMMENTS

"The way a brand strategy ought to be. They are looking at the highest level of what the brand means, as opposed to offering just positioning statements and taglines. And it's well done as an application."

12
comprehensive brand strategies

DESIGN FIRM: DESIGN GUYS, MINNEAPOLIS

CREATIVE DIRECTOR: STEVE SIKORA
DESIGNERS: JOHN MOES, GARY PATCH, ANNE PETERSON, TOM RIDDLE, DAWN SELG, JERRY
STENBACK, SCOTT THARES, JAY THEIGE
PHOTOGRAPHERS: DARRELL EAGER, JIM ERICKSON, TODD HAFERMANN, LARS HANSEN, EARL
KENDALL
WRITERS: JAY KASKEL, STEVE SIKORA
TYPEFACE: AVANT GARDE
CLIENT: TARGET CORPORATION

MICHAEL GRAVES IN-STORE BRANDING SYSTEM

Our objective was two-fold: to make credible the idea of a world-class architect/designer developing products for a discount chain; and to express the initiative in terms that would resonate with the mass market. Working across media we were able to push for consistency of message and aesthetic. Our greatest challenges were technical—such as matching Graves Blue, which didn't exist in any color system.

JURORS' COMMENTS

"The application is brilliant. They really made the Target brand work through even the simplest of products."

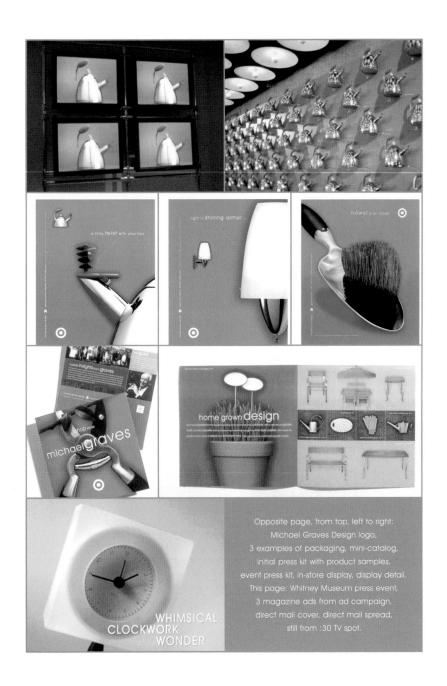

Opposite page, from top, left to right:
Michael Graves Design logo,
3 examples of packaging, mini-catalog,
initial press kit with product samples,
event press kit, in-store display, display detail.
This page: Whitney Museum press event,
3 magazine ads from ad campaign,
direct mail cover, direct mail spread,
still from :30 TV spot.

WHIMSICAL
CLOCKWORK
WONDER

12

comprehensive brand strategies

DESIGN FIRM: RIGSBY DESIGN, HOUSTON

CREATIVE DIRECTOR, ART DIRECTOR: LANA RIGSBY
DESIGNERS: THOMAS HULL, RAUL PAVÓN, LANA RIGSBY, PAMELA ZUCCKER
PHOTOGRAPHER: NICHOLE SLOAN
WRITERS: LANA RIGSBY, JESSE KORNBLUTH/EDITORIAL DIRECTOR FOR AMERICA ONLINE;
SCOTT OMELIANUK, TED ALLEN, *ESQUIRE*
STYLISTS: LYNN MITCHELL, SUSAN PRITCHETT,
PAGE SCHNEIDER, KRISTIN VALENTINO
PRINTER: H. MacDONALD PRINTING | BLANCHETTE PRESS
PAPER: STRATHMORE ELEMENTS
TYPEFACE: HELVETICA NEUE
CLIENT: STRATHMORE/INTERNATIONAL PAPERS

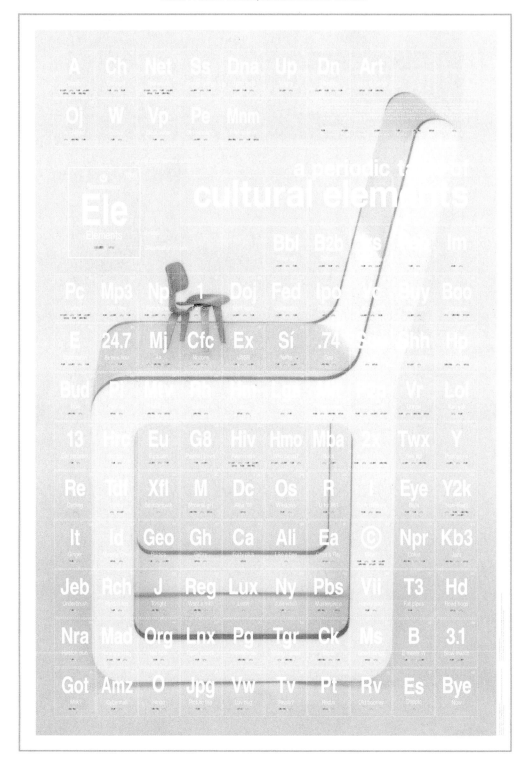

Strathmore Elements' initial debut in 1994 was the most successful product launch in paper history. By 2001 sales were lagging, the brand was tired. Rigsby Design's challenge was to reposition the product and reinvigorate the Elements brand. Our approach was to create a series of elegant, edgy collectibles that communicate through a combination of stylish images and provocative editorial content.

JURORS' COMMENTS

"Very witty. Really fun. Well-designed and thoughtful."

12

comprehensive brand strategies

DESIGN FIRM: THE MODERNS, LTD., NEW YORK

CREATIVE DIRECTORS: ADRIAN PULFER, A3; JANINE JAMES, THE MODERNS
DESIGNERS: RYAN MANSFIELD, JEREMIAH SIMPSON, A3; SARA MEARS, CANACE PULFER,
CHRISTIAN ROBERTSON, KEVIN SZELL, THE MODERNS
PHOTOGRAPHERS: ANDREW BOHAN, ERIK OSTLING, CONNIE SAGAN, TINA WEST
ILLUSTRATORS: CRAIG FRAZIER, ROBERT NEUBECKER
WRITERS: LYNN DANGEL, NED LEVINSOHN, KRISTEN RUMBLE
TYPEFACES: HUMANIST, META, SABON
PRINTER: SLATER GRAPHICS
CLIENT: IDEA EXCHANGE

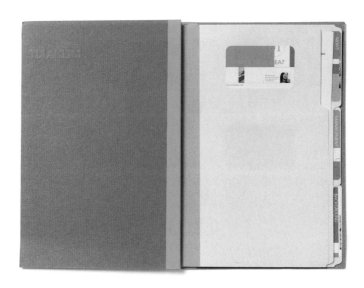

IDEA EXCHANGE BRAND STRATEGY

An internet-based company specializing in the commerce of ideas
retained The Moderns, in collaboration with A3, to develop an
effective brand strategy for ideaexchange.com. Our goal was to give
back to customers the human experience they give up online. The website
and all promotion pieces—environmental graphics to printed materials—
explain and illustrate a complex concept using a visual language that
clearly reflects the online existence of the company. All components
were designed to nurture invention and promote idea submissions and
purchases at the exchange. We developed a multi-layered look and feel—
integrating geometric grids, typography, symbology, illustration,
photography, dimensional colorful forms, materials and finishes.

JURORS' COMMENTS

"A particularly human way of building a brand, played out in
wonderful photography."

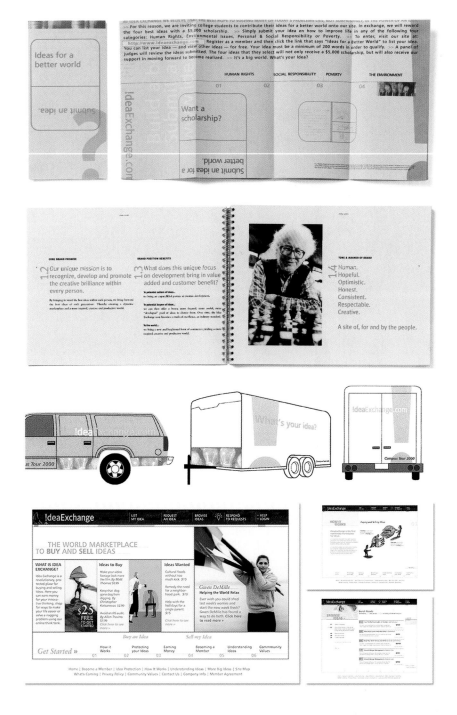

DESIGN FIRM: GENSLER, NEW YORK

DESIGN DIRECTOR: JOHN BRICKER
DESIGNERS: JAMIE BRIZZOLARA, JEAN KOEPPEL, BETH NOVITSKY
WRITER: PETER BARRY
CLIENT: SAM GOODY / MUSICLAND GROUP, INC.

12
comprehensive brand strategies

Simply About Me. (SAM)

Strategy
Personalization. SG understands that everyone is different. Through that, it is allowing and helping me to become me. It's empowering me.

Tone of voice
Understanding, non-judgmental, authentic, irreverent, witty, fun.

Tagline
Simply about me.

- -

Living Entertainment

Strategy
Passionate opinions. Young people feel passionate about the arts and entertainment, especially music and movies. It's not only very subjective, but a big part of my life and who I am. I live and breathe entertainment.

Tone of voice
Honest, witty, cutting-edge.

Tagline
Live it.

- -

All paths lead to Sam.

Strategy
Embracing Sam Goody as the place where young, creative minds meet. Demonstrate this by using "road trip" imagery and visual references to travel routes, subway graphics, maps, highway signs, etc.

Tone of voice
Youthful, chatty, energetic.

Tagline
Minds meet at Sam.
Meet me at Sam.

SAM GOODY BRAND STRATEGY

Sam Goody's goal was to capture a larger share of the huge, lucrative "Gen Y" market—teens and young adults 14 to 24 years old. To do this, they needed to re-energize their brand to speak to a younger audience. Gensler developed a long-term vision and strategy for the brand based on lifestyle rather than product—a big change for Sam Goody. Out of this strategy grew several approaches to brand positioning and tone of voice, each of which suggested a different graphic vocabulary.

JURORS' COMMENTS

"Not only is this really good thinking, but it's really well described—especially the theme of personalization and what it means to the customer experience."

12

comprehensive brand strategies

juror

lee green

IBM THINKPAD DESIGN, IBM.

LEE GREEN, IBM, SOMERS, NEW YORK

LEE GREEN IS THE DIRECTOR OF CORPORATE IDENTITY AND DESIGN FOR IBM CORPORATION.
HE HAS RESPONSIBILITY FOR IBM'S WORLDWIDE PRODUCT DESIGN, INDUSTRIAL DESIGN,
IDENTITY PROGRAMS, GRAPHICS, PACKAGING AND INTERNET DESIGN. GREEN HAS PLAYED A
PIVOTAL ROLE IN RECENT BRANDING AND DESIGN INITIATIVES INCLUDING THE LAUNCH OF
IBM'S E-BUSINESS IDENTITY PROGRAM, THE NEW TECHNOLOGY BRANDING PROGRAM AND
THE REDESIGN OF IBM'S DESKTOP, MOBILE AND SERVER PRODUCTS. HE ALSO LEADS THE
CORPORATION'S EFFORTS IN THE AREA OF "ADVANCED CONCEPT DESIGN." GREEN HAS
PUBLISHED NUMEROUS ARTICLES AND CASE STUDIES ON A VARIETY OF DESIGN AND IDENTITY
TOPICS, AND HAS TAUGHT DESIGN COURSES AND LECTURED ON DESIGN AT STANFORD
UNIVERSITY, HARVARD, MIT AND RIT.

12
comprehensive brand strategies
juror

nathan shedroff

1

NATHAN SHEDROFF'S WORLD WEBSITE, NATHAN SHEDROFF, 2001–PRESENT.

2

HERMAN MILLER RED WEBSITE, HERMAN MILLER, 2001.

FURNITURE MATRIX FOR THE HERMAN MILLER RED WEBSITE INFORMATION DESIGN, 2001.

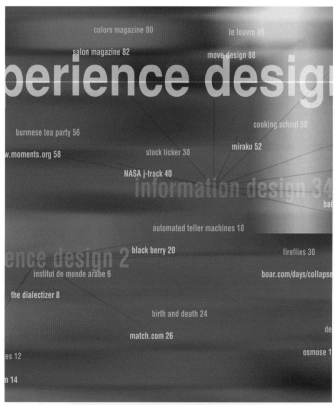

1

2

NATHAN SHEDROFF, SAN FRANCISCO

NATHAN SHEDROFF DEVELOPS EXPERIENCE AND BRAND STRATEGIES FOR A VARIETY OF
COMPANIES IN VARIOUS MEDIA, INCLUDING PRINT, DIGITAL, ONLINE AND PRODUCT DESIGN.
HE CO-FOUNDED VIVID STUDIOS—A DECADE-OLD COMPANY, ONE OF THE PIONEERS OF INTERACTIVE
MEDIA—AND WORKED WITH RICHARD SAUL WURMAN AT UNDERSTANDING BUSINESS.
SHEDROFF EARNED A BS IN INDUSTRIAL DESIGN, WITH EMPHASIS IN AUTOMOBILE DESIGN,
FROM ART CENTER COLLEGE OF DESIGN IN PASADENA, CALIFORNIA.
SHEDROFF OFTEN TEACHES AND SPEAKS AT INTERNATIONAL COLLEGES AND PROFESSIONAL
SEMINARS. HE IS ON THE STEERING COMMITTEE FOR AIGA BRAND EXPERIENCE AND CO-PRODUCES
AIGA BRAND FUTURE SCENARIOS WORKSHOPS WITH DAVIS MASTEN.

12
comprehensive brand strategies
juror

ann willoughby

AMERICAN HISTORY: LEE JEANS, LEE JEANS, 2000.

ANN WILLOUGHBY, WILLOUGHBY DESIGN GROUP, KANSAS CITY
AS A MEMBER OF AIGA BRAND EXPERIENCE LEADERSHIP BOARD, ANN WILLOUGHBY IS
WORKING ON INITIATIVES TO EXPOSE MEMBERS TO FRESH PERSPECTIVES ON PROMOTING AND
BUILDING EFFECTIVE BRANDS. WILLOUGHBY IS THE FOUNDING PARTNER AND CREATIVE
DIRECTOR OF KANSAS CITY-BASED WILLOUGHBY DESIGN GROUP AND HER ONGOING CLIENTS
INCLUDE LEE COMPANY, HALLMARK AND INTERSTATE BRANDS CORPORATION. WILLOUGHBY'S
HOLISTIC APPROACH TO DESIGN AND BUSINESS IS REFLECTED IN THE UNIQUE STUDIO
ENVIRONMENT SHE HAS CREATED, DESIGNED TO FUNCTION AS A COLLABORATIVE SPACE WHERE
DESIGNERS WORK ALONGSIDE ENTREPRENEURS AND CEOS TO VISUALIZE NEW BUSINESS
MODELS AND RETAIL CONCEPTS. THE OFFICE, COMPLETE WITH A MEDITATION ROOM
AND AN OFFSITE DESIGN-BARN RETREAT, HELPS ATTRACT AND RETAIN TOP CREATIVE TALENT
AND BRINGS BLUE-CHIP CLIENTS TO KANSAS CITY.

13
book design: 50 books/50 covers

SELECTED WORKS REPRESENT THE YEAR'S BEST-DESIGNED BOOKS AND BOOK COVERS.

JURORS
RICHARD ECKERSLEY, UNIVERSITY OF NEBRASKA PRESS, LINCOLN, NEBRASKA;
CARIN GOLDBERG, CARIN GOLDBERG DESIGN, NEW YORK;
RICHARD HULL, BRIGHAM YOUNG UNIVERSITY, PROVO, UTAH;
JENNIFER MORLA, MORLA DESIGN, SAN FRANCISCO;
PAUL SAHRE, OFFICE OF PAUL SAHRE, NEW YORK;

13

book design: 50 books/50 covers

AIGA INVITED ACCLAIMED BOOK DESIGNER RICHARD ECKERSLY
TO REFLECT UPON THE SELECTIONS MADE BY
THIS YEAR'S "AIGA 50 BOOKS/50 COVERS" COMPETITION JURY

Perhaps the most controversial issue in the judging of this year's "AIGA 50 Books/50 Covers" competition was that of innovation. Many of the rejected books and covers were castigated for their timidity and lack of experiment. This was attributed to market insecurity and a resultant conservatism that has eroded the confidence and authority of the designer. With particular reference to covers, concern was expressed at the growing and pernicious influence of commercial distributors and bookstore chains. It was also suggested that a changing of the guard among art directors has left the unseasoned and diffident barely in control. Given the harshness of this judgment, it's hardly surprising that the jury restricted its selection of covers to fewer than the allotted 50. It seems to me that the quality of covers from the university presses has improved in recent years—perhaps in an effort to compete with the commercial houses—but the general trend is away from the strongly conceptual and toward the decorative—sometimes aesthetically pleasing, often nebulously generic.

I am much less comfortable when the word "innovation" is applied to book design. Books and covers are such different animals that I question whether they even should be elided into a single show. Covers are advertisements that must push themselves forward in the jostle of a gaudy marketplace. Books are receptacles of thought, and should be driven by language unimpeded by the fripperies of fashionable design. Book typography may whisper, bellow or cajole, and, certainly, it may be innovative—but only as the text demands.

Books are driven by convention, by a common language shared by author and reader. Even the most experimental typography—the eccentric chapbooks of the Russian Suprematists, Tschichold's *New Typography*, Dada—honors convention in the breach. Conventions change for better or worse, and some may grow as tight and brittle as corsets in a thrift store. When that happens, the designer may attempt to make repairs that appear innovative, but often are derived from an older model. Hanging punctuation, for example—a refreshing characteristic of press advertising in the 1960s—was used by scribes long before Gutenberg.

Perhaps true innovation in typography only occurs as a reflection of innovative language. The acquisitiveness and daring of Elizabethan English demanded an equivalent typography. Experiment was joined with unity of purpose »

and publishers were deaf to "can't" or "mustn't." In contrast, the hierarchy within today's publishing houses where editor, marketing manager and designer are each prescribed a separate and limited function, tends towards rigidity.

The computer allows refinements of typographical detail, those impossible or very difficult to achieve with metal type, but the constraints of modern style discourage many of the freedoms with language that allowed the Renaissance compositor to produce beautiful pages. It was once common to use ad hoc, contractions, abbreviations and symbols to adjust the spacing in the line. Terminal hyphens were sometimes legion, apparently without complaint from the reader. Even a title page might be broken into bits of words in a fruit salad of styles and sizes that would send a modern editor into fits. The early typographers sought an aesthetic unity that transcended consistency. Now we value consistency for its own sake.

I don't suggest that we should attempt only to emulate the typography of the past—though for certain texts this would be no bad thing—rather, that we should seek an equivalent vibrancy to express this moment in time. The development of electronic publishing is still waiting for authors to exploit its potential. When that happens, the impact on language and its typography may be as profound as it was in the 16th century. In the meantime, examples of good book design in a variety of styles, some looking forward and some back, continue to appear among AIGA's 50 books.

The number of entries for this year's show was smaller than last but the university presses increased their overall submissions—which is puzzling since scholarly publishing has been affected by an insecure economy at least as painfully as have the commercial houses. Predictably, the largest number of books was entered in the special trade category. Many of these are large-format illustrated books, often lavishly produced.

Stinehour Press' *Commonplace Books'* features elegant typography that exactly matches the subject matter and the printing renders the gorgeous blacks of the letterpress originals in a way that is nothing short of masterly. Another large-format book that was much admired is Chicago University Press' *On European Ground,*[2] which records the vestiges of war and its incumbent horrors—rendered all the more poignant because of the deliberate »

PG 372[1]

PG 402[2]

understatement of the design. In direct contrast, Stefan Sagmeister's *Made You Look*,[3] which the author/designer describes as "another self-indulgent design monograph," never stands still. Text, typography and the examples of Sagmeister's work are propelled by the same hyperactive wit. It's like watching a demonstrative conductor who also understands the music. PG 387

Another irreverent author-designed book appears in the general trade category—Chip Kidd's *The Cheese Monkeys*,[4] published by Knopf. As with the Sagmeister, the innovative typography grows naturally out of the subject. I particularly enjoyed the jacket that wraps vertically over the front cover—more like a cuff than a jacket—the stamping on the fore-edge that reads "Good Is Dead" and the copyright notice run in a single line across eight pages. PG 437

The children's book is another contentious area, where marketing strategy appears often to run counter to good design sense. Is the market defined by the demands of the parent or the child? Do young children respond more to abstraction or to detail? The entries incline in all directions, but the best of them share a common characteristic: they do not condescend. A notable example is Steedman's edition of *Pinocchio*,[5] in which illustrations, admirably matched by typography, retrieve Collodi's classic text from the cartoon status imposed by Disney. As Pinocchio eventually comes to understand, lying is a serious business. PG 362

Another children's edition that neither condescends nor patronizes is *Love that Dog*,[6] published by Joanna Cotler Books. This is the only book of poetry in the show. Legibly typeset in an intimate format, it suggests that quality one hopes a child might come to expect of a volume of verse: that it is a receptacle for valuable things. PG 416

The work of the private presses may sometimes suggest affectation of a different sort, a cloying preciosity. This could never be said of the work of Walter Hamady at the Perishable Press, whose *Nullity* and *Salutations 1995*[7] are included among this year's 50 books. Physically rooted in the crafts yet untrammeled by convention, they address both the perennial and the immediate in their language and their physical form, and may be the most palpable expressions of the existential now among the many excellent books included in the show. □ PG 391

13

book design: 50 books/50 covers

SYP TEAM: TOM ANDREWS, TARA BODDEN, ANNE BODEL, KAT CASCONE,
JOHNSON CHOW, JULES ELLINGSON, VASILIA EMMANOUILIDES, ALLISON KOCH,
PATTY K. LaDUKE, JORDAN LAZOVIK, LISA MAULHARDT, TODD McPHERSON,
LYNDA PREBLE, JON RITT, JoANNA SCHULL, JOE STITZLEIN, ROBERT STONE,
KEITH YAMASHITA, LIZ SUTTON, TODD HOLCOMB, AURA OSLAPAS,
SUSAN SCHUMAN; STONE YAMASHITA PARTNERS, SAN FRANCISCO
TRIM SIZE: 7 1/4 X 8 3/4 INCHES
PAGES: 298 QUANTITY PRINTED: 1,500
TYPEFACES: INTERSTATE, MRS. EAVES
PRINTER: COLORBAR
PAPER: UTOPIA II BOOK MATTE 80 LB., UTOPIA II GLOSS 60 LB. COVER,
CANSON SATIN TRANSLUCENT 29 LB. TEXT, CANSON SATIN RED 27 LB. TEXT,
CANSON SATIN TRANSLUCENT 48 LB. TEXT, LITMUS BLUE, LITMUS UNIVERSAL ORANGE,
POPSET CURIOUS CRYOGEN WHITE 80 LB. COVER, BUCKRAM BLUE COVER
BINDER: COLORBAR
METHOD OF BINDING: CASEBOUND, MICRO-PERFORATED, FRENCH-FOLD
PUBLISHER: STONE YAMASHITA PARTNERS

CHEMISTRY (AND THE CATALYSTS FOR SEISMIC CHANGE)

We help CEOs and leadership teams take their companies through eras of extreme change. The purpose of this book was to take ideas, lessons, truths and examples gleaned from our experience, and weave them into a consistent, engaging story. We chose the metaphor of chemistry to talk about the "work of change."

The biggest parameter was our own desire not to go overboard on the design merely because we could. We tried to be deliberate about where we innovated in the design, always pursuing the goal of making the content more engaging.

The thing that seems to delight readers most is the fact that the pages are French-folded and perforated. Break the perf, and every page opens up to reveal more content inside.

CREATIVE DIRECTOR: ROBERT PRIEST, PRIEST MEDIA, NEW YORK
DESIGNERS: PETER B. CURY, ROBERT PRIEST, PRIEST MEDIA, NEW YORK
ILLUSTRATOR: CHRISTOPH NIEMANN (COVER)
PRODUCTION COORDINATOR: MARK HEFLIN
TRIM SIZE: 9 1/4 X 12 1/4 INCHES
PAGES: 432
QUANTITY PRINTED: 3,000
COMPOSITOR: DAI NIPPON
TYPEFACE: AVENIR
PRINTER: DAI NIPPON
PAPER: BIBEREST 135 G/M²
METHOD OF BINDING: SMYTHE-SEWN
PUBLISHER: AMILUS, INC.

AMERICAN ILLUSTRATION 20

Each of the recent annuals made significant improvements to the book, so our challenge with this one was to go a step further to create a package that would have universal appeal, not just for art directors and illustrators. The stipulation that each page should feature a single piece of art (we had proposed this notion for the first annual in 1982) allows the reader uncluttered access to the work. Christoph Niemann's response to the cover (and inside illustrations) was brilliant. His exquisite technique combined with his whimsical sense of humor gives the book its individuality.

DESIGNER: STUART HENLEY, STUART HENLEY GRAPHIC DESIGN, HONOLULU, HAWAI'I
DESIGN ASSISTANT: JUNG KIM, STUART HENLEY GRAPHIC DESIGN, HONOLULU, HAWAI'I
COVER ART: ROGER WHITLOCK
PRODUCTION COORDINATORS: WAYNE KAWAMOTO, JIM REIS
TRIM SIZE: 5 1/2 X 8 1/2 INCHES
PAGES: 240
QUANTITY PRINTED: 25,000
COMPOSITOR: STUART HENLEY
TYPEFACES: MRS. EAVES, UNIVERS
PRINTER: MCNAUGHTON & GUNN, INC.
PAPER: WRITERS NATURAL 60 LB. TEXT, CIS 10 PT.
METHOD OF BINDING: PERFECT-BOUND
EDITOR: MICHAEL PULELOA
PUBLISHER: UNIVERSITY OF HAWAI'I MANOA BOARD OF PUBLICATIONS

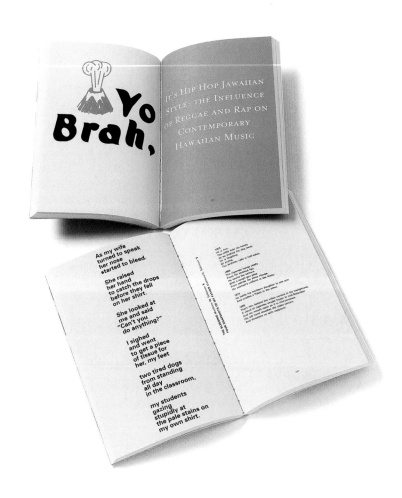

HAWAI'I REVIEW 56

The goal was to create a solution encouraging different reading styles and to make the text accessible to a wider audience. The introductory pages encourage reading rather than "selecting." The first lines of each poem and the first paragraphs of each essay form an additional text impressing upon the reader the character of the book. The geometric and strange organic black shapes that appear throughout the book are recognized by some readers who are familiar with Hawai'i, baffling others at the same time. With an eclectic mix of images and texts it is hoped that something new can be discovered with every reading.

DESIGNER: DOUGLAS FITCH, BROOKLYN, NEW YORK
ILLUSTRATOR: DOUGLAS FITCH
PHOTOGRAPHER: KATHERINE BORDEAUX
PRODUCTION COORDINATOR: DAVID JANIK
TRIM SIZE: 6 X 6 INCHES
PAGES: 160
QUANTITY PRINTED: 1,000
COMPOSITOR: DAVID JANIK
TYPEFACE: MATRIX
PRINTER: DAVID SCHULMAN, KROMAR PRINTING
PAPER: MOHAWK FLAX 70 LB. TEXT
METHOD OF BINDING: PERFECT-BOUND, FOAM COVER, DIE-CUT, WITH DOUBLE-STICK PAPER,
HAND APPLIED TO BOOK
JACKET PRINTER: INDUSTRIAL PLASTICS
AUTHORS: DOUGLAS FITCH, RICHARD EOIN NASH
PUBLISHER: MULTI-ART INTERNATIONAL

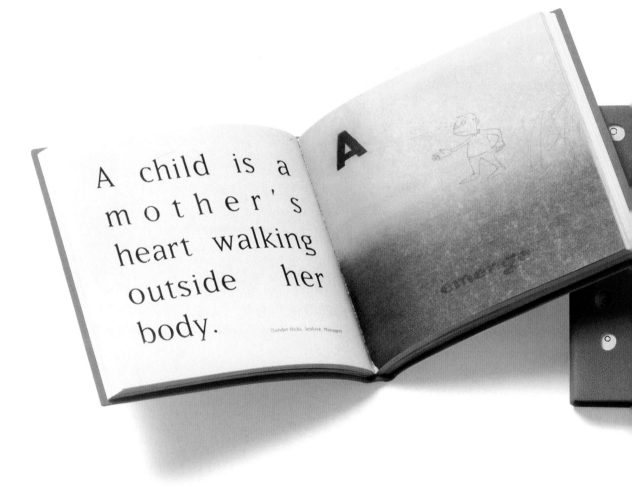

ORGANS OF EMOTION

Whereas the exhibition "Organs of Emotion" was about ideas for a new anatomy based on human emotions, this book, the catalogue accompanying the exhibition, is about depicting emotions in the language of art. As such, the cover is intended to represent a kind of outer tissue for these invented emotional organs, with the book inside being a bladder of ideas. The holes in the cover are meant to facilitate osmosis of those ideas, and come partially removed to encourage interaction with the book's absorbee.

What I like is that it looks like a feeling and it feels the way it looks.

13
book design: 50 books/50 covers

ART DIRECTORS: PAUL KEPPLE, HEADCASE DESIGN, PHILADELPHIA;
NANCY AUSTIN, TEN SPEED PRESS, BERKELEY, CALIFORNIA
DESIGNER: PAUL KEPPLE, HEADCASE DESIGN, PHILADELPHIA
PRODUCTION COORDINATOR: HAL HERSHEY
TRIM SIZE: 5 1/2 X 7 INCHES
QUANTITY PRINTED: 30,000 (*WRITE RIGHT!*), 11,500 (*REWRITE RIGHT!*)
TYPEFACES: AVENIR, MONOLINE SCRIPT, SURBURBAN
PRINTER: TRANSCONTINENTAL PRINTING INC.
AUTHOR: JAN VENOLIA
EDITOR: KATHRYN HASHIMOTO
PUBLISHER: TEN SPEED PRESS

WRITE RIGHT! AND *REWRITE RIGHT!* COVERS

The challenge was to take a relatively dry and intimidating subject—
writing proper prose and grammar—and make it seem fun and friendly.
Because these are guidebooks, we wanted the covers to be functional as
well as visually appealing. We decided to make the covers reference
charts of the various terms and symbols used throughout the books.
Lively typefaces and rich colors were used to give them some visual punch.

13
book design: 50 books/50 covers

DESIGNERS: FRANÇOISE MOULY, ART SPIEGELMAN, NEW YORK
ILLUSTRATORS: CHARLES BURNS, KIM DEITCH, IAN FALCONER, JULES FEIFFER,
CROCKETT JOHNSON, KAZ, MARTIN HANDFORD, JACQUES de LOUSTAL, BARBARA McCLINTOCK,
RICHARD McGUIRE, CLAUDE PONTI, FRANÇOIS ROCA, MARC ROSENTHAL, MAURICE SENDAK,
POSY SIMMONDS, ART SPIEGELMAN, LEWIS TRONDHEIM
INCLUDING TEXT BY: PAUL AUSTER, DAVID SEDARIS
PRODUCTION COORDINATORS: RUIKO TOKUNAGA, HARPERCOLLINS; FRANÇOISE MOULY,
NOVA REN SUMA, RAW
TRIM SIZE: 9 1/4 X 13 1/8 INCHES
PAGES: 64
QUANTITY PRINTED: 55,000
PRINTER: OCEANIC GRAPHIC PRINTING
PAPER: JAPANESE WOODFREE WHITE 140 G/M²
METHOD OF BINDING: CASE-BOUND, SECTION-SEWN WITH SEPARATED ENDS, FULLY CASED
WITH PLC OVER BOARD, SQUARE-BACKED
EDITORS: FRANÇOISE MOULY, ART SPIEGELMAN
PUBLISHER: HARPERCOLLINS PUBLISHERS/JOANNA COTLER BOOKS

LITTLE LIT: STRANGE STORIES FOR STRANGE KIDS

The challenge in editing and producing the _Little Lit_ anthology was to gather contributions by the top artists and writers working today and encourage them to do their best work while appealing to children. The challenge in designing the book was to establish an overarching look while giving each individual style its due. We designed breathy headers and bouncy page numbers. The contents spread was handled by superimposing one enlarged detail from the cover onto many small details from the inside. The cover was perfect for a book of strange stories. We had to pressure Charles Burns into giving us a "cute" monster, as he wasn't sure he had it in him. He certainly did.

13
book design: 50 books/50 covers

DESIGNER: JERRY KELLY, JERRY KELLY LLC, NEW YORK
PHOTOGRAPHER: BOB LORENSZON
PRODUCTION COORDINATOR: SARAH FUNKE
TRIM SIZE: 6 X 9 INCHES
PAGES: 96
QUANTITY PRINTED: 1,000
COMPOSITOR: JERRY KELLY
TYPEFACE: MILLER
PRINTER: THE STUDLEY PRESS
PAPER: COUGAR OPAQUE 70 LB. TEXT
BINDER: MUELLER TRADE BINDERY
METHOD OF BINDING: PERFECT-BOUND, PAPERBACK
AUTHOR: SARAH FUNKE
PUBLISHER: GLENN HOROWITZ BOOKSELLER

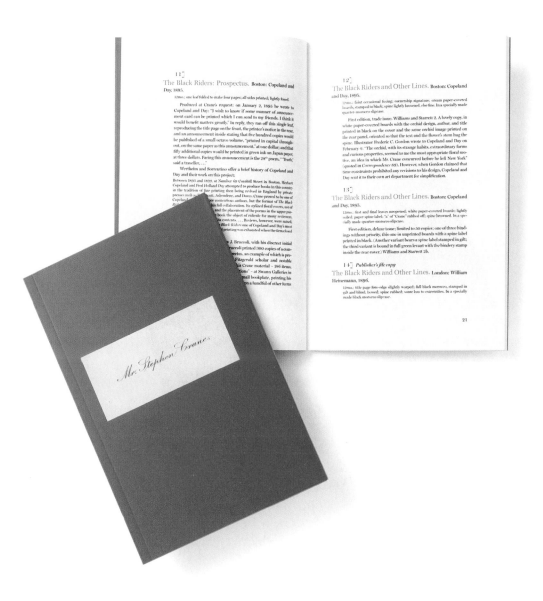

STEPHEN CRANE

The objective was to make a readable, interesting design for a listing
of old books. By using two colors throughout, some rules and a handsome
typographic layout—together with a sprinkling of full-color illustrations—
we achieved the desired look. I'm happiest with the way the type falls
on the page and the quality of the printing. The intended audiences
were book collectors and students of American literature.

13
book design: 50 books/50 covers

CREATIVE DIRECTOR: LANA RIGSBY, RIGSBY DESIGN, HOUSTON
DESIGNERS: LANA RIGSBY, PAMELA ZUCCKER, RIGSBY DESIGN, HOUSTON
PHOTOGRAPHER: TERRY VINE
TRIM SIZE: 7 3/4 X 6 BOOK IN 8 1/8 X 6 3/8 BOX
PAGES: 56
TYPEFACES: CLARENDON, SCALA, TRADE GOTHIC
PRINTER: H. MACDONALD PRINTING | BLANCHETTE PRESS
PAPER: FOX RIVER STARWHITE VICKSBURG ARCHIVA 80 LB. TEXT
METHOD OF BINDING: SIDE-SEWN BOOK
WITH DEBOSSED TISSUE COVER; INSERTED INTO CUSTOM CLAMSHELL BOX
WRITER: LANA RIGSBY
TRANSLATIONS: RAUL PAVON

25 RETRATOS: TERRY VINE IMÁGENES MEXICANAS

This book is photographer Terry Vine's portrait of the central-Mexican village of San Miguel de Allende. The intimate images offer a peek at festivals, holy days and "diversiones" seldom seen by outsiders—from cockfights to quincinaeras to crucifixions. Notations at the bottom of each page, plus a map in the center of the book, offer an insider's guide to the best locations for obscure and often exotic games and rituals throughout Mexico.

DESIGNER: GARY TOOTH, EMPIRE DESIGN STUDIO, NEW YORK
TRIM SIZE: 5 X 7 INCHES
QUANTITY PRINTED: 1,500
TYPEFACES: ROSEWOOD, UNIVERS
PAPER: FRENCH PAPER COMPANY CEMENT GREEN 80 LB. COVER
PRINTER: O'KEEFE PRINTING, LTD.
AUTHOR: MARY DINABURG
PUBLISHER: DINABURG ARTS/SAKS FIFTH AVENUE

REFLECTIONS: SAKS FIFTH AVENUE PROJECT ART COVER

The book *Reflections* is a collection of art installations that used the windows at Saks Fifth Avenue stores as a venue. The cover had to represent a diverse collection of artists. By listing the artists names on the cover, no one individual was featured too prominently but all were included. By printing "reflections" backwards it puts the reader on the inside of the windows, looking out.

CREATIVE DIRECTOR: ANDREW BLAUVELT, WALKER ART CENTER, MINNEAPOLIS
DESIGNER: LINDA BYRNE, WALKER ART CENTER, MINNEAPOLIS
PRODUCTION COORDINATOR: EUGENIA BELL
TRIM SIZE: 8 X 10 INCHES
PAGES: 368
QUANTITY PRINTED: 8,500
TYPEFACES: AKZIDENZ GROTESK, KNOCKOUT SERIES, WALBAUM
PRINTER: DR. CANTZ'SCHE DRUCKEREI
PAPER: MUNKEN LYNX 115/150 G/M², SIGNA SET YELLOW 120 G/M², BVS GLOSS 115 G/M²,
SIGNA SET CHERRY 80 G/M², SALAPRINT CG 135 G/M²
METHOD OF BINDING: SMYTHE-SEWN, END-GLUED, FLUSH TRIMMED
EDITOR: KAREN JACOBSON
PUBLISHERS: TATE, WALKER ART CENTER

ZERO TO INFINITY: ARTE POVERA 1962–1972

This catalogue documents an exhibition that examines the work of 14 Italian artists who explored a wide range of common materials to create extraordinary works. The book deploys a range of graphic devices without mimicking specific historical styles. The tactile nature of the artists' works is referenced, for example, in the range of papers used throughout the book, each delineating a different section (essays, timeline, artworks, back-matter). The flush-cut treatment of the cover not only exposes the construction of these sections, but also emphasizes the object-like quality of the book.

Large horizontal images were turned on edge to save space, which in turn enhanced the physicality of the book by shifting its orientation.

DESIGNER: JUDITH STEEDMAN, STEEDMAN DESIGN, VANCOUVER
ILLUSTRATOR: IASSEN GHIUSELEV
TRIM SIZE: 7 5/8 X 11 INCHES
PAGES: 156
QUANTITY PRINTED: 5,500
TYPEFACE: MINION, POETICA
PRINTER: GRAFICHE AZ
PAPER: ACID FREE
METHOD OF BINDING: SMYTHE-SEWN, HARDCOVER WITH JACKET
AUTHOR: CARLO COLLODI
PUBLISHER: SIMPLY READ BOOKS

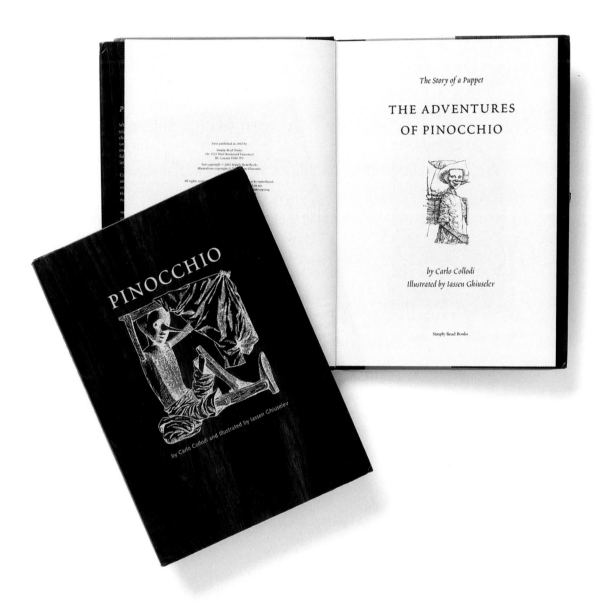

PINOCCHIO

The primary challenge with the design of this book was to reintroduce the richness and complexity of the classic tale of Pinocchio to an audience informed primarily by the Disney version. The recognizable wooden puppet is carved out of the dark, solid wood cover to foreshadow that for this moralistic tale about the challenges of life; the text clearly states: "the wood out of which Pinocchio is carved is humanity itself." In this way, the cover is at once recognizable and surprising. The body of the book is proportioned and set in a contemporary reworking of a traditional book layout, to speak to the tale's enduring history and to forefront Ghiuselev's illustrations.

13
book design: 50 books/50 covers

DESIGNER: PAUL BUCKLEY, NEW YORK
ILLUSTRATOR: ANDREW DAVIDSON
PRODUCTION COORDINATOR: DOLORES M. REILLY
TRIM SIZE: 5 1/2 X 8 7/16 INCHES
QUANTITY PRINTED: 18,000
TYPEFACES: CLARENDON, DEAR JOHN, HELVETICA, SONGOTHIC
PAPER: SEBAGO 2000, 50 LB.
PRINTER: CORAL GRAPHICS
AUTHOR: JOHN STEINBECK
PUBLISHER: PENGUIN

TRAVELS WITH CHARLEY AND *THE PEARL* COVERS

John Steinbeck is an American treasure, and as such, these titles have been packaged numerous times. I needed this new box-set edition to look classic without looking overly retro and dated. I also wanted these covers to stand the test of time and hopefully still look handsome many years from now.

DESIGNER: CHIP KIDD, ALFRED A. KNOPF, INC., NEW YORK
ILLUSTRATOR: CHARLES M. SCHULZ
PHOTOGRAPHER: GEOFF SPEAR
PRODUCTION COORDINATORS: ANDY HUGHES, SERENA PARK
TRIM SIZE: 8 1/2 X 7 INCHES
PAGES: 336
QUANTITY PRINTED: 168,000
COMPOSITOR: TOPPAN PRINTING CO.
TYPEFACES: CENTURY SCHOOLBOOK, TRADE GOTHIC
PRINTER: TOPPAN PRINTING CO.
PAPER: JAPANESE ART MATTE 128 G/M²
METHOD OF BINDING: SMYTHE-SEWN
AUTHOR: CHARLES M. SCHULZ
EDITOR: CHIP KIDD
PUBLISHER: PANTHEON BOOKS

PEANUTS

For a single book to do Schulz's work justice it would have to be about four times as long as this one.

That was the bittersweet conclusion I came to while figuring out what this book was going to be, and once I accepted it (however grudgingly), I was able to give myself limits and parameters (maximum page count for what we wanted to sell it for, etc.) that enabled me to finish. Otherwise I'd still be working on it.

It's deeply flawed, which is entirely my fault—not the subject's or anyone else's—but at least it serves as a proper introduction to what I feel is one of the great single literary works of the second half of the 20th century.

DESIGNER: FRANK VIVA, VIVA DOLAN COMMUNICATIONS AND DESIGN INC., TORONTO
ILLUSTRATOR: FRANK VIVA
PHOTOGRAPHER: RON BAXTER SMITH
PRODUCTION COORDINATOR: HIRAM PINES
TRIM SIZE: 6 X 9 1/2 INCHES
PAGES: 40
QUANTITY PRINTED: 34,000
COMPOSITOR: RICHARD HUNT
TYPEFACE: GROTESQUE MT
PRINTERS: LOGISTIQUE, VASTI IMPRESSION
PAPER: ARJO WIGGINS CURIOUS COLLECTION
METHOD OF BINDING: SMYTHE-SEWN, PERFECT-BOUND
EDITOR: FRANK VIVA
PUBLISHER: ARJO WIGGINS

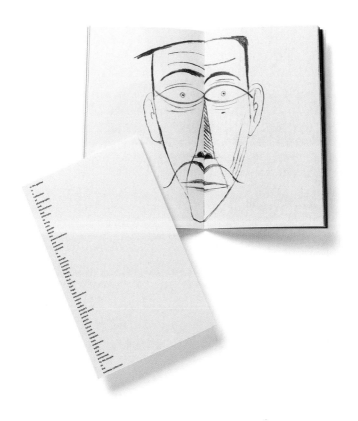

IN THE GUTTER

To help launch the Curious Collection, a new brand of fine papers from Arjo Wiggins, we created this printed brochure to strengthen the campaign targeting the advertising and graphic design communities.

We identified 3 goals: firstly to show the 4 paper lines under the Curious Collection umbrella; secondly to reinforce the brand we introduced through an integrated system of swatch books; and thirdly to minimize the cost of printing plate changes and information management in 14 languages.

We came up with the theme "in the gutter." Each image interacts with the physical gutter rather than avoiding it.

DESIGNER: MIKE SAVITSKI, SAVITSKI DESIGN, ANN ARBOR, MICHIGAN
PRODUCTION AND DESIGN MANAGER: ALICE NIGOGHOSIAN,
WAYNE STATE UNIVERSITY PRESS, DETROIT
TRIM SIZE: 18 X 13 INCHES
PAGES: 256
QUANTITY PRINTED: 4,000 REGULAR EDITIONS, 300 LIMITED EDITIONS
TYPEFACE: FAIRFIELD
PRINTER: UNIVERSITY LITHOPRINTERS
PAPER: MOHAWK SUPERFINE 100 LB. TEXT
BINDER: ROSWELL BINDERY
METHOD OF BINDING: SMYTHE-SEWN
JACKET PRINTER: INDUSTRIAL PRINTING
AUTHOR: BRIAN LEIGH DUNNIGAN
PUBLISHER: WAYNE STATE UNIVERSITY PRESS

ontier Metropolis

ring Early Detroit, 1701–1838   *Brian Leigh Dunnigan*

Frontier Metropolis was published by Wayne State University Press to celebrate Detroit's 300th birthday. It chronicles the city's pre-photographic history using more than 280 maps, artifacts and documents from collections all over the world.

Premium uncoated paper was selected to reflect the warm, tactile qualities of the original maps depicted in the book. The 18- by 13-inch page size and 300-line color separations allowed for large, highly detailed reproductions but also meant a physically challenging volume to navigate. To aid the reader, the dates of each work and figure numbers were placed in the outer margin for easy reference.

13
book design: 50 books/50 covers

CREATIVE DIRECTOR: MARTHA KENNEDY, HOUGHTON MIFFLIN CO., NEW YORK
DESIGNER: LAURIE ROSENWALD, ROSENWORLD.COM, NEW YORK
ILLUSTRATOR: LAURIE ROSENWALD
PRODUCTION COORDINATOR: JILL LAZER
TRIM SIZE: 5 5/8 X 9 1/2 INCHES
QUANTITY PRINTED: 12,500
TYPEFACE: BULMER
PAPER: QUEBECOR LIBERTY CREAM-WHITE ANTIQUE 50 LB. TEXT
PRINTER: PLYMOUTH COLOR
AUTHOR: JOSEPH EPSTEIN
PUBLISHER: HOUGHTON MIFFLIN CO.

SNOBBERY: THE AMERICAN VERSION COVER

The only hurdle I faced was limiting myself to just one solution;
I tried about 80 different ideas, because it was such a funny subject
and one so close to my heart.

    The part I am happiest with? The nose. It's hard to find a good
one, you know.

13

book design: 50 books/50 covers

SENIOR DESIGNER: M. KRISTEN BEARSE, ALFRED A. KNOPF, INC., NEW YORK

PRODUCTION COORDINATOR: KATHY GRASSO

TRIM SIZE: 5 1/2 X 8 1/4 INCHES

PAGES: 400

QUANTITY PRINTED: 9,000

COMPOSITORS: M. KRISTEN BEARSE, NORTH MARKET STREET GRAPHICS

TYPEFACES: AKZIDENZ GROTESK, CLARENDON, GILL SANS, PLANTIN, ZAPF DINGBATS

PRINTER: R. R. DONNELLEY & SONS

PAPER: STRATEGIC ANTIQUE CREAM 50 LB. TEXT

BINDER: R. R. DONNELLEY & SONS

METHOD OF BINDING: HARDCOVER, BURST

JACKET DESIGNER: ARCHIE FERGUSON

JACKET PRINTER: CORAL GRAPHICS

AUTHOR: KURT THOMETZ

EDITOR: ERROU MCDONALD

PUBLISHER: PANTHEON BOOKS

LIFE TURNS MAN UP AND DOWN

The challenge of the interior design of this book was to unify the author's collection of African open-air market pamphlets as a coherent volume whilst maintaining their individual characteristics. In some cases, we reproduced the entire pamphlet and in other cases, we only used a couple of pages or a group of pages.

To capture the look and feeling of the pamphlets we used several "dirty" blank pages as backgrounds—to give an aged-newsprint effect—and limited ourselves to the three colors that were used on the covers of the originals (pink, blue and green). To meet budgetary constraints we could only print one color per signature, so the pagination had to be precise.

CREATIVE DIRECTORS: STEVEN GUARNACCIA, SUSAN HOCHBAUM, MONTCLAIR, NEW JERSEY
DESIGNER: SUSAN HOCHBAUM, MONTCLAIR, NEW JERSEY
PHOTOGRAPHER: JAMES SHANKS
TRIM SIZE: 4 7/8 X 6 5/8 INCHES
PAGES: 256
QUANTITY PRINTED: 10,000
TYPEFACES: DIN, MONOLINE SCRIPT
PRINTER: IMAGO
PAPER: JAPANESE MATTE 157 G/M²
METHOD OF BINDING: PERFECT-BOUND
AUTHOR: STEVEN GUARNACCIA
EDITOR: ALAN RAPP
PUBLISHER: CHRONICLE BOOKS

BLACK AND WHITE

Black and White is a book of contrasts from the natural world and man-made culture, including nuns and convicts, skeletons and saddle shoes, mourning masks and Rorschach tests.

 The design challenge was to sustain variety and visual interest over 250 pages, despite a restricted palette. Sequencing, scale and composition—always important—became the crucial elements in totally immersing the reader in black-and-whiteness. The cover and chapter title typography provided a graphic and conceptual counterpoint to the imagery. Exaggerating scale and bleeding pages helped the book feel larger than its trim size.

CREATIVE DIRECTORS: KATHY FREDRICKSON, CHERYL TOWLER WEESE, GAIL WIENER,
STUDIO BLUE, CHICAGO
DESIGNERS: JAKE GARDNER, INGA NADEN, KAYO TAKASUGI, SUE WALSH,
CHERYL TOWLER WEESE, GAIL WIENER, STUDIO BLUE, CHICAGO
TYPOGRAPHIC PHOTOGRAPHY: MATT SIMPSON, GAIL WIENER
PRODUCTION COORDINATOR: SARAH GUERNSEY
TRIM SIZE: 8 1/2 X 12 INCHES
PAGES: 272
TYPEFACES: GOTHIC 13, HTF CHAMPION, NEWS GOTHIC
PRINTER: AMILCARE PIZZI
PAPER: LARIUS
METHOD OF BINDING: FLEXI-BOUND, PAPER OVER THIN BOARD
AUTHORS: ELIZABETH SIEGEL, DAVID TRAVIS
PUBLISHERS: THE ART INSTITUTE OF CHICAGO, THE UNIVERSITY OF CHICAGO PRESS

TAKEN BY DESIGN: PHOTOGRAPHS FROM THE INSTITUTE OF DESIGN, 1937-1971

The seminal photography program at Chicago's Institute of Design was begun by Moholy-Nagy in the 1930s and developed by photographic greats Harry Callahan and Aaron Siskind into the 1970s.

We tried to capture the school's philosophy of documentation and experimentation in this catalogue—pairing large documentary images of the school with graphic, straightforward typography, while using our own photographs of light and type for titles and chapter openers. Titles wrap the book's spine and pages, and book boards are thin and flexible, referencing the school's time- and motion-based work.

13

book design: 50 books/50 covers

DESIGNER: GREER ALLEN, NEW HAVEN, CONNECTICUT
PHOTOGRAPHER: FLETCHER MANLEY
PRODUCTION COORDINATOR: JON QUAY
TRIM SIZE: 9 1/2 X 11 7/8 INCHES
PAGES: 100
QUANTITY PRINTED: 2,025
COMPOSITOR: ANN M. MORAN
TYPEFACES: HADRIANO, POLIPHILUS
PRINTER: THE STINEHOUR PRESS
PAPER: MOHAWK SUPERFINE EGGSHELL 100 LB. TEXT,
STRATHMORE RHODODENDRON BLACK 80 LB. COVER
BINDER: MUELLER TRADE BINDERY
METHOD OF BINDING: SMYTHE-SEWN, PAPERBACK, APPLIED SCORED JACKET WITH FULL FLAPS
AUTHOR: EARLE HAVENS
EDITOR: JAMES MOONEY
PUBLISHER: THE BEINECKE RARE BOOK AND MANUSCRIPT LIBRARY, YALE UNIVERSITY

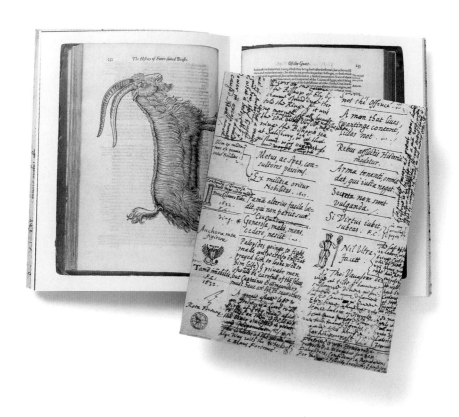

*COMMONPLACE BOOKS: A HISTORY OF MANUSCRIPTS AND
PRINTED BOOKS FROM ANTIQUITY TO THE TWENTIETH CENTURY*

The volume aims to set forth the origins of the commonplace book using Yale's broad Osborn collection to expound the genre and to invite scholars to use these books in their research.

To impart a heightened reality to the illustrated leaves, the printer scanned for duotones directly from the books—at life-size where possible—so the reader would come to feel, "I'm holding the actual thing in my hand!" The type, while remaining legible—even gutsy—was never allowed, in density or in scale, to challenge the pictures.

The occasional surround of eminently dull black allowed smaller illustrations to avoid seeming lost on the larger pages— while encouraging them to pop out.

43

book design: 50 books/50 covers

CREATIVE DIRECTORS: PAUL NEALE, ANDREW STEVENS, GRAPHIC THOUGHT FACILITY, LONDON
DESIGNERS: HUW MORGAN, PAUL NEALE, ANDREW STEVENS, GRAPHIC THOUGHT FACILITY, LONDON
PHOTOGRAPHER: HUW MORGAN
PRODUCTION COORDINATORS: HUW MORGAN, PAUL NEALE
TRIM SIZE: 148 1/2 X 210 MM
PAGES: 64
QUANTITY PRINTED: 3,000
COMPOSITOR: PAUL NEALE
TYPEFACES: HELVETICA NEUE, TIMES NEW ROMAN
PRINTER: STAMPERIA ARTISTICA NAZIONALE
PAPER: ZANDERS IKONO GLOSS 170 G/M², MEDLEY PURE WHITE 90 G/M²
METHOD OF BINDING: PERFECT-BOUND, CLEAR PLASTIC COVER
JACKET DESIGNERS: PAUL NEALE, ANDREW STEVENS
AUTHOR: EMILY KING
PUBLISHER: GABRIELE CAPELLI EDITORE

GTF-BITS WORLD

The publisher gave us a very open brief: write and design a book about Graphic Thought Facility's interests.

Being used to the discipline of working to tighter briefs, (we hardly ever produce self-authored work) we re-defined the challenge as: how can we present our commercial work to a broader audience that is more than just another design monograph of squared-up images?

We laid out ten years of work on the floor and wheeled a homemade "copy-camera" over it, shooting sections to a fixed scale.
Back in the design studio we converted a Casio wristwatch-camera to scan 35mm contact sheets for the contextual images for inclusion in the book.

I am happy that we managed to create a sense of theatre from the two-dimensional content.

DESIGNER: WALTER HAMADY, THE PERISHABLE PRESS LIMITED, MOUNT HOREB, WISCONSIN
PRODUCTION COORDINATOR: WALTER HAMADY
TRIM SIZE: 7 X 11 INCHES
PAGES: 52
QUANTITY PRINTED: 100
COMPOSITOR: WALTER HAMADY
TYPEFACE: SPEIDOTYPE BOLD 517J
PRINTER: WALTER HAMADY
PAPER: HAHNEMUHLE BIBLIO AND GUTENBERG, EVERGREEN SCRIPT
METHOD OF BINDING: HAND-SEWN BOARDS
AUTHOR: KENNETH BERNARD
PUBLISHER: THE PERISHABLE PRESS LIMITED

NULLITY

Every book poses the special question of how to convert the integrity
of meaning from idea to physical artifact with the guiding gnomon of
appropriateness. The solution has to do with egolessness in listening,
love and respect of text, and a crafting that allows for the dignity of
risk. The audience is fellow-subversives who absolutely love to read
books and who are addicted sensualists devoted to the extension of text.

ART DIRECTOR: JOHN FULBROOK III, SIMON & SCHUSTER, NEW YORK
DESIGNER: RODRIGO CORRAL, RODRIGO CORRAL DESIGN, NEW YORK
ILLUSTRATOR: ALEXA MULVIHILL
PRODUCTION COORDINATOR: JULIE PRIMAVERA
TRIM SIZE: 6 1/2 X 9 3/4 INCHES
QUANTITY PRINTED: 11,000
TYPEFACES: ROCKWELL, TRADE GOTHIC
PAPER: CUSTOM, COATED ONE SIDE, 80 LB.
PRINTER: PHOENIX
AUTHOR: TED HELLER
PUBLISHER: SCRIBNER

FUNNYMEN COVER

I was approached with the problem of designing a jacket for a 1950s period book that was supposed to have a retro style. I chose to focus on two period characters in the story who were different from each other in many external ways, but were also very much the same person. I chose one simple, streamlined period illustration to represent both characters, and divided it.

DESIGNER: SUSAN L. MITCHELL, FARRAR, STRAUS AND GIROUX, NEW YORK
COVER ART: "THE VEGETABLE GARDENER," BY GIUSEPPE ARCIMBOLDO
PRODUCTION COORDINATOR: PETER RICHARDSON
TRIM SIZE: 5 X 7 1/2 INCHES
PAGES: 176
QUANTITY PRINTED: 19,000
COMPOSITOR: STRATFORD PRINTING SERVICES
TYPEFACES: BERTHOLD SCRIPT, FIRST GRADER, GRANJON, KUENSTLER SCRIPT,
ROCOCO ORNAMENTS #1
PRINTER: R. R. DONNELLEY & SONS
PAPER: GLATFELTER B-18 CREAM 55 LB. TEXT
METHOD OF BINDING: NOTCH BINDING
JACKET PRINTER: PHOENIX COLOR
AUTHOR: JIM CRACE
PUBLISHER: FARRAR, STRAUS AND GIROUX

THE DEVIL'S LARDER

The challenge in designing books is always the same for me: exercising restraint in my text layout to allow the author's words to emerge without sacrificing overall design "oomph." My choice of ornamentation reflected the "devil's appetite" theme of the 64 short fictions. With a limited budget, I worked closely with my production manager to juggle costs, thus enabling us to afford a second color for the first signature and colorfully printed endpapers. My favorite design element is the naughty red "s" in the title.

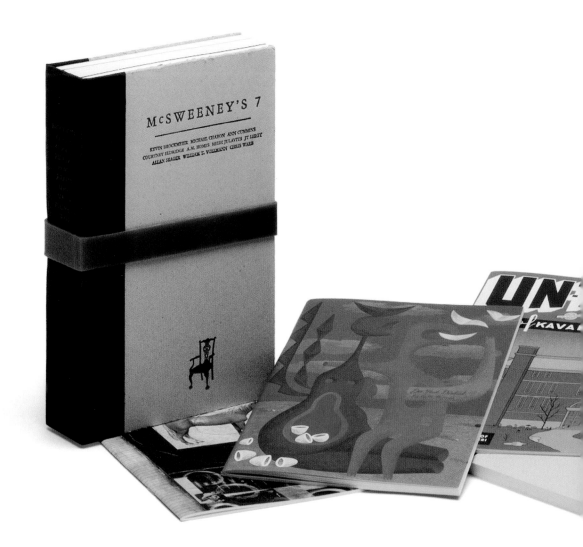

Giving each story in this issue of *McSweeney's* its own binding and cover is a great way to work with lots of artists at once and to make ten books when you're supposed to be making one. The outer cover is just raw board with the type letterpressed into it. We wanted to have a thick rubber band holding the booklets together, but the printer, Oddi Printing of Reykjavik, felt they might buckle within the band, and recommended using a hardcover shell with the books slipped inside. We love the result; it looks like a book in mid-process, before binding—very raw. As always, it was a true collaboration between Oddi Printing, Elizabeth Kairys (who commissioned all the illustrations) and the authors.

13
book design: 50 books/50 covers

ART DIRECTORS: DAVE EGGERS, ELIZABETH KAIRYS, *MCSWEENEY'S*, SAN FRANCISCO
DESIGNER: DAVE EGGERS, *MCSWEENEY'S*, SAN FRANCISCO
ILLUSTRATORS: MELINDA BECK, TIM BOWER, ELIZABETH KAIRYS, SHARON LEONG,
KATHERINE STREETER, CHRIS WARE, ERIC WHITE
PRODUCTION COORDINATOR: ARNI SIGURDSSON, ODDI PRINTING
TRIM SIZE: 5 1/2 X 8 1/4 INCHES
PAGES: 335
QUANTITY PRINTED: 15,000
TYPEFACE: GARAMOND 3
PRINTER: ODDI PRINTING
PAPER: BOOK DESIGN SMOOTH 120 G/M², MUNKEN LYNX 170 G/M², KAPPA 2.5 MM
(BINDERS BOARDS)
BINDER: ODDI PRINTING
METHOD OF BINDING: SADDLE-STITCHED, RUBBER BAND
AUTHORS: KEVIN BROCKMEIER, MICHAEL CHABON, ANN CUMMINS, COURTNEY ELDRIDGE,
A.M. HOMES, HEIDI JULAVITS, JT LEROY, ALLAN SEAGER, WILLIAM T. VOLLMAN
EDITOR: DAVE EGGERS
PUBLISHER: *MCSWEENEY'S*

ART DIRECTOR: LORRAINE WILD, LORRAINE WILD GRAPHIC DESIGN, LOS ANGELES
DESIGNERS: ROBERT RUEHLMAN, AMANDA WASHBURN,
LORRAINE WILD, LORRAINE WILD GRAPHIC DESIGN, LOS ANGELES
PHOTOGRAPHER: PAULA GOLDMAN
PRODUCTION COORDINATOR: LORRAINE WILD
TRIM SIZE: 8 1/2 X 11 INCHES
PAGES: 464
QUANTITY PRINTED: 3,000
TYPEFACES: CHOLLA, FOUNDRY SANS
PRINTER: DR. CANTZ'SCHE DRUCKEREI
PAPER: ZANDERS IKONOFIX
METHOD OF BINDING: HARDCOVER WITH TIPPED-IN PAPER
EDITORS: CINDY BURLINGHAM, BRUCE WHITEMAN
PUBLISHERS: GETTY PUBLICATIONS,
UCLA GRUNWALD CENTER FOR THE GRAPHIC ARTS,
UCLA HAMMER MUSEUM

THE WORLD FROM HERE: TREASURES OF THE GREAT LIBRARIES IN LOS ANGELES

This catalogue was for an exhibition of great books from publicly accessible collections in Los Angeles. The books were organized into a set of broad themes, and then chronologically within those themes; it was this categorizing that set the major design parameter for the book. We reshot every book that was to be depicted in the catalogue, and we tried to emphasize the physicality of the books as objects.

The entire book is one large checklist, with every book in the show listed, and the books that are depicted are signed with a silhouette of their shape to key the reader to the caption that accompanies the book. Process color backgrounds are used to differentiate the major organizational categories.

13

book design: 50 books/50 covers

ART DIRECTOR: STEVE TOLLESON, TOLLESON DESIGN, SAN FRANCISCO
DESIGNER: CRAIG CLARK, TOLLESON DESIGN, SAN FRANCISCO
PRODUCTION COORDINATOR: ELLEN ELFERING
TRIM SIZE: 10 1/4 X 9 1/2 INCHES
PAGES: 272
QUANTITY PRINTED: 2,500
TYPEFACES: SCALA, TRADE GOTHIC
PRINTER: TOPPAN
PAPER: OFF-SHORE, COATED TEXT #2 GRADE
BINDER: TIM JAMES, TAURUS BOOKBINDING
METHOD OF BINDING: SMYTHE-SEWN, THREE-PIECE CASE-BOUND
JACKET PRINTER: PRESS ARTS
AUTHORS: NEIL FEINEMAN, STEVE REISS
PUBLISHER: HARRY N. ABRAMS

THIRTY FRAMES PER SECOND: THE VISIONARY ART OF THE MUSIC VIDEO

We had to translate the movement and energy of the music video format to print and also organize the catalog of music video directors and their work.

We made the format similar to a letterbox screen, designing each page to have its own unique personality. A number of different fonts were used to help express motion.

The most difficult parameter was translating the video screen shots into print. Many could not be blown up to a large size, and for printing purposes, the RGB imagery needed to be converted to CMYK, so maintaining color consistency and image quality was an issue.

The plexiglass cover—with its resemblance to a CD case and a television screen—elevates the book to an entirely different level.

13
book design: 50 books/50 covers

DESIGNER: FRANC NUNOO-QUARCOO, NUNOO-QUARCOO DESIGN, BALTIMORE
PHOTOGRAPHER: DAN MEYERS
TRIM SIZE: 9 X 12 INCHES
QUANTITY PRINTED: 3,000
TYPEFACES: MONOTYPE CENTURY EXPANDED, MONOTYPE FUTURA
PAPER: IKONO SILK
PRINTER: ODDI PRINTING
AUTHOR: MAURICE BERGER
EDITORS: MAURICE BERGER, JOHN FARMER, ANTONIA GARDNER
PUBLISHER: CENTER FOR ART AND VISUAL CULTURE, UMBC

FRED WILSON: OBJECTS AND INSTALLATIONS, 1979-2000 COVER

The cover design for *Fred Wilson: Objects and Installations, 1979-2000* was conceived to have the viewer focus entirely on the artist and his art. With one image dominating both the front and back cover, the use of the spine of the book as the informational zone becomes critical. Dan Meyer's superb photograph of the artist's piece "Guarded View" assisted immeasurably in completing this process.

CREATIVE DIRECTOR: JOHN FONTANA, DOUBLEDAY, NEW YORK
ART DIRECTOR: RODRIGO CORRAL, DOUBLEDAY, NEW YORK
DESIGNER: RODRIGO CORRAL, DOUBLEDAY, NEW YORK
PHOTOGRAPHER: DAN BIBB
TRIM SIZE: 5 5/8 X 8 1/8 INCHES
QUANTITY PRINTED: 15,000
TYPEFACE: TRADE GOTHIC
PRINTER: CORAL GRAPHICS
AUTHOR: DAVID GRAND
PUBLISHER: DOUBLEDAY/NAN A. TALESE BOOKS

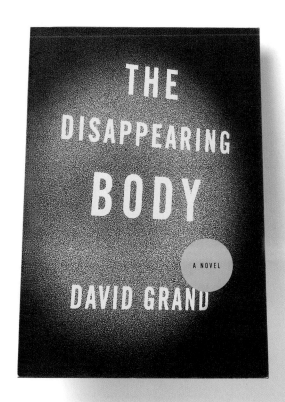

THE DISAPPEARING BODY COVER

I was approached with the problem of designing a jacket for a noir thriller, that wasn't supposed to look like a noir thriller. I chose strong title typeface, Trade Gothic, to illustrate the title's image, rather than creating a separate and literal illustrative translation of the title—since all that needed to be "seen" was in the words of the title itself: disappearing.

13
book design: 50 books/50 covers

ART DIRECTOR: ANGUS HYLAND, PENTAGRAM DESIGN INC., LONDON
DESIGNERS: ANGUS HYLAND, PENTAGRAM DESIGN INC., LONDON; PADDIE CRAMSIE
PHOTOGRAPHERS: RENE BURRI, MARC RIBOUD, GEORGE RODGER,
MAGNUM PHOTOS; HELGE SKODVIN, MILLENNIUM; GEORGIUS KAFALAS, MODELS PLUS;
CP MCDONOUGH, PHOTONICA; DIDIER GAILLARD, RON ROSENSTOCK,
RICHARD WAITE, SPECIAL PHOTOGRAPHERS COMPANY; MICHAEL WILDSMITH
PAGES: 821; QUANTITY PRINTED: 53,300; TYPEFACE: UNIVERS
PRINTER: OFFSET PAPERBACK MANUFACTURERS
PAPER: PATHFINDER NATURAL 50 LB.
BINDER: OFFSET PAPERBACK MANUFACTURERS
METHOD OF BINDING: PERFECT-BOUND, SLIPCASE
JACKET DESIGNER: ANGUS HYLAND
JACKET PRINTER: OFFSET PAPERBACK MANUFACTURERS
PUBLISHERS: GROVE PRESS (U.S.), CANONGATE BOOKS (U.K.)

THE BOOKS OF THE BIBLE AND *THE POCKET CANONS*

Canongate Books published 12 extracts from the authorized version of the *King James Bible* in pocket book form. To broaden market appeal and make these well-known pieces of text more relevant to a contemporary audience, we decided to design these books as if they were for modern fiction.

A striking language of black-and-white photography was employed and combined with a strong graphic grid and a clear sans serif type-face. The tonal balance and typography holds the whole series together.

The tonally dark photographs were chosen from stock photography to avoid a particular photographer's style. Iconographic imagery was used such as a nuclear explosion for *Revelation* and a road receding into the distance for *Exodus*.

CREATIVE DIRECTOR: STEFAN SAGMEISTER, SAGMEISTER, INC., NEW YORK
DESIGNERS: HJALTI KARLSSON, STEFAN SAGMEISTER, SAGMEISTER, INC., NEW YORK
PHOTOGRAPHER: KEVIN KNIGHT (COVER)
PRODUCTION COORDINATOR: STEFAN SAGMEISTER
TRIM SIZE: 6 3/4 X 9 1/2 INCHES
PAGES: 294
QUANTITY PRINTED: 12,000
TYPEFACE: HANDWRITTEN
PRINTER: DAI NIPPON
PAPER: FLOOR PAPER, MATTE-COATED
METHOD OF BINDING: SMYTHE-SEWN, SEPARATE PLASTIC SLIPCASE
AUTHOR: PETER HALL
EDITOR: CHEE PEARLMAN
PUBLISHER: BOOTH-CLIBBORN EDITIONS

MADE YOU LOOK

Made You Look contains practically all the work we ever designed, including the bad stuff. It was published as a paperback contained in a red-tinted transparent slipcase.

    Removing the book from the slipcase causes the mood of the dog to worsen considerably; bending it results in "made you look" (or in the other direction "dog food") showing up on the fore edge.

    Peter Hall wrote a very detailed text (for a design book) and I included handwritten excerpts from my diary and many comments from our dear clients.

DESIGNERS: RUTH LINGEN, NEW YORK;
ALEXANDER S. C. ROWER, THE CALDER FOUNDATION, NEW YORK
ILLUSTRATOR: ALEXANDER CALDER
TRIM SIZE: 6 1/2 X 9 1/2 INCHES
PAGES: 14
QUANTITY PRINTED: 500
COMPOSITOR: RUTH LINGEN
TYPEFACE: NICHOLAS COCHIN
PRINTER: RUTH LINGEN
PAPER: SOMERSET BOOK WOVE SOFT WHITE 115 G/M²
METHOD OF BINDING: HAND-SEWN PAMPHLET STITCH WITH WRAPPER
AUTHOR: ELMER E. SCOTT
PUBLISHER: THE CALDER FOUNDATION

THE P-CULIAR DOG OR THE PIDDLING PUP

The design challenge of *The P-culiar Dog or The Piddling Pup* was to create a book in 2001 that looks and feels as if it was from circa 1925. We achieved this by using type, printing techniques and binding materials that were used at the time. Also, the credits appear on the colophon page rather than the title page, so the surprise is discovered at the end of the book.

We are happiest about maintaining the playful, informal feeling of Calder's original maquette.

ART DIRECTOR: MICHAELA SULLIVAN, HOUGHTON MIFFLIN CO., NEW YORK
DESIGNER: ARCHIE FERGUSON, NEW YORK
ILLUSTRATOR: JOHN JAMES AUDUBON
PRODUCTION COORDINATOR: RITA CULLEN
TRIM SIZE: 5 1/2 X 8 1/2 INCHES
QUANTITY PRINTED: 11,000
TYPEFACES: CLAREDON BOLD CONDENSED, ENGRAVERS, ESCRITA
PAPER: WHITE UNCOATED LINEN
PRINTER: HENRY SAWYER
AUTHOR: JOHN GREGORY BROWN
PUBLISHER: HOUGHTON MIFFLIN CO.

AUDUBON'S WATCH COVER

This is a slightly creepy but romantic novel with some love, death
(maybe murder) and, of course, an unacknowledged artist included.
It seemed obvious to use one of Audubon's drawings, especially a raven,
the symbol of death. The challenge was to use it in a way that it didn't
look like it was from a field guide while maintaining the integrity of
the art and possibly adding some of the darker qualities of the writing
to it in the process. I like the tactile quality of the final piece.
The ratty old binding, slightly sloppy design and antiquated fonts all
thrown together imprecisely create something that looks elegant and rich.

13
book design: 50 books/50 covers

DESIGNER: JORDAN CRANE, RED INK, LOS ANGELES
ILLUSTRATORS: JORDAN CRANE (COVER, INDEX); NICK BERTOZZI, BRIAN BIGGS, MAT
BRINKMAN, BRIAN CHIPPENDALE, DAVID CHOE, GREG COOK, JORDAN CRANE, TOM DEVLIN,
JASON, ULF K., DAVE KIERSH, MEGAN KELSO, JAMES KOCHALKA, PAUL LYONS, PAUL POPE,
PSHAW, BRIAN RALPH, RON REGE JR., STEVEN WEISSMAN, KURT WOLFGANG
PRODUCTION COORDINATOR: JORDAN CRANE
TRIM SIZE: 7 X 10 INCHES
PAGES: 472
QUANTITY PRINTED: 2,000
TYPEFACE: HAND-DRAWN BY JORDAN CRANE
PRINTER: QUEBECOR
PAPER: LARGE BOOK: TINTED 60 LB. TEXT, CORNWALL 12 PT.; TWO SMALLER BOOKS:
WILLIAMSBURGH REPLY TINTED 7 PT., BYRONIC EGGSHELL BROCADE FINISH; DUST JACKET:
FRENCH CONSTRUCTION WHITEWASH 70 LB. TEXT; DIE CUT: 1/4 INCH CORRUGATED
BINDERS: JORDAN CRANE, BROOKE COREY, TOM DEVLIN, HANNAH MILLER, JOHN PHAM,
STACY DOLIN, QUEBECOR
METHOD OF BINDING: SQUARE-BOUND, HAND SCORED AND GLUED DUST JACKETS
JACKET PRINTER: JORDAN CRANE, FIREHOUSE
EDITOR: JORDAN CRANE
PUBLISHER: RED INK

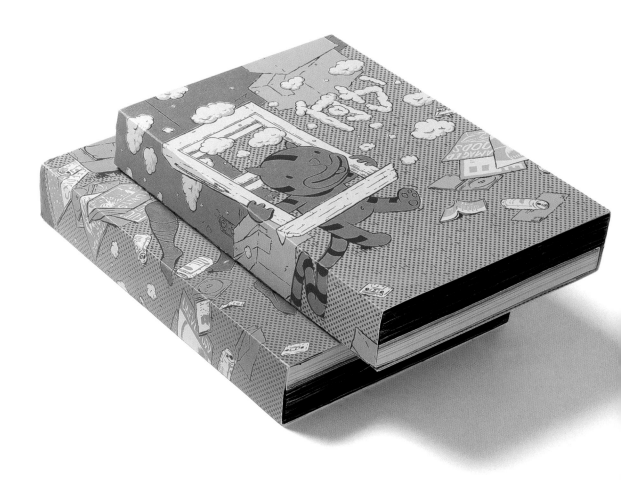

NON NO. 5

Because of the diversity of art and storytelling used by the comics in
this collection, the primary challenge was to unify without taking away
from the individual voice of each story. Two stories were too long for
the main book, and were printed in books of their own, and the same
identity problem—unified versus individual—was presented. I used a
two-color patterned cover—based on a single shape that is derived from
the book's content—with the same colors being used again on the inside,
the darker color as line art. Thus, maintaining their individuality
through design and layout, the books nonetheless appear to be a set
when presented together.

13
book design: 50 books/50 covers

DESIGNER: WALTER HAMADY, THE PERISHABLE PRESS LIMITED, MOUNT HOREB, WISCONSIN
ILLUSTRATOR: JOHN WILDE
PRODUCTION COORDINATOR: WALTER HAMADY
TRIM SIZE: 7 1/2 X 11 INCHES
PAGES: 124
QUANTITY PRINTED: 95
COMPOSITOR: WALTER HAMADY
TYPEFACE: GILL SANS
PRINTER: WALTER HAMADY
PAPER: AIKOI HANDMADES, TWINROCKER HANDMADES
METHOD OF BINDING: HANDSEWN IN HEAVY TWINROCKER "TINKERTAPE"
AUTHORS: WALTER HAMADY, JOHN WILDE
PUBLISHER: THE PERISHABLE PRESS LIMITED

SALUTATIONS 1995

Every book poses the special question of how to convert the integrity of meaning from idea to physical artifact with the guiding gnomon of appropriateness. The solution has to do with egolessness in listening love and respect of text, and a crafting that allows for the dignity of risk. The audience is fellow-subversives who absolutely love to read books and who are addicted sensualists devoted to the extension of text.

ART DIRECTOR: JOHN GALL, VINTAGE BOOKS, NEW YORK
DESIGNER: CHIN-YEE LAI, CHIN-YEE LAI DESIGN, FOREST HILLS, NEW YORK
PHOTOGRAPHER: SIMON LEE
TRIM SIZE: 5 3/16 X 8 INCHES
QUANTITY PRINTED: 6,000
TYPEFACE: BASKERVILLE OPTI
PRINTER: CORAL GRAPHICS
AUTHOR: ABIGAIL THOMAS
PUBLISHER: VINTAGE BOOKS

SAFEKEEPING: SOME TRUE STORIES FROM A LIFE COVER

Safekeeping is an autobiography, composed of short stories, which depicts events and moments of significance in the author's life. Though tumultuous, her life also seems to be her most treasured experience. The image of a glass storage jar sprang to mind when I asked myself the question: "How would people store their most valuable possessions?"

13
book design: 50 books/50 covers

DESIGNER: RENATE GOKL, CHICAGO
PHOTOGRAPHER: ERIK GOULD
TRIM SIZE: 11 X 11 INCHES
PAGES: 48
QUANTITY PRINTED: 2,500
COMPOSITOR: RENATE GOKL
TYPEFACE: BELL GOTHIC
PAPER: UTOPIA TWO 80 LB. TEXT, CHAMPION CARNIVAL 80 LB. COVER
PRINTER: MERIDIAN PRINTING
METHOD OF BINDING: PERFECT-BOUND WITH TOP-GROMMETING
EDITOR: LIISA SILANDER
PUBLISHER: MUSEUM OF ART, RHODE ISLAND SCHOOL OF DESIGN

A VIEW BY TWO: CONTEMPORARY JEWELRY

We had to design a 48-page exhibition catalogue featuring 14 artists'
works, including an essay/interview with the curator, artists' biographies,
a checklist and front matter. The challenge was to integrate the
disparate parts into a unified whole, and to create a flow avoiding
creating many little separate chunks of information.

We designed a system whereby the spreads of artists' plates and
bios could be interwoven with the essay/interview. This allowed the
curator's perspective and voice to accompany one's viewing of the work.
The unifying size of the transparencies created a natural parallel between
the various artists while the formal grid structure became a scaffold upon
which positive and negative space defined discrete areas of information.
Minimal use of a hairline rule also helped articulate boundaries.

13
book design: 50 books/50 covers

CREATIVE DIRECTOR: ANDREW BLAUVELT, WALKER ART CENTER, MINNEAPOLIS
DESIGNER: ALEX DEARMOND, WALKER ART CENTER, MINNEAPOLIS
PRODUCTION COORDINATOR: LISA MIDDAG
TRIM SIZE: 5 3/4 X 6 5/8 INCHES
PAGES: 128
QUANTITY PRINTED: 3,000
TYPEFACES: ELECTRA, NEUZEIT GROTESK
PRINTER: SHAPCO
PAPER: FINCH FINE VANILLA 80 LB. TEXT, PRODUCTOLITH DULL 80 LB. COVER
BINDER: TRAFFIC WORKS
METHOD OF BINDING: LOOP SADDLE STITCH, METAL RING BINDER
JACKET PRINTER: TRAFFIC WORKS
AUTHORS: DIANE GLANCY, DAVID HAYNES, PATRICIA HEMPL, NORAH LABINER, WANG PING,
GEORGE RABASA, BART SCHNEIDER, JULIE SCHUMACHER
EDITORS: PAMELA JOHNSON, KATHLEEN MCLEAN
PUBLISHER: WALKER ART CENTER

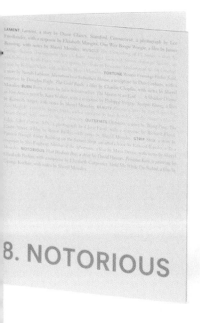

AMERICAN TABLEAUX

Instead of producing a single gallery guide for "American Tableaux," we produced eight different booklets, suggesting the plurality of interpretive possibilities contained within the exhibition. A new gallery guide is available each month during the eight-month run of the show, and finally bound into a single notebook.

    All the books were produced out of two press sheets, which determined the trim size. We used different paperstocks to articulate the difference between the writings and artworks. The translucent binder that houses the collection allows the front of a booklet to serve as a "cover" for the bound volume. This "non-cover/cover" treatment, the striped color scheme and the looped staples are three details that are particularly rewarding.

13
book design: 50 books/50 covers

DESIGN FIRM: VINTAGE BOOKS, NEW YORK

ART DIRECTOR: JOHN GALL, VINTAGE BOOKS, NEW YORK
DESIGNERS: NED DREW, NEWARK, NEW JERSEY; JOHN GALL, VINTAGE BOOKS, NEW YORK
ILLUSTRATORS: NED DREW, JOHN GALL
TRIM SIZE: 5 3/16 X 8 1/4 INCHES
QUANTITY PRINTED: 10,000
TYPEFACES: ALTERNATE GOTHIC, BODONI OLD FACE
PRINTER: CORAL GRAPHICS
AUTHOR: KOBO ABE
PUBLISHER: VINTAGE BOOKS

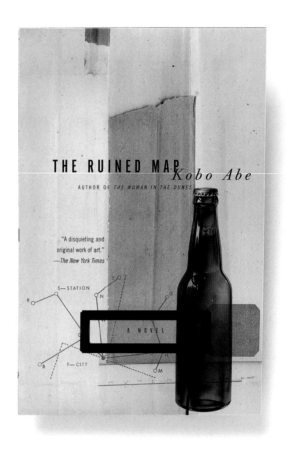

THE RUINED MAP AND *THE BOX MAN* COVERS

The Box Man and *The Ruined Map* are two titles in a series of redesigned
backlist covers for the author Kobo Abe. The designs and illustrations
are the result of a collaborative process between Ned Drew and myself.
They were produced via e-mail correspondence. A piece of art was sent
back and forth—with each person adding something to the collage—until
we reached a mutually agreed upon conclusion. This method, created by
Ned, utilizing imagery from the book (the surreal stories concern a detective
and man who wanders around Tokyo wearing a large box on his head) enabled
us to come up with unexpected and oddly juxtaposed artwork that
paralleled the often bizarre and dreamlike worlds created in Abe's books.

ART DIRECTOR: JOHN GALL, VINTAGE BOOKS, NEW YORK
DESIGNERS: NED DREW, NEWARK, NEW JERSEY; JOHN GALL, VINTAGE BOOKS, NEW YORK
ILLUSTRATORS: NED DREW, JOHN GALL
TRIM SIZE: 5 3/16 X 8 1/4 INCHES
QUANTITY PRINTED: 10,000
TYPEFACES: ALTERNATE GOTHIC, BODONI OLD FACE
PRINTER: CORAL GRAPHICS
AUTHOR: KOBO ABE
PUBLISHER: VINTAGE BOOKS

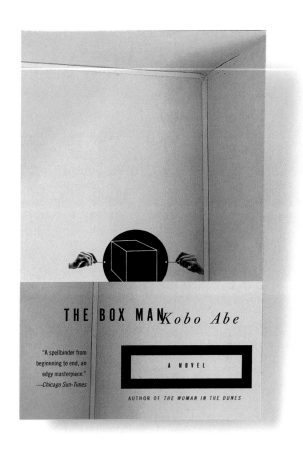

ART DIRECTOR: JOHN FULBROOK III, SIMON & SCHUSTER, NEW YORK
DESIGNER: KEVIN BRAINARD, SIMON & SCHUSTER, NEW YORK
PRODUCTION COORDINATOR: OLGA LEONARDO
TRIM SIZE: 5 7/8 X 8 15/16 INCHES
QUANTITY PRINTED: 34,000
TYPEFACES: SCRIPPS COLLEGE OLDSTYLE, TRAJAN
PAPER: TOMAHAWK 80 LB.
PRINTER: CORAL GRAPHICS
AUTHOR: CHLOE HOOPER
PUBLISHER: SCRIBNER

A CHILD'S BOOK OF TRUE CRIME COVER

The greatest difficulty I encountered with the design of this book cover was the complexity of the novel itself, which tells three stories simultaneously.

The design was influenced by a series of old children's books provided by the author and my love for the tactile quality of old books. It was also influenced by the eighth paragraph into the novel: "At the bottom of the cliffs, black swans sang mournfully. The stately birds dipped their necks in and out of the water, arching, straining: an ocean of questions marks."

13
book design: 50 books/50 covers

ART DIRECTOR: JOHN GALL, VINTAGE BOOKS, NEW YORK
DESIGNER: JAMIE KEENAN
PHOTOGRAPHER: MARC ATKINS, PANOPTIKA
PRODUCTION COORDINATOR: CLAIRE BRADLEY ONG
TRIM SIZE: 5 3/16 X 8 1/4 INCHES
QUANTITY PRINTED: 17,500
TYPEFACE: BASKERVILLE
PRINTER: CORAL GRAPHICS
AUTHOR: MOSES ISEGAWA
PUBLISHER: VINTAGE BOOKS

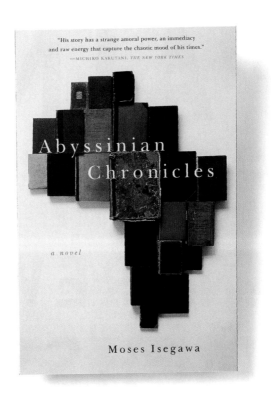

ABYSSINIAN CHRONICLES COVER

I liked the idea that *Abyssinian Chronicles* is a grand book in terms of location, timescale (and spine width) and the variety of serious subjects like poverty, war and AIDS, yet derives from the viewpoint of a young Ugandan boy.

In the same way, the cover is meant to convey the scale of the book's reach, without losing sight of its basis in individual characters.

ART DIRECTOR: CAROL DEVINE CARSON, ALFRED A. KNOPF, INC., NEW YORK
DESIGNER: EVAN GAFFNEY, EVAN GAFFNEY DESIGN, NEW YORK
TRIM SIZE: 6 1/4 X 9 1/2 INCHES
QUANTITY PRINTED: 50,000
TYPEFACE: ITC CONDUIT
PRINTER: CORAL GRAPHICS
AUTHOR: ANDREW VACHSS
PUBLISHER: ALFRED A. KNOPF INC.

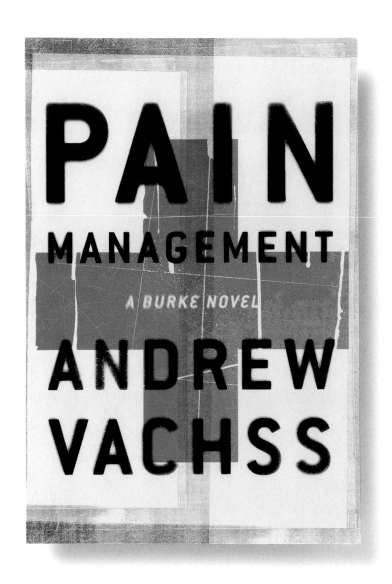

PAIN MANAGEMENT: A BURKE NOVEL COVER

This is a thriller in which medicine plays an important part, but it's not of the familiar "medical thriller" genre, so the expected images of creepy doctors and close-ups of needles were immediately ruled out. The red cross, an emblem of medical rescue, is treated like a battered wound to convey the central contradiction of the story—that a good-Samaritan drug trade exists to help chronic-pain-suffering patients obtain illegal drugs the medical establishment refuses to provide for them.

DESIGNER: JOHN GALL, VINTAGE BOOKS, NEW YORK
COVER ART: "LE SIEUR GAUTIER," ANATOMIE DE LA TETE EN TABLEAUX IMPRIMES, 1748,
BIBLIOTHEQUE NATIONALE DE FRANCE, PARIS (FRONT COVER);
"DEMOURS," TRAITE DES MALADIES DES YEUX (DETAIL), 1818,
DUKE UNIVERSITY HISTORY OF MEDICINE COLLECTIONS (SPINE)
TRIM SIZE: 5 3/16 X 8 1/4 INCHES
QUANTITY PRINTED: 15,000
TYPEFACES: FILOSOFIA, SACKERS GOTHIC
PRINTER: CORAL GRAPHICS
AUTHOR: SHELLEY JACKSON
PUBLISHER: VINTAGE BOOKS

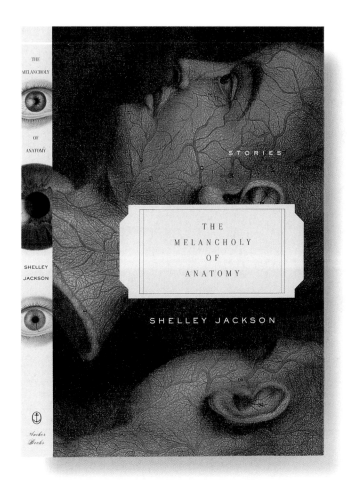

THE MELANCHOLY OF ANATOMY COVER

The Melancholy of Anatomy is a debut collection of stories, each one based on some part of the body or the result of a bodily function. Titles include: "Egg," "Heart," "Sperm," "Phlegm," "Hair" and "Fat." Rather than be specific to the surreal book, I wanted to use 17th- and 18th-century anatomical drawings, which are already suitably bizarre, to create a sort of *Gray's Anatomy* from an alternate world.

13
book design: 50 books/50 covers

DESIGNER: JILL SHIMABUKURO, UNIVERSITY OF CHICAGO PRESS, CHICAGO
PHOTOGRAPHER: ALAN COHEN
PRODUCTION COORDINATOR: SYLVIA HECIMOVICH
TRIM SIZE: 9 X 10 INCHES
PAGES: 130
QUANTITY PRINTED: 3,000
COMPOSITOR: JILL SHIMABUKURO
TYPEFACES: ADOBE GARAMOND, EUROPA ARABESQUE, META
PRINTER: MERIDIAN
PAPER: GLENEAGLE DULL 80 LB. TEXT
METHOD OF BINDING: SMYTHE-SEWN, HARDCOVER
AUTHOR: ALAN COHEN
PUBLISHER: UNIVERSITY OF CHICAGO PRESS

ON EUROPEAN GROUND

The challenge: How could I present 90-or-so photographs—each perfectly square and similar in appearance—in an engaging way, without betraying the photographer's intent? And what should I do with those dreaded footnotes?

With the help of the photographer, a hierarchy of images was decided upon. Some worked better as part of a group; others were more meaningful on their own. Solid-bleed pages were peppered throughout to indicate shifts in time and terrain.

Soft-colored footnotes were moved into the thumb margins, where they quietly, but effectively, get the job done.

This collection of images rewards in proportion to the time spent perusing it. My goal was to create a framework that facilitates this process of discovery.

13
book design: 50 books/50 covers

CREATIVE DIRECTORS: KATHY FREDRICKSON, GARRETT NIKSCH, CHERYL TOWLER WEESE,
STUDIO BLUE, CHICAGO
DESIGNERS: GARRETT NIKSCH WITH INGA NADEN, STUDIO BLUE, CHICAGO
PHOTOGRAPHER: BARBARA CRANE
PROJECT MANAGER: MATT SIMPSON
PRODUCTION COORDINATORS: MATT SIMPSON, KATHY FREDRICKSON
TRIM SIZE: 10 1/2 X 11 1/4 INCHES
PAGES: 64
QUANTITY PRINTED: 3,000
TYPEFACES: GOTHIC 13, NEWS GOTHIC
PRINTER: MERIDIAN PRINTING
PAPER: JOB PARILUX SILK 115 LB. TEXT
BINDER: MIDWEST EDITIONS
METHOD OF BINDING: SMYTHE-SEWN, PERFECT-BOUND, HARDCOVER
AUTHOR: SARAH MCNEAR
PUBLISHER: LASALLE BANK PHOTOGRAPHY COLLECTION

BARBARA CRANE: CHICAGO LOOP

Chicago Loop is the second book in a series on LaSalle Bank's contemporary photography collection. Photographer Barbara Crane's working method-a series of contact prints with consistent dimensions, reprinted at actual size—became the model for the book's design; her insistent frame appears repeatedly and establishes the book's grid. We dramatized Crane's small, rather quiet images with black backgrounds and gloss varnish, and reversed the plate section's foreground/background relationship on the cover.

ART DIRECTOR: CAROL DEVINE CARSON, ALFRED A. KNOPF INC., NEW YORK
DESIGNER: GABRIELE WILSON, ALFRED A. KNOPF INC., NEW YORK
PHOTOGRAPHER: KAMIL VOJNAR
TRIM SIZE: 5 5/8 X 8 1/4 INCHES
QUANTITY PRINTED: 5,000
TYPEFACE: REQUIEM
PAPER: CLARION BOOK ANTIQUE CREAM
PRINTER: CORAL GRAPHICS
AUTHOR: WILLIAM H. GASS
PUBLISHER: ALFRED A. KNOPF, INC.

TESTS OF TIME COVER

Gass' essays are conceptual, abstract and beautiful. I wanted a cover that would complement his discussion of what makes great art, literature and science timeless. An old book jacket torn, to reveal an image of the constellations beneath, in conjunction with classical typography made for an effective solution.

DESIGNER: JOHN FULBROOK III, SIMON & SCHUSTER, NEW YORK
PHOTOGRAPHER: BROWN BROTHERS
PRODUCTION COORDINATOR: OLGA LEONARDO
TRIM SIZE: 6 1/2 X 9 3/4 INCHES
QUANTITY PRINTED: 20,800
TYPEFACE: GIRALDON (HANDSET BY DAN X. SOLO)
PAPER: CUSTOM, COATED ONE SIDE, 80 LB.
PRINTER: CORAL GRAPHICS
AUTHOR: JAMIE O'NEIL
PUBLISHER: SCRIBNER

AT SWIM, TWO BOYS COVER

I had to create a mood of 1916 Dublin, where two boys fall in love while one teaches the other to swim.

I used handset 1916 typography, and tried to depict the sense of "jumping in"—a quality these two brave boys must have felt—while maintaining the gritty, aged look of old Dublin.

I am happy with the pause that is created between the two parts of the title—*At Swim…Two Boys*—almost as if it was two titles. I also love the photo (it was hard to find art from Ireland in 1916).

ART DIRECTOR: SARA LOVE
DESIGNER: RICHARD MCGUIRE, WORK IS PLAY, INC., NEW YORK
ILLUSTRATOR: RICHARD McGUIRE
PRODUCTION COORDINATOR: SARA LOVE
TRIM SIZE: 7 X 12 INCHES
QUANTITY PRINTED: 55,000
TYPEFACES: FUTURA, HAND LETTERING, SUBURBAN
PRINTER: PHOENIX COLOR GROUP
PUBLISHER: GRAPHIC ARTISTS GUILD, INC.

GRAPHIC ARTISTS GUILD HANDBOOK:
PRICING & ETHICAL GUIDELINES, 10TH EDITION COVER

For the cover, I wanted to create a narrative with a single image to show the circuitry of the profession: Client, Briefing, Deadline, Inspiration, Execution, Delivery and Pay Day.

CREATIVE DIRECTORS: FABRIZIO GILARDINO, MONTREAL; ORANGEFLUX, WHEATON, ILLINOIS
DESIGNERS: MATT FEY, STEVE GARIEPY, FABRIZIO GILARDINO, KRISTINA MEYER, ED WANTUCH
ILLUSTRATORS: STEVE GARIEPY, FABRIZIO GILARDINO, ED WANTUCH
PHOTOGRAPHERS: KRISTINA MEYER, ED WANTUCH
PRODUCTION COORDINATOR: FABRIZIO GILARDINO
TRIM SIZE: 8 X 9 1/2 INCHES
PAGES: 48   QUANTITY PRINTED: 600
TYPEFACES: CLARENDON, SAMUEL, UNIVERS
PRINTER: GINETTE NAULT ET DANIEL BEAUCAIRE IMPRIMEURS
METHOD OF BINDING: PERFECT-BOUND
JACKET DESIGNER: FABRIZIO GILARDINO
JACKET PRINTER: HAND-SILKSCREENED BY JULIE DOUCET
AUTHORS: FABRIZIO GILARDINO, ORANGEFLUX
PUBLISHER: L'OIE DE CRAVAN

LOUD {BRUYANT} HYBRID COMMODITY

Loud(Bruyant) is a theoretical and visual reflection on the role of graphic design.

Fabrizio Gilardino: My essay, *Catastrophe Au Salon Macao*, is both a political statement and an aesthetic one. I wanted to be as far away as possible from the classic coffee-table book on graphic design: nice to look at and convenient to forget when clients call. It is also a fulfillment of our desire to create hybrid products.

OrangeFlux: Such products fuse design, art, music and literature to create a new expression. For *Esperanto Marmalade*, we each played graphic instruments on a long scroll, improvising as the music moved us. It became our visual recording, a live graphic jam session.

DESIGNER: DAVID DRUMMOND, SALAMANDER HILL DESIGN, ATHELSTAN, QUEBEC
PHOTOGRAPHER: DAVID DRUMMOND
PRODUCTION COORDINATOR: SUZANNE McADAM
TRIM SIZE: 6 1/8 X 9 1/4 INCHES
QUANTITY PRINTED: 564
TYPEFACES: BAVER BODONI, BLISS
PAPER: JENSON GLOSS 80 LB.
PRINTER: UNIVERSITY OF TORONTO PRESS
AUTHOR: DAVID E. MERCER
PUBLISHER: McGILL-QUEEN'S UNIVERSITY PRESS

KIERKEGAARD'S LIVING-ROOM:
BETWEEN FAITH AND HISTORY IN PHILOSOPHICAL FRAGMENTS COVER

This book deals with the relation between faith and history in Kierkegaard's *Philosophical Fragments*. According to the author, there is a fundamental lack of clarity among scholars on this subject. It is like having an elephant in your living room and not addressing the very fact of its presence. I thought that using the shadow of an elephant cast against a living-room wall would add to the surreal quality of this notion.

ART DIRECTOR: JOHN FULBROOK III, SIMON & SCHUSTER, NEW YORK
DESIGNERS: JOHN FULBROOK III, SIMON & SCHUSTER, NEW YORK; MARKUS MAZZA
ILLUSTRATOR: CHRISTOPH NIEMANN
PRODUCTION COORDINATOR: JULIE PRIMAVERA
TRIM SIZE: 5 1/8 X 7 1/2 INCHES
QUANTITY PRINTED: 8,000
TYPEFACES: BANK GOTHIC, HELVETICA NEUE
PAPER: CUSTOM, COATED ONE SIDE, 80 LB.
PRINTER: CORAL GRAPHICS
AUTHOR: ERIK JONSSON
PUBLISHER: SCRIBNER

INNER NAVIGATION: WHY WE GET LOST AND HOW WE FIND OUR WAY COVER

Christoph Niemann's illustration shows a maze where the negative (inner) space creates the shape of a person running. I supported it with a traffic signal reference and clean type.

The smart, energetic illustration harmonizes with the necessary type. The result embodies the themes of the book in many ways.

DESIGNER: ROBERTO DE VICQ DE CUMPTICH, RVC DESIGN, NEW YORK
PRODUCTION COORDINATOR: MICHAEL SIBERT
TRIM SIZE: 5 X 7 INCHES
QUANTITY PRINTED: 8,000
TYPEFACE: HELVETICA NEUE
PRINTER: PHOENIX
AUTHOR: FRANÇOISE SAGAN
PUBLISHER: ECCO

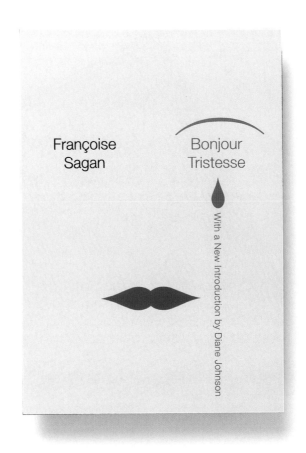

BONJOUR TRISTESSE COVER

Bonjour Tristesse is a classic novel, written more than 50 years ago; it was one of my mother's favorite books. Redesigning a classic is always a problem.

In Otto Preminger's movie of this book, the credits unfold over an image of Jean Seberg applying make up in front a vanity mirror. This image captures the essence of the novel. A girl discovers her sexuality and uses it to keep her father from remarrying and, in doing so, becomes cynical and unfulfilled. Saul Bass created a wonderful poster for the movie using the face of a young woman with a single tear falling. I just updated this image.

I am pleased with the spare nature of the cover—just type, parentheses and a teardrop.

ART DIRECTOR: ROSEANNE SERRA, PENGUIN PUTNAM, INC., NEW YORK
DESIGNER: EVAN GAFFNEY, EVAN GAFFNEY DESIGN, NEW YORK
COVER ART: FROM THE INTRODUCTION OF *AWAKENING FROM DELUSION*,
WRITTEN BY THE EMPEROR YONGZHENG (OUTER COVER); FROM A SERIES OF FANTASY
PAINTINGS COMMISSIONED BY THE EMPEROR YONGZHENG (INNER COVER)
PRODUCTION COORDINATOR: DOLORES M. REILLY
TRIM SIZE: 5 5/16 X 8 INCHES
QUANTITY PRINTED: 20,000
TYPEFACES: BODONI AS, CORNIVUS, ELDORADO, HELVETICA, NOBEL, OCRB, UNIVERS
PAPER: MANDO 70, 40 LB.
PRINTER: CORAL GRAPHICS
AUTHOR: JONATHAN D. SPENCE
PUBLISHER: PENGUIN

TREASON BY THE BOOK COVER
The challenge was to take a subject that would scare off many readers—
a Chinese political scandal from centuries ago—and package it like a
contemporary thriller without cheapening the content.

13
book design: 50 books/50 covers

ART DIRECTOR: TRACEY SHIFFMAN, TRACEY SHIFFMAN DESIGN, SANTA MONICA, CALIFORNIA
DESIGNERS: TRACEY SHIFFMAN WITH ANNABELLE GOULD,
TRACEY SHIFFMAN DESIGN, SANTA MONICA, CALIFORNIA
PRODUCTION COORDINATOR: STEVE SEARS
TRIM SIZE: 8 X 12 INCHES
PAGES: 184
COMPOSITOR: ANNABELLE GOULD
TYPEFACE: DAX, DESIGNED BY HANS REICHEL
METHOD OF BINDING: SMYTHE-SEWN, PAPER OVER BOARD WITH A DUST JACKET
JACKET DESIGNER: TRACEY SHIFFMAN
AUTHOR: GEORGE H. MARCUS
PUBLISHER: THE MONACELLI PRESS

LE CORBUSIER: INSIDE THE MACHINE FOR LIVING

"No attention was ever given to the environment in which a man lives: day-to-day existence, those moments and those hours spent in the streets, the squares, in his room, day after day, from infancy till death—all those places potentially inspiring, constituting as they do the context within which our consciousness develops from the moment we open our eyes to life…. I gave to the home its fundamental importance. I called it a 'machine for living.'" (Le Corbusier on "The Construction of Dwellings," 1920.)

Le Corbusier's all-encompassing ideas on architecture, interior spaces and the design of furniture were the catalyst from which the design of this publication germinated.

13
book design: 50 books/50 covers

CREATIVE DIRECTOR: BARBARA WERSBA, THE BOOKMAN PRESS,
SAG HARBOR, NEW YORK
DESIGNER: JERRY KELLY, JERRY KELLY LLC, NEW YORK
PRODUCTION COORDINATOR: JERRY KELLY
TRIM SIZE: 6 1/8 X 9 INCHES
PAGES: 20
QUANTITY PRINTED: 200
COMPOSITOR: JERRY KELLY
TYPEFACES: DELLA ROBBIA, KOCH ANTIQUA
PRINTER: E. H. ROBERTS
PAPER: COUGAR OPAQUE NATURAL 70 LB. TEXT, FRENCH MARBLED PAPER
BINDER: JERRY KELLY
METHOD OF BINDING: HAND-SEWN
AUTHOR: JANET FLANNER
PUBLISHER: THE BOOKMAN PRESS

ISADORA

The special challenge of this book was trying to capture something of the feel of Isadora Duncan's time: the Art-Deco period. The uncommon Della Robbia typeface (with Koch Antiqua display) captured something of this slightly eccentric era: both types are from the 1920s and both are somewhat unusual in form. The project had a tight budget, so we used a relatively inexpensive paper and only one black-and-white illustration, but splurged with a second color throughout and a nice binding paper. Since I hand-bound the books myself I was able to keep down the cost of the pasted label and hand sewing.

13
book design: 50 books/50 covers

DESIGNER: STEFAN G. BUCHER, 344 DESIGN, PASADENA, CALIFORNIA
PHOTOGRAPHER: CRAIG CUTLER (COVER)
PRODUCTION COORDINATOR: MARK HEFLIN
TRIM SIZE: 9 1/4 X 12 1/4 INCHES
PAGES: 432
QUANTITY PRINTED: 3,000
TYPEFACE: HELVETICA
PRINTER: DAI NIPPON
PAPER: BIBEREST MATTE-COATED 135 G/M²
BINDER: DAI NIPPON
METHOD OF BINDING: SMYTHE-SEWN, HARDCOVER
AUTHOR: ALISON MORLEY
EDITORIAL CONSULTANT: PEGGY ROALF
PUBLISHER: AMILUS, INC.

AMERICAN PHOTOGRAPHY 17

American Photography displays the year's best photography, as selected by a jury of photo editors, art directors and designers.

The cover traditionally uses an image from the year's crop of winning entries. In this case I chose Craig Cutler's condiments for their bold, graphic look (and because I've always liked those little ketchup packages with the rubbery flexography). I silk-screened all the typography and design elements onto a clear vinyl slipcover, leaving the photograph itself untouched.

The only constraints were the traditional 9 1/4 by 12 1/4 hardcover format and that the images had to be shown un-cropped at a minimum height of 5 inches. Beyond that I was given carte blanche. So my main challenge was controlling my desire to show off.

43
book design: 50 books/50 covers

CREATIVE DIRECTORS: ALISON HAHN, NIGEL SMITH, HAHN SMITH DESIGN, TORONTO
DESIGNER: DEREK BARNETT, HAHN SMITH DESIGN, TORONTO
PHOTOGRAPHERS: BRIAN BOYLE, VOLKER SEDING
PRODUCTION COORDINATOR: NORAH JACKSON
TRIM SIZE: 5 1/2 X 8 3/4 INCHES
PAGES: 76
QUANTITY PRINTED: 1,500
COMPOSITOR: HAHN SMITH DESIGN & ARCHETYPE
TYPEFACE: DANTE BY GIOVANNI MARDERSTEIG
PRINTER: ST. JOSEPH/M.O.M. PRINTING
PAPER: MONADNOCK ASTROLITE 80LB. TEXT
METHOD OF BINDING: SMYTHE-SEWN, CLOTH SPINE, PAPER WRAP HARDCOVER
JACKET DESIGNERS: DEREK BARNETT, NIGEL SMITH
AUTHORS: ULANA BALUK, ELIZABETH MCLUHAN
PUBLISHER: ROYAL ONTARIO MUSEUM

THE FINAL SLEEP/LE DERNIER SOMMEIL

We created this catalogue as a parallel experience to an installation by artist Spring Hurlbut at the Royal Ontario Museum.

We used a number of strategies to try to reflect the aura of the exhibition that was about the relationship between curating, collecting, museology, tradition, popular culture and physical space. Primarily we inverted the typical "architecture" of the book/catalogue. We opened with an engaging image section and placed the curatorial essays at the end of the book.

We used the traditional qualities of book design such as classical typography, uncoated paper and simple binding techniques. To capture the intensity of the curation and the artist's obsession with organization, we also included a map and detailed listing of the many and diverse objects on display.

DESIGNER: ALICIA MIKLES, HARPERCOLLINS PUBLISHERS, NEW YORK
ILLUSTRATOR: WILLIAM STEIG
PRODUCTION COORDINATOR: RUIKO TOKUNAGA
TRIM SIZE: 5 1/4 X 7 1/2 INCHES
PAGES: 112
QUANTITY PRINTED: 25,000
TYPEFACES: AGARAMOND, FUTURA
PRINTER: QUEBECOR
PAPER: GLATFELTER OFFSET 70 LB.
METHOD OF BINDING: BURST
JACKET PRINTER: CORAL GRAPHICS
AUTHOR: SHARON CREECH
EDITOR: JOANNA COTLER
PUBLISHER: HARPERCOLLINS PUBLISHERS/JOANNA COTLER BOOKS

LOVE THAT DOG

Love That Dog is a novel told in verse for an intended audience of children, aged 8 to 12. Unusual text formats are employed in the book; the text takes on the shape of the subject of the poem, for example. It was my job to realize the author's ideas typographically and aesthetically, while giving the book a cohesive feel. I printed the text in Pantone blue rather than the standard black to give it a scholastic feel, as if Jack, the protagonist, was writing his poems in blue ink.

For the jacket, I used three Pantone colors, plus black. The soft colors were enhanced by matte-finishes. William Steig's wonderful line art of a dog completed the package.

13

book design: 50 books/50 covers

CREATIVE DIRECTOR: STEPHEN DOYLE, DOYLE PARTNERS, NEW YORK
DESIGNER: ROSEMARIE TURK, DOYLE PARTNERS, NEW YORK
PHOTOGRAPHER: VICTOR SCHRAGER
PRODUCTION COORDINATOR: MICHAEL GERBINO
TRIM SIZE: 9 X 11 3/4 INCHES
PAGES: 132
QUANTITY PRINTED: 4,000
TYPEFACES: GARAMOND, ORATOR
PRINTER: DAI NIPPON
METHOD OF BINDING: SMYTHE-SEWN
AUTHOR: A.S. BYATT
PUBLISHER: GRAPHIS

BIRD HAND BOOK

The book is about language: the language of photography and the language that humans use to relate to these delicate, ethereal creatures. The design of the book allows the photographs and the essay to flaunt their unique eccentricities while coming together in an elegant and visually entertaining way. We tried to allow Victor Schrager's photographs to resonate with luminosity and strangeness and A.S. Byatt's essay to act the way it reads—a gorgeously written patchwork of man's attempt to harness with words the mystery of birds.

13
book design: 50 books/50 covers

CREATIVE DIRECTOR: CAROLINE HERTER, HERTER STUDIO, SAN FRANCISCO
ART DIRECTOR: PAMELA GEISMAR, CHRONICLE BOOKS, SAN FRANCISCO
DESIGNER: JANA ANDERSON, STUDIO A, SAN FRANCISCO
PHOTOGRAPHER: DEBORAH SAMUEL
PRODUCTION COORDINATOR: TERA KILLIP
TRIM SIZE: 10 1/4 X 12 1/4 INCHES
PAGES: 112
QUANTITY PRINTED: 15,000
TYPEFACES: FRUTIGER, MRS. EAVES
PRINTER: C & C OFFSET
PAPER: JAPANESE MATTE 157 G/M²
BINDER: C & C OFFSET
METHOD OF BINDING: SMYTHE-SEWN, HARDCOVER
AUTHOR: DEBORAH SAMUEL
EDITOR: KATHLEEN ERICKSON
PUBLISHER: CHRONICLE BOOKS

DOG

My challenge as the designer of this book was, first and foremost, to give credence to the exquisite photos that I was so fortunate to work with. The design needed to give a fresh, non-distracting venue for the photos to breathe and tell their story.

13
book design: 50 books/50 covers

DESIGNER: JAMES COSTELLO, COSTELLO COMMUNICATIONS, INC., CHICAGO
TRIM SIZE: 7 3/8 X 10 1/2 INCHES
PAGES: 80
QUANTITY PRINTED: 1,500
COMPOSITOR: KIER DAVIS
TYPEFACES: FILOSOFIA, MINION, TRADE GOTHIC
PRINTERS: ACE GRAPHICS, ROHNER LETTERPRESS
PAPER: WEYERHAEUSER COUGAR OPAQUE 70 LB. TEXT,
MOHAWK ULTRAFELT SOFT WHITE 100 LB. COVER
BINDER: BOOKLET BINDERY
METHOD OF BINDING: PERFECT-BOUND
EDITOR: DR. JACOB LASSNER
PUBLISHER: SPERTUS INSTITUTE FOR JEWISH STUDIES

CAIRO'S BEN EZRA SYNAGOGUE

This book examines the historic and cultural significance of letter
fragments from the late ninth century, found at the Ben Ezra Synagogue
in Cairo, Egypt. Our challenge was to make an academic text, intended
mainly for students and researchers, visually interesting and inviting
for a general audience.

With a limited budget, our efforts focused on making
typography—a critical factor in the design—along with innovative use
of color and texture, particularly evident on the cover. The mosaic
patterns, reminiscent of the synagogue interior, are symbolic of the
fragments of transcripts that were pieced together to provide a glimpse
into medieval Jewish life.

13
book design: 50 books/50 covers

DESIGNER: CHRISTINE PUN, CALIFORNIA POLYTECHNIC STATE UNIVERSITY,
SAN LUIS OBISPO, CALIFORNIA
PRODUCTION COORDINATOR: MARY LAPORTE
TRIM SIZE: 6 X 8 INCHES
PAGES: 152
QUANTITY PRINTED: 400
TYPEFACES: AMERICAN TYPEWRITER, CLARENDON, CENTURY SCHOOLBOOK
PRINTER: POOR RICHARD'S PRESS
PAPER: FRENCH PAPER COMPANY SPECKLETONE CHOCOLATE 100 LB. COVER
METHOD OF BINDING: PERFECT-BOUND
AUTHORS: MIKE CLEARWATER, MONICA DELMARTINI, ROBIN L. FRANKLIN,
KRISTIANNE HUNTSBERGER, ERIN JO MARTIN, MARNIE L. PARKER, CANDI PEMBERTON,
MOLLY REID, ZAC SAWDEY, BRIDGER WRAY, CAROL FRANCES WULFF
EDITORS: JENNIE FIELDS, STEPHANIE YANG
PUBLISHER: CALIFORNIA POLYTECHNIC STATE UNIVERSITY

BYZANTIUM VOL. 11

Byzantium is published by Cal Poly's English Department. It showcases winning entries from the school's literary contest. Because of the nature of the project, I wanted to create something visually exciting yet with a quiet elegance. The idea was to design the book so those who own it will cherish it. Delicate design elements and deep solid colors help create the idea that *Byzantium* contains something precious.

13
book design: 50 books/50 covers

ART DIRECTORS: PATRICK SEYMOUR, CATARINA TSANG, TSANG SEYMOUR DESIGN INC., NEW YORK
DESIGNERS: VICTORIA LATIMER ROAN,
PATRICK SEYMOUR, TSANG SEYMOUR DESIGN INC., NEW YORK
PRODUCTION COORDINATOR: CHRISTOPHER ZICHELLO
TRIM SIZE: 10 X 11 INCHES
QUANTITY PRINTED: 9,000
TYPEFACE: TRADE GOTHIC
PRINTER: STAMPERIA VALDONEGA S.R.L.
AUTHORS: MARGIT ROWELL, DEBORAH WYE, WITH ESSAYS BY JARED ASH, NINA GURIANOVA,
GERALD JANECEK
PUBLISHER: MUSEUM OF MODERN ART

THE RUSSIAN AVANT-GARDE BOOK 1910–1934 COVER

When we first began to work on this cover, we had just completed the page layouts and felt very strongly that these books should not be represented through an appropriation of the Constructivist language typically associated with the Russian avant-garde period. We ultimately returned to something that one of the curators stressed to us during an afternoon that we were invited to look through the books: that these were objects of use—intended to be handled, read, carried in the pocket and passed on to others. We have tried to capture this quality in a simple, bold, legible gesture that is representative of the medium through which the artists in this book chose to communicate.

13
book design: 50 books/50 covers

DESIGNER: DMITRY KRASNY, DEKA DESIGN, NEW YORK
IMAGES: MAX ERNST, ANDREAS GURSKY, HENRI MATISSE, RICHARD SERRA
PHOTOGRAPHERS: ADAM BARTOS, ROBERT DAMORA, TIMOTHY GREENFIELD-SANDERS,
KOSHIBA, JACEK MARCZEWSKI, JOCK POTTLE, JOSHUA WHITE, KAREN WILLIS
PRODUCTION COORDINATOR: CLAIRE COREY
TRIM SIZE: 5 3/4 X 8 1/2 INCHES (BOOK BLOCK), 5 3/4 X 9 1/2 INCHES (OVERHANGING COVER)
PAGES: 34
QUANTITY PRINTED: 7,500
TYPEFACES: FRANKLIN GOTHIC, THE MIX
PRINTER: PRINTRICATE
PAPER: ZANDERS IKONO DULL 100 LB. TEXT, 3-COLOR SILKSCREEN ON HAND-BRUSHED
ALUMINUM VENEER LAMINATED TO 120 PT. BOARD
METHOD OF BINDING: JAPANESE-FOLD PAGES, PERFECT-BOUND
AUTHORS: REBECCA STOKES, MARK SWARTZ
PUBLISHER: MUSEUM OF MODERN ART

MoMA BUILDS—CAPITAL CAMPAIGN

The *MoMA Builds* book provides members as well as current and future
contributors of the Museum of Modern Art with a remarkable preview of
the new building. We chose materials and production techniques that
reference the structure of the future edifice. The brushed aluminum cover
and metallic silver ink correspond to the same metal of the museum
exterior. Abundant white space throughout the pages and the use of
tinted varnish relate to the airy gallery interiors and the glass
atrium. The book with its overhanging cover and the Japanese-folded
pages highlights the process of construction and pays homage to
Japanese architect Yoshio Taniguchi.

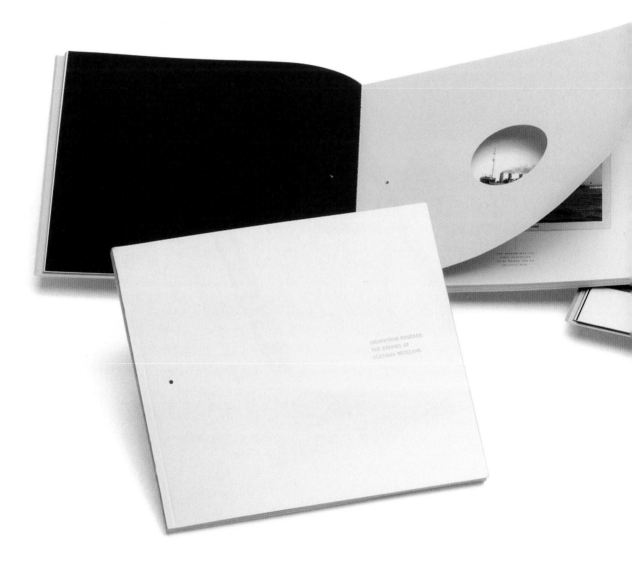

IDENTIFYING COURAGE, THE STORIES OF ALABAMA VETERANS

Since 1900, the state of Alabama has enlisted more military volunteers per capita than any other state in the Union. This book tells the stories of some of those who lost either their life or their youth to combat.

We chose to shoot additional photography to supplement that which the families provided, which avoided a *Time/Life* feel, and gave us the opportunity to focus instead on each individual's personal story: the drill sergeant that volunteered for Vietnam because his boys were dying "as quickly as you strike a match, and blow it out"; a 19-year-old kid that would have avoided the draft had he made the college baseball team; and a Coca-Cola delivery man whose dream of being a pilot cost him his life.

13
book design: 50 books/50 covers

ART DIRECTORS: MARION ENGLISH, PAT POWELL, SLAUGHTERHANSON, BIRMINGHAM, ALABAMA
DESIGNER: MARION ENGLISH, SLAUGHTERHANSON, BIRMINGHAM, ALABAMA
PHOTOGRAPHERS: DON HARBOR (PRINCIPAL), MITCH EPSTEIN (BLINDSPOT STOCK),
PERSONAL ARCHIVE PHOTOS
PRODUCTION COORDINATOR: TONY PIZZO
TRIM SIZE: 10 X 9 INCHES
PAGES: 148
QUANTITY PRINTED: 1,250
COMPOSITORS: DOUG BENSON, SLAUGHTERHANSON
TYPEFACES: HELVETICA, NEWS GOTHIC, TRADE GOTHIC, VENETIAN
PRINTER: THE STINEHOUR PRESS
PAPER: ZANDERS IKONO DULL SATIN 100 LB. TEXT, TRANSILWRAP ORIENTED POLYESTER .003
(FLYSHEET), FRENCH PAPER CO. BLACK SPECKLETONE 70 LB. TEXT (LETTERPRESS INSETS),
CHROMOLUX 700 12 PT. COVER
BINDER: ACME BOOKBINDING
METHOD OF BINDING: PERFECT-BOUND, PAPERBACK, DRAWN-ON DOUBLE GATEFOLD
WITH 8 1/2 INCH FLAPS COVER, BLIND DEBOSS FRONT COVER, SINGLE HOLE DRILL
AUTHORS: THE ALABAMA VETERANS MEMORIAL FOUNDATION, SARA DEVINE,
KRISTIN HENSON, DAN MONROE, DAVE SMITH
PUBLISHER: R. BOOZER PRESS

13
book design: 50 books/50 covers

ART DIRECTOR: AVA WEISS, HARPERCOLLINS PUBLISHERS, NEW YORK
DESIGNERS: BYRON BARTON, SARASOTA, FLORIDA; SYLVIE LE FLOCH, HARPERCOLLINS
PUBLISHERS, NEW YORK
ILLUSTRATOR: BYRON BARTON
PRODUCTION COORDINATOR: LISA WONG
TRIM SIZE: 9 X 9 INCHES
PAGES: 40
QUANTITY PRINTED: 18,000
COMPOSITOR: TIEN WAH PRESS
TYPEFACE: AVANT GARDE GOTHIC
PRINTER: TIEN WAH PRESS
PAPER: NYMOLLA MATTE 135 G/M²
METHOD OF BINDING: THREAD-SEWN
AUTHOR: BYRON BARTON
PUBLISHER: GREENWILLOW BOOKS

MY CAR

When I was in high school, in the 1940s, a kid could buy a beat-up 1930
Model A Ford or a 1936 Ford V8, fix it up and have a nice car to ride
around in. I could fix almost anything that went wrong with my car.
Today, I hardly ever look under the hood of my Jeep, and I hope I don't
ever have to change a flat tire. Things change.
      The first books I did, in the 1970s, I pre-separated the colors
of the artwork to black half tones on acetate sheets. Years later,
I graduated to painting in full color using vinyl or gouache paints.
In making this book, I worked on an Apple computer using Adobe Photoshop
and Macromedia Director.

13
book design: 50 books/50 covers

DESIGNER: RUDY VANDERLANS, EMIGRE, SACRAMENTO, CALIFORNIA
PHOTOGRAPHER: RUDY VANDERLANS
PRODUCTION COORDINATOR: RUDY VANDERLANS
TRIM SIZE: 9 X 12 INCHES
PAGES: 176
QUANTITY PRINTED: 5,000
TYPEFACES: EMIGRE SOLEX, EMIGRE VENDETTA
PRINTER: QUINNESSENTIALS, REGAL PRINTING
PAPER: ROSEBUD BY RAINBOW ENDS, MUNKEN PRINT UNCOATED 100 G/M², JAPANESE NPI
MATTE ARTPAPER 157 G/M² AND 128 G/M², 3 MM BOARD WRAPPED IN SAIFU F-197 CLOTH
METHOD OF BINDING: SMYTHE-SEWN, HARDCOVER
JACKET PRINTER: REGAL PRINTING
AUTHOR: RUDY VANDERLANS
PUBLISHER: GINGKO PRESS

SUPERMARKET

I had traveled to the Southern California desert region many times and
wanted to create a photographic record that would show both my love for
the desert environment and the concerns I have for its exploitation.
Its audience includes those interested in the Southern California
environment, landscape photographers and those interested in photographer
and artists' books.

    I'm happy with the design and production of this book, because
it turned out as I had imagined it. Much of the credit for this,
however, should go to my publisher, Gingko Press, who allowed me
complete artistic freedom in making this book.

DESIGNER: IVAN CHERMAYEFF, CHERMAYEFF & GEISMAR, INC., NEW YORK
ILLUSTRATOR: IVAN CHERMAYEFF
PHOTOGRAPHER: RICH FAHEY
PRODUCTION COORDINATOR: LARS MÜLLER
TRIM SIZE: 6 1/2 X 9 7/16 INCHES
PAGES: 256
QUANTITY PRINTED: 4,000
COMPOSITORS: INTEGRAL, LARS MÜLLER
TYPEFACES: FRANKLIN GOTHIC, GARAMOND
PRINTER: STÄMPFLI AG
PAPER: THALO WERKDRUCK 120 G/M², BIBER ALEGRO 150 G/M²
BINDER: BUCHBINDEREI BURKHARDT AG
METHOD OF BINDING: CLOTH-BOUND, HARDCOVER
AUTHOR: LARS MÜLLER
PUBLISHER: LARS MÜLLER

SUSPECTS, SMOKERS, SOLDIERS AND SALESLADIES: COLLAGES BY IVAN CHERMAYEFF

It is always difficult to design a book, or anything else for that matter, about one's own work. In addition, I had to use an affordable format for full-color and maintain a pace whilst showing the works as large as possible.

Color fidelity, binding and paper stocks are vitally important, which is why the book was published in Switzerland and looked after at every stage by its author and publisher Lars Müller, who cares as much about quality as I do.

ART DIRECTOR: JOHN FULBROOK III, SIMON & SCHUSTER, NEW YORK
DESIGNER: MICHAEL I. KAYE, NEW YORK
PRODUCTION COORDINATOR: OLGA LEONARDO
TRIM SIZE: 5 7/8 X 8 15/16 INCHES
QUANTITY PRINTED: 13,000
TYPEFACE: DIN MITTELSCHRIFT
PAPER: CUSTOM, COATED ONE SIDE, 80 LB.
PRINTER: PHOENIX
AUTHOR: MARTHA SOUTHGATE
PUBLISHER: SCRIBNER

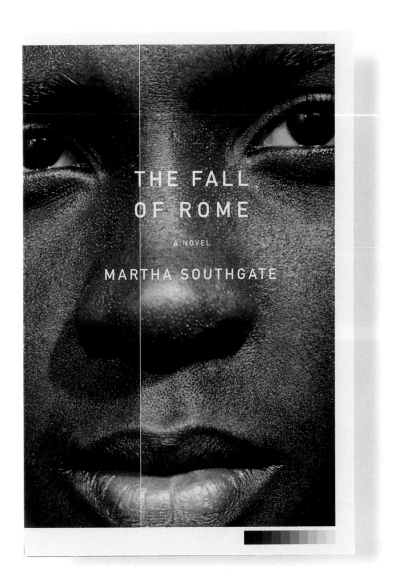

THE FALL OF ROME COVER

In a novel of race and class, a lone African-American confronts the inevitable tensions of attending an all-white boarding school. The close up cropping of the boy's face on the jacket creates an uncomfortable tension, while engaging the reader with piercing eyes. The type moves back and forth over the white line running down the center of the jacket, echoing the moving race lines of the novel. Moreover, the boy is literally being framed by white and a black-and-white color bar, continuing the race theme.

DESIGNERS: CORNELIA BLATTER, MARCEL HERMANS, COMA, BROOKLYN, NEW YORK
PHOTOGRAPHY: FROM THE RIETVELD SCHRÖDER ARCHIVE
PRODUCTION COORDINATOR: COMA
TRIM SIZE: 7 9/16 X 8 11/16
PAGES: 120
QUANTITY PRINTED: 3,000
COMPOSITOR: COMA
TYPEFACE: GOTHIC 720
PRINTER: VEENMAN DRUKKERS
PAPER: GRAFISCH PAIER ARCTIC THE SILK 130 G/M²,
PROOST EN BRANDT INVERCOTE CREATO MAT 240 G/M²
BINDER: BINDERIJ HEXSPOOR
METHOD OF BINDING: OTABIND
AUTHOR: IDA VAN ZIJL
EDITOR: MILOU HALBESMA
PUBLISHER: CENTRAAL MUSEUM

RIETVELD IN UTRECHT

The challenge was to design a consumer-friendly international architectural guide that would heighten awareness of 20 lesser-known Gerrit Rietveld buildings in the Utrecht area.

Our solution included the following devices: large numbers and street names as guidance throughout book, connecting projects to the map; red and white (and spot varnish) dividers for the two languages, referencing the colors of the Rietveld chair; and a grid taken from one of his buildings and reused in different ways.

ART DIRECTOR: JARED EBERHARDT, BOOK, BOOK, BOOK, LONG BEACH, CALIFORNIA
DESIGNERS: MALCOLM BUICK, AARON DRAPLIN, JARED EBERHARDT, RUBY LEE
ILLUSTRATORS: STEPHEN BLISS, JASON BRASHILL, NOAH BUTKISS, CHIMP, JOHN COPELAND,
MARK GONZALES, EVAN HECOX, ANDY JENKINS, DAVE KINSEY, SCOTT LEONHARDT,
GEOFF McFETRIDGE, ANDY MUELLER, MARK REUSH, WOO ROBERTS, STRUGGLE INC.
PHOTOGRAPHERS: BLOTTO, JEFF CURTES, GEOFF FOSBROOK, JON FOSTER, MARK GALLUP,
TREVOR GRAVES, SCOTT NEEDHAM, VINCENT SKOGLUND, VIANNEY TISSEAU,
ALEX WILLIAMS, HIRO YAMADA, KEVIN ZACHER
PRODUCTION COORDINATOR: JARED EBERHARDT
TRIM SIZE: 9 1/2 X 11 INCHES; PAGES: 256; QUANTITY PRINTED: 25,000
COMPOSITOR: JARED EBERHARDT
TYPEFACES: COOPER BLACK, HELVETICA BOLD, HELVETICA CONDENSED, HELVETICA MEDIUM
PRINTER: TOPPAN PRINTING CO.
PAPER: SATIN KINFUJI 128 G/M², YUPO LIGHTWEIGHT 84.7 G/M²,
WOODFREE UNCOATED 120 G/M², NEWSPRINT 48.8 G/M²
METHOD OF BINDING: FLEXIBOUND
JACKET DESIGNER: JARED EBERHARDT; JACKET PRINTER: TOPPAN PRINTING CO.
AUTHORS: JARED EBERHARDT, EVAN ROSE, KEVIN WILKINS
EDITOR: ELIZABETH FARRELLY
PUBLISHER: BOOTH-CLIBBORN EDITIONS

BLOWER, SNOWBOARDING INSIDE OUT

The most challenging part of this project was trying to represent the
feeling of snowboarding to snowboarders while still keeping it
accessible to outsiders. The structure of *Blower* is meant to be both
linear and non-linear. It's intended to take you through a day of
snowboarding, the progression of the sport itself and the history of
snowboard design. It is organized so that you can start anywhere, move
forward or backward and still it makes sense; if you get stuck, there's
an index which gives brief but potent insight into what you have seen.

DESIGNER: CHIP KIDD, CHIP KIDD DESIGN, NEW YORK
PHOTOGRAPHER: GEOFF SPEAR
TRIM SIZE: 6 X 8 INCHES
QUANTITY PRINTED: 15,000
TYPEFACE: NEWS GOTHIC
PRINTER: CORAL GRAPHICS
AUTHOR: HENRY PETROSKI
PUBLISHER: ALFRED A. KNOPF, INC.

PAPERBOY: CONFESSIONS OF A FUTURE ENGINEER COVER

For this memoir of a boyhood in 1950s Queens, I initially went the traditional route and used several of the author's personal photos of the time. The editor felt the result was adequate but standard The editor-in-chief thought it was just plain boring. "Why not make it. look like a newspaper?" he wisely asked. So I did.

I should also point out here that this the fifth book I've worked on for this author, and they all look completely different—a testament to his faith in the pluralism of design.

13

book design: 50 books/50 covers

DESIGNER: CHIN-YEE LAI, CHIN-YEE LAI DESIGN, FOREST HILLS, NEW YORK
PHOTOGRAPHERS: TOM BARIL, TIB SWANSTOCK
TRIM SIZE: 5 1/2 X 8 1/4 INCHES
QUANTITY PRINTED: 15,000
TYPEFACE: PERPETUA
PRINTER: CORAL GRAPHICS
AUTHOR: SANDRA M. GILBERT
PUBLISHER: W. W. NORTON

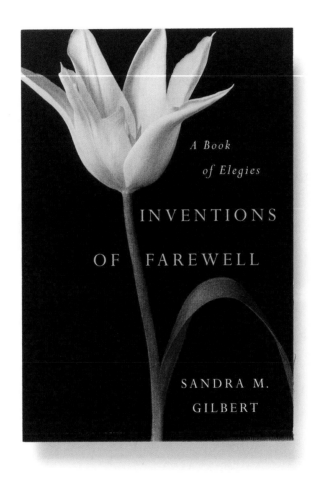

INVENTIONS OF FAREWELL COVER

Since a book cover usually conveys the theme of the book, when I began the jacket for *Inventions of Farewell*, I was confronted by the challenge of finding an image that conveys the concept of death. From several photographs, I chose an image of a single white tulip because I was struck by its lonely serenity, as well as its unyielding and silent strength.

GYMNASIUM

The photographs in the gymnasium were taken primarily in western Pennsylvania between 1988 and 2000, though many people looking at them think their quirky compositions date them from the turn of the 20th century. When editing and sequencing the book, I wanted to resist any antique design conceits and, instead, present the images in a clean and direct manner. Eleanor Caponigro and I designed two different dust jackets for the book: one a blowup of an image that wraps entirely around the book and is oddly abstracted by only seeing portions of the whole when viewing the book from different angles; the other a more constructivist homage with an image reproduced numerous times on the front and back of the jacket.

DESIGNER: JACK WOODY, TWIN PALMS PUBLISHERS, SANTA FE, NEW MEXICO
PHOTOGRAPHER: LUKE SMALLEY
PRODUCTION COORDINATORS: TOM LONG, JACK WOODY
TRIM SIZE: 8 X 10 3/4 INCHES
PAGES: 168
QUANTITY PRINTED: 4,000
TYPEFACES: BK ITC KABEL BOOK, M ITC KABEL MEDIUM, SYNTAX
PRINTER: OCEANIC GRAPHIC PRINTING
PAPER: WHITE MATTE-COATED 180 G/M²
METHOD OF BINDING: SEWED, CASE-BOUND
AUTHOR: LUKE SMALLEY
PUBLISHER: TWIN PALMS PUBLISHERS

DESIGNER: CHIP KIDD, CHIP KIDD DESIGN, NEW YORK
TRIM SIZE: 6 X 8 INCHES
QUANTITY PRINTED: 25,000
TYPEFACE: CORVINUS (CUSTOMIZED)
PRINTER: CORAL GRAPHICS
AUTHOR: DAVID RACKOFF
PUBLISHER: DOUBLEDAY

FRAUD COVER

The difference between this jacket and most of the jackets I design is that the author is a close friend, which always makes it a little dicey. Luckily he instantly got it.

The major conceit in these essays is that the writer feels he is in over his head and not qualified to write about whatever he's writing about. So the jacket just reflects what a frustrated reader with a red marker pen would do upon totally agreeing with him.

13
book design: 50 books/50 covers

DESIGNER: CHIP KIDD, CHIP KIDD DESIGN, NEW YORK
ILLUSTRATOR: CHRIS WARE
PHOTOGRAPHER: GEOFF SPEAR
PRODUCTION COORDINATOR: JOHN FULBROOK
TRIM SIZE: 4 3/4 X 7 1/2 INCHES
PAGES: 275
QUANTITY PRINTED: 27,000
COMPOSITOR: CHIP KIDD
TYPEFACES: APOLLO, BODONI
PRINTER: CORAL GRAPHICS
PAPER: HAMMERMILL WINTER 85 LB.
METHOD OF BINDING: SMYTHE-SEWN, HARDCOVER
JACKET DESIGNER: SOME GUY
AUTHOR: CHIP KIDD
PUBLISHER: SCRIBNER

THE CHEESE MONKEYS
This one was a nightmare. The author is a total asshole.

CREATIVE DIRECTOR: JOHN FONTANA, DOUBLEDAY, NEW YORK
ART DIRECTOR: RODRIGO CORRAL, DOUBLEDAY, NEW YORK
DESIGNER: RODRIGO CORRAL, DOUBLEDAY, NEW YORK
PHOTOGRAPHER: BROWN BROTHERS
TRIM SIZE: 6 1/8 X 9 1/8 INCHES
QUANTITY PRINTED: 20,000
TYPEFACES: CLARENDON CONDENSED, SCRIPT, TRADE GOTHIC
PRINTER: CORAL GRAPHICS
AUTHOR: COLSON WHITEHEAD
PUBLISHER: DOUBLEDAY

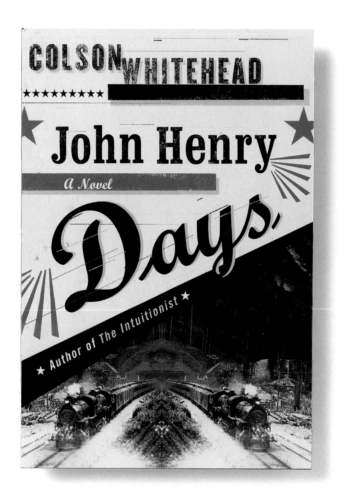

JOHN HENRY DAYS COVER

This, the second novel by a promising new author, is about the legend
of John Henry—a black laborer with superhuman strength and stamina—
which has since had an impact on generations of Americans.

I chose historical photography to reflect the life of John Henry
and festival-inspired, letter-pressed type and ornamentation to invoke
a spirit of celebration of his myth.

richard eckersley

STRAVINSKY RETROSPECTIVES BOOK COVER, UNIVERSITY OF NEBRASKA PRESS, 1987.

RICHARD ECKERSLEY, UNIVERSITY OF NEBRASKA PRESS, LINCOLN, NEBRASKA
RICHARD ECKERSLEY BEGAN HIS DESIGN CAREER AS A JUNIOR AT LUND HUMPHRIES,
THE PUBLISHER OF *TYPOGRAPHICA* AND *THE PENROSE ANNUAL*, WHERE E. McKNIGHT KAUFFER
HAD ONCE BEEN ART DIRECTOR. MUCH OF THE WORK WAS BOOKS AND CATALOGUES,
BY WHICH HE LEARNED THE RUDIMENTS OF TYPOGRAPHY. SUBSEQUENTLY HE JOINED THE
STATE-SPONSORED KILKENNY DESIGN WORKSHOPS IN IRELAND. AFTER SIX YEARS THERE,
ECKERSLEY TOOK A TEACHING POSITION IN THE UNITED STATES, AND IN 1981 APPLIED FOR
A JOB AT THE UNIVERSITY OF NEBRASKA PRESS. HE IS STILL THERE.

13
book design: 50 books/50 covers
juror

carin goldberg

1
CATALOG, STEWART, TABORI AND CHANG, 2001.

2
TYPE DIRECTOR'S CLUB 45 CALL FOR ENTRIES POSTER AND *TDC 20 DESIGN ANNUAL*,
THE TYPE DIRECTOR'S CLUB, 1999.

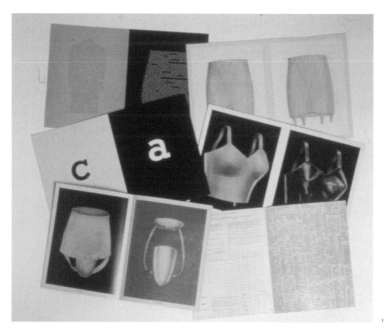

1

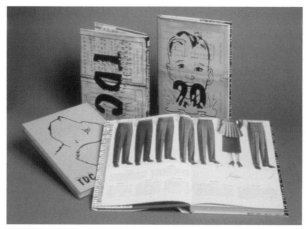

2

CARIN GOLDBERG, CARIN GOLDBERG DESIGN, NEW YORK

CARIN GOLDBERG BEGAN HER DESIGN CAREER IN THE DESIGN DEPARTMENT AT CBS TELEVISION,
UNDER THE TUTELAGE OF LOU DORFSMAN, AND LATER MOVED ON TO CBS RECORDS,
(NOW SONY) WHERE SHE WORKED UNDER THE TUTELAGE OF HENRIETTA CONDAK AND
PAULA SCHER. HAVING HAD ENOUGH OF SEXIST, BUREAUCRATIC AND INCESTUOUS CORPORATE
LIFE, GOLDBERG STARTED HER OWN BUSINESS. SHE CONTINUED TO DESIGN ALBUM COVERS,
FOR ARTISTS INCLUDING MADONNA AND THE WALLFLOWERS, AND LAUNCHED
THE FIRST SERIES OF COVERS FOR THE NEWLY RESURRECTED NONESUCH RECORDS.
GOLDBERG IS CURRENTLY A DESIGN CONSULTANT AT TIME INC. CUSTOM PUBLISHING WHERE
SHE DESIGNS PROTOTYPES FOR MAGAZINES. AS WELL AS DESIGNING COUNTLESS
BOOK JACKETS FOR OTHERS, SHE CONCEIVED, WROTE AND DESIGNED THE BOOK *CATALOG*
(STEWART, TABORI & CHANG, 2001).

"SANTA'S CL   HRISTMAS CARD,"

RICHARD HULL, BRIGHAM YOUNG UNIVERSITY   UTAH
RICHARD HULL STUDIED GRAPHIC DESIGN AT BRIGHAM YOUNG UNIVERSITY—WHERE HE
NOW DIRECTS THE ILLUSTRATION PROGRAM IN THE DEPARTMENT OF VISUAL ARTS.
BEFORE BECOMING A TEACHER, HULL WORKED FOR MANY YEARS AS A GRAPHIC DESIGNER
BACK IN THE DAYS OF HOT LEAD TYPE, RUBBER CEMENT AND RULING PENS. HE HAS
BEEN ILLUSTRATING FOR MORE THAN 30 YEARS IN THE WORLD OF CHILDREN'S PUBLISHING.
HIS CLIENTS INCLUDE: ATHENEUM, AN IMPRINT OF SIMON & SCHUSTER BOOKS FOR YOUNG
READERS; DOUBLEDAY, AN IMPRINT OF RANDOM HOUSE; MACMILLAN/MCGRAW HILL,
SCHOOL BOOK DIVISION; WILLIAM SADLIER, INC.; *RANGER RICK* MAGAZINE; AND HARPERCOLLINS.

jennifer morla

CAPP STREET PROJECT CATALOGUE 1991–1993, CAPP STREET PROJECT, 1995.

JENNIFER MORLA, MORLA DESIGN, SAN FRANCISCO

JENNIFER MORLA IS PRESIDENT AND CREATIVE DIRECTOR OF MORLA DESIGN LOCATED IN
SAN FRANCISCO. OVER THE PAST 18 YEARS SHE HAS COLLABORATED WITH LEVI'S,
THE NEW YORK TIMES, APPLE COMPUTER, MTV, SWATCH AND CHRONICLE BOOKS. IN ADDITION,
SHE HAS CREATED NUMEROUS POSTER AND IDENTITY CAMPAIGNS FOR EXPERIMENTAL ART
ORGANIZATIONS AND MUSEUMS. WITH OVER 500 AWARDS FOR EXCELLENCE IN GRAPHIC
DESIGN, MORLA HAS BEEN ACKNOWLEDGED BY VIRTUALLY EVERY ORGANIZATION IN THE FIELD.
MORLA HAS HAD SOLO EXHIBITIONS AT SFMOMA AND DDD GALLERY IN JAPAN, AND
HER WORK IS A PART OF THE PERMANENT COLLECTIONS OF THE MOMA IN NEW YORK,
SFMOMA AND THE SMITHSONIAN AMERICAN ART MUSEUM.

paul sahre

OMON RA BOOK COVER, FARRAR, STRAUS AND GIROUX, 1997.

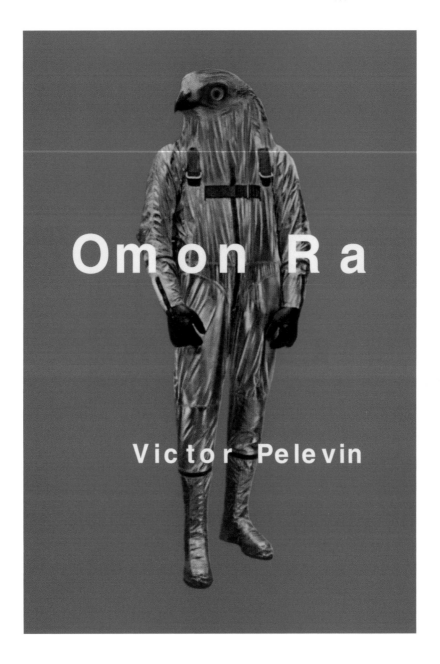

PAUL SAHRE, OFFICE OF PAUL SAHRE, NEW YORK

PAUL SAHRE IS A GRAPHIC DESIGNER AND EDUCATOR WHOSE WORK EXPLORES THE DIVE
GENCE BETWEEN DESIGN AND ART. HE HAND-PRINTS POSTERS FOR NONPROFIT INSTITUTIONS
SUCH AS THE FELLS POINT CORNER THEATRE, IN BALTIMORE AND THE SOHO REPERTORY
THEATRE, IN NEW YORK. HE ALSO DESIGNS BOOK COVERS FOR BEACON PRESS, KNOPF,
VINTAGE, LITTLE, BROWN, VERSO AND OTHER PUBLISHERS. SAHRE TEACHES GRAPHIC DESIGN
AND TYPOGRAPHY AT PARSONS SCHOOL OF DESIGN AND THE SCHOOL OF VISUAL ARTS.
ALL OF THIS, WHILE OVERSEEING THE OPERATION OF HIS OWN DESIGN OFFICE IN NEW YORK
CITY. HE RECEIVED A BFA AND MFA IN GRAPHIC DESIGN FROM KENT STATE IN OHIO.

barbara de wilde

MARTHA STEWART BABY SPECIAL ISSUE, MARTHA STEWART LIVING OMNIMEDIA, 2000.

BARBARA DE WILDE, MARTHA STEWART OMNIMEDIA, NEW YORK.
BARBARA DE WILDE IS CURRENTLY THE DESIGN DIRECTOR AT *MARTHA STEWART LIVING*
MAGAZINE. AFTER THE SUCCESSFUL LAUNCH OF *MARTHA STEWART BABY* AND
MARTHA STEWART HOLIDAY, SHE BEGAN WORKING WITH HOEFLER TYPE FOUNDRY TO
DEVELOP TWO NEW FONTS FOR MSL FOR THE REDESIGN OF THE MAGAZINE.
PRIOR TO HER WORK FOR MARTHA STEWART LIVING OMNIMEDIA, DE WILDE WORKED AS A
GRAPHIC DESIGNER IN THE BOOK PUBLISHING AND MUSIC PACKAGING INDUSTRIES.
HER WORK FOR THE KNOPF PUBLISHING GROUP, FARRAR, STRAUS AND GIROUX,
HARPERCOLLINS AND LITTLE, BROWN HAS BEEN PUBLISHED IN *EYE*, *PRINT*, *TIME*, *VANITY FAIR*
AND *I.D.* MAGAZINES, AND SELECTED FOR DISPLAY BY THE COOPER-HEWITT NATIONAL
DESIGN MUSEUM, AIGA, ART DIRECTORS CLUB AND SOCIETY OF PUBLICATION DESIGNERS.

american institute of graphic arts

AIGA

aiga purpose

THE PURPOSE OF AIGA IS TO SET THE NATIONAL AGENDA FOR THE ROLE OF DESIGN IN ITS ECONOMIC, SOCIAL, POLITICAL AND CULTURAL CONTEXTS. AIGA IS THE OLDEST AND LARGEST MEMBERSHIP ASSOCIATION FOR PROFESSIONALS ENGAGED IN THE DISCIPLINE, PRACTICE AND CULTURE OF DESIGNING. AIGA WAS FOUNDED IN 1914 AND NOW REPRESENTS MORE THAN 15,000 DESIGNERS THROUGH NATIONAL ACTIVITIES AND LOCAL PROGRAMS DEVELOPED BY 46 CHAPTERS AND MORE THAN 100 STUDENT GROUPS.

AIGA SUPPORTS THE INTERESTS OF PROFESSIONALS, EDUCATORS AND STUDENTS WHO ARE ENGAGED IN THE PROCESS OF DESIGNING, REGARDLESS OF WHERE THEY ARE IN THE ARC OF THEIR CAREERS. THE DISCIPLINES REPRESENTED IN THE PROFESSION INCLUDE BRAND STRATEGY, ILLUSTRATION, INFORMATION ARCHITECTURE, BOOK DESIGN, TYPE DESIGN, DESIGN FOR NEW MEDIA, FILM AND TELEVISION, AND DESIGN CRITICISM.

AIGA SERVES AS A HUB OF THOUGHT-LEADERSHIP AND ACTIVITY FOR THE DESIGNING COMMUNITY. THE ASSOCIATION IS COMMITTED TO STIMULATING THINKING ABOUT DESIGN THROUGH THE EXCHANGE OF IDEAS AND INFORMATION, THE ENCOURAGEMENT OF CRITICAL ANALYSIS AND RESEARCH, AND THE ADVANCEMENT OF EDUCATION AND ETHICAL PRACTICE.

USING CONFERENCES, COMPETITIONS, EXHIBITIONS, PUBLICATIONS AND WEBSITES, AIGA INSPIRES, EDUCATES AND INFORMS DESIGNERS, HELPING THEM TO REALIZE THEIR TALENTS AND TO ADVOCATE THE VALUE OF DESIGN AMONG THE MEDIA, THE BUSINESS COMMUNITY, GOVERNMENTS AND THE PUBLIC.

AIGA IS A NATIONAL NOT-FOR-PROFIT EDUCATIONAL ORGANIZATION INCORPORATED UNDER SECTION 501 (C)(3) OF THE INTERNAL REVENUE CODE IN THE STATE OF NEW YORK.

creative leadership campaign

CREATIVE LEADERSHIP CAMPAIGN
CONTRIBUTIONS TO AIGA'S BUILDING AND PROGRAM FUNDS SINCE JANUARY 1, 2000

IF YOU WOULD LIKE TO JOIN THE LEADERSHIP CIRCLE THAT IS COMMITTED TO ADVANCING
THE PROFESSION, YOU MAY MAKE TAX-DEDUCTIBLE CONTRIBUTIONS TO:
AIGA DESIGN EXPERIENCE FUND
AIGA NATIONAL DESIGN CENTER FUND
AIGA RESEARCH AND DEVELOPMENT FUND
AIGA SCHOLARSHIP FUND

SPONSORS ($10,000+)

PENTAGRAM DESIGN INC.
EDWARD R. TUFTE

DONORS ($5,000–$9,999)

CARBONE SMOLAN AGENCY
STEPHEN DOYLE
ROBERT GREENBERG
ROGER HAYES
GONG SZETO

CONTRIBUTORS ($3,000–$4,999)

ADAMSMORIOKA
TIM LARSEN
CLEMENT MOK
EMILY OBERMAN
MARGARET YOUNGBLOOD

SUPPORTERS ($1,000–$2,999)

DANA ARNETT
ALEX BERNHARDT
MARIA BESONEN
LYNDA DECKER
TIMOTHY EATON
BILL GRANT
ERIC HANSON
KIT HINRICHS
PEGGY LAURITSEN
MONICA LITTLE
ERIC MADSEN
DAVE MALONE
MICHAEL MANWARING
JENNIFER MORLA
JASON OTERO
RIPSAW, INC.
BRUCE RUBIN
LANCE RUTTER
MARY SCOTT
SAM SHELTON
BETH SINGER
TOM TRIPLETT
MICHAEL VANDERBYL

FRIENDS (UP TO $1,000)

DOUG AKAGI
BOB AUFULDISH
LESLIE BECKER
PENNY BENDA

JOHN BIELENBERG
MICHAEL BIERUT
SIMON BLATTNER
AGNES BOURNE
PATRICIA BRUNING
REBECCA CLARK
BRIAN COLLENTINE
BRIAN COLLINS
MICHAEL CRONAN
PAUL CURTIN
JO DAVISON
MELANIE DOHERTY
SUSANNA DULKINYS
MARC ENGLISH
MARK FOX
JANET FROELICH
JONATHAN GOUTHIER
BRIAN GRAHAM
ALLAN HAAG
KEN HANSON
ROBERT HAYDEN
MIRKO ILIC
THOMAS INGALLS
INITIO
CHRISTINA JACKSON
BIRGIT KELLEY
TAMERA LAWRENCE
PEGGY LOAR
ELLEN LUPTON
MICHAEL MABRY
JOCK McDONALD
DAVID MECKEL
GRANT POUND
DOUGLAS POWELL
CHRISTOPHER PULLMAN
GERALD REIS
MICHAEL ROTH
MICHAEL SCHWAB
RICH SILVERSTEIN
SAM SMIDT
JENNIFER STERLING
AUDREY TALBOTT
JOEL TEMPLIN
LUCILLE TENAZAS
LOUISE VENINGA
HEATHER WEST
PAUL WHARTON
DENISE WOOD

aiga 2002 activities

aiga 2002 activities

january

"365: AIGA ANNUAL DESIGN EXHIBITION 22," PART 1, DECEMBER 6, 2001–FEBRUARY 8, 2002

THE WINNING SELECTIONS OF SIX OF AIGA'S ANNUAL DESIGN COMPETITIONS—BRANDING
APPLICATIONS, PACKAGING, ENVIRONMENTAL GRAPHICS, EXPERIENCE DESIGN, INFORMATION
GRAPHICS, AND DESIGN AND TYPOGRAPHY—WERE EXHIBITED TO DEMONSTRATE ASPECTS
OF THE DESIGN PROCESS, THE ROLE OF THE DESIGNER AND THE VALUE OF DESIGN.
THE EXHIBITION—WHICH DREW MORE THAN 4,000 VISITORS—WAS DESIGNED BY TWO TWELVE
ASSOCIATES, WHO TOOK THEIR INSPIRATION FROM THE 3, 6 AND 5 LETTERFORMS, TRANSFORM-
ING THEM INTO 3-DIMENSIONAL CURVACEOUS DISPLAY UNITS.
PRESENTING SPONSOR: AQUENT

DESIGN FORUM: "ILLUSTRATION"

A NODE DEVOTED TO ILLUSTRATION LAUNCHED ON AIGA'S ONLINE DESIGN FORUM, WITH
CHRISTOPH NIEMANN AS ITS MODERATOR. "ILLUSTRATION" IS AN ONLINE FORUM BUILT TO
BRIDGE THE GAP BETWEEN THE OFTEN SEPARATE WORLDS OF DESIGN
AND ILLUSTRATION. IT'S A PLACE FOR CRITICISM, COMMENTARY AND DIALOGUE
BETWEEN ILLUSTRATORS AND DESIGNERS—AN EXPLORATION OF THE EVOLVING ROLE
ILLUSTRATION PLAYS IN TODAY'S PUBLISHING ENVIRONMENT.

february

"365: AIGA ANNUAL DESIGN EXHIBITION 22," PART 2, FEBRUARY 21–APRIL 26, 2002

THE SECOND INSTALLMENT OF AIGA'S ANNUAL DESIGN EXHIBITION WAS COMPRISED
OF SELECTIONS FROM THE REMAINING FIVE AIGA ANNUAL DESIGN COMPETITIONS:
ADVERTISING AND PROMOTIONAL, BRANDING STRATEGIES AND CONCEPTS, EDITORIAL DESIGN,
DESIGN AND ILLUSTRATION, AND DESIGN FOR FILM AND TELEVISION.
THE 103 WINNING SELECTIONS OF THE YEAR 2000 WERE ALSO POSTED ON AIGA'S WEBSITE.
THE EXHIBITION OF AIGA'S ANNUAL DESIGN COMPETITIONS EXTENDS A LEGACY
THAT BEGAN MORE THAN 85 YEARS AGO AND IS WIDELY RECOGNIZED AS THE MOST
SELECTIVE STATEMENT ON DESIGN EXCELLENCE TODAY.
PRESENTING SPONSOR: AQUENT

LOOP: AIGA JOURNAL OF INTERACTION DESIGN EDUCATION, NUMBER 4

FEBRUARY'S ISSUE OF LOOP FEATURES 18 INTERACTIVE MEDIA PROJECTS SUBMITTED
BY EDUCATORS AND STUDENTS FROM INTERACTIVE PROGRAMS AROUND THE COUNTRY.
WHAT EMERGES IS A SNAPSHOT OF THE CURRENT STATE OF TEACHING IN
INTERACTIVE MEDIA AS WELL AS A GLIMPSE OF THE TALENTED YOUNG INDIVIDUALS
WHO ARE CREATING TOMORROW'S MEDIA TODAY.

march

"VOICE: AIGA NATIONAL DESIGN CONFERENCE", MARCH 21–23, 2002

"VOICE," AIGA'S NINTH BIENNIAL NATIONAL DESIGN CONFERENCE—POSTPONED LAST FALL
IN THE AFTERMATH OF THE SEPTEMBER 11 TRAGEDY—TOOK PLACE IN WASHINGTON, DC, MARCH
21–23, 2002. TWELVE HUNDRED DESIGNERS GATHERED IN THE NATION'S CAPITAL
TO EXPLORE DESIGN'S POWER TO EFFECT CHANGE IN ITS SOCIAL AND POLITICAL CONTEXTS.
SOCIALLY ENGAGED AND IDIOSYNCRATIC VOICES, INCLUDING SIMPSONS' CREATOR
MATT GROENING, DESIGNER AND AUTHOR DAVE EGGERS, THE ONION WRITER JOE GARDEN AND
ACTIVIST ILLUSTRATOR SUE COE, WERE INVITED TO DEMONSTRATE THEIR POTENCY
AS CREATIVE PRACTITIONERS AND AS HUMAN BEINGS. PRESENTATION TRANSCRIPTS,
PHOTOGRAPHS AND A DISCUSSION BOARD ARE POSTED ON AIGA'S WEBSITE.

aiga 2002 activities

april

AIGA DESIGN: BUSINESS E-NEWSLETTER

AIGA LAUNCHED *AIGA DESIGN: BUSINESS*—A MONTHLY E-NEWSLETTER THAT ADDRESSES
ISSUES OF STUDIO AND PRACTICE MANAGEMENT FOR DESIGNERS.

may

"STRATHMORE GRAPHICS GALLERY EXHIBITION," MAY 16—31, 2002

THIS EXHIBITION SHOWCASED THE WINNERS OF THE "STRATHMORE GRAPHICS GALLERY
DESIGN COMPETITION"—A COLLECTION INCLUDING LETTERHEADS, ENVELOPES,
BUSINESS CARDS, REPORT COVERS, MEMOS, NOTE CARDS, LABELS, TAGS AND OTHER
COMPONENTS PRINTED ON STRATHMORE PAPER.
PRESENTING SPONSOR: STRATHMORE

june

"ROADSHOW: DUTCH GRAPHIC DESIGN 1990—2001," JUNE 27—AUGUST 23, 2002

"ROADSHOW," CURATED BY TOON LAUWEN, REPRESENTED THE DIVERSITY OF DUTCH DESIGN
OVER THE LAST DECADE. THE EXHIBITION INCLUDED POSTERS, BOOKS, CATALOGUES,
BROCHURES, HOUSE STYLES, ANNUAL REPORTS, LETTER FONTS, MAGAZINES AND WEBSITES BY 70
DESIGNERS AND DESIGN STUDIOS—BOTH RECOGNIZED AND EMERGING TALENTS.

AIGA|AQUENT SURVEY OF DESIGN SALARIES, 2002

AIGA PUBLISHED ITS ANNUAL SURVEY OF DESIGN SALARIES IN A BROCHURE DESIGNED
BY CROSBY ASSOCIATES AND ON THE AIGA WEBSITE.
PRESENTING SPONSOR: AQUENT

july

DESIGN FORUM: "PROFESSIONAL PRACTICES"

A NODE DEVOTED TO ETHICS AND PRACTICES LAUNCHED ON AIGA'S ONLINE
DESIGN FORUM, WITH SAM SHELTON AS ITS MODERATOR. "PROFESSIONAL PRACTICES" FOCUSES
ON IMPORTANT ISSUES DESIGNERS FACE DAILY, FROM THE PRAGMATIC
MATTERS OF MANAGEMENT TO THE PURSUIT OF DESIGN EXCELLENCE AND INTEGRITY.
DESIGNERS PARTICIPATE IN THIS FORUM TO SEEK BEST PRACTICES,
SHARE SUCCESS STORIES AND ADDRESS THE CHALLENGES OF THE PROFESSION.

aiga 2002 activities

august

365: AIGA YEAR IN DESIGN 22

365 IS AIGA'S PRESENTATION OF THE BEST IN AMERICAN DESIGN. IT FEATURES THE CUTTING-EDGE PROJECTS THAT WERE SELECTED BY INDIVIDUAL EXPERT JURIES IN A SUITE OF 13 COMPETITIONS. CONCEIVED BY AIGA IN CONJUNCTION WITH CHICAGO-BASED DESIGN GROUP STUDIO BLUE, *365: AIGA YEAR IN DESIGN 22* IS A TRULY STUNNING RECORD OF A YEAR'S DESIGN ACTIVITY IN THE U.S. A CRITICAL ESSAY THAT RECORDS THE JUDGING PROCESS AND SITUATES THE WINNING WORK IN A CONTEXTUAL FRAMEWORK INTRO-DUCES EACH SECTION OF THE BOOK. FEATURED PIECES ARE FURTHER AMPLIFIED BY PROJECT STATEMENTS AND EXTENSIVE DESIGN AND PRODUCTION CREDITS. IN ADDITION, AIGA'S 2001 MEDALISTS—SAMUEL ANTUPIT AND PAULA SCHER—ARE PROFILED IN INSIGHTFUL BIOGRAPHICAL ESSAYS AND RETROSPECTIVE PORTFOLIOS.

september

"AIGA 50 BOOKS/50 COVERS OF 2001 EXHIBITION," SEPTEMBER 13—OCTOBER 25, 2002

SINCE 1923, THE "AIGA 50 BOOKS/50 COVERS" COMPETITION HAS RECOGNIZED EXCELLENCE IN BOOK DESIGN AND PRODUCTION. BOOKS AND BOOK COVERS DESIGNED DURING 2001 WERE ENTERED INTO CATEGORIES RANGING FROM TRADE, REFERENCE AND JUVENILE BOOKS TO UNIVERSITY AND MUSEUM PUBLICATIONS, AND INCLUDED LIMITED EDITION AND SPECIAL-FORMAT BOOKS. THE EXHIBITION WAS DESIGNED BY CHERMAYEFF & GEISMAR.

AIGA TRANSITIONS

AIGA TRANSITIONS WAS CREATED FOR STUDENT MEMBERS TO HELP THEM WITH SPECIFIC ISSUES PERTAINING TO THEIR DESIGN EDUCATION AND THEIR EVENTUAL TRANSITION TO THE PROFESSIONAL DESIGN WORLD.

october

"GAIN: AIGA NATIONAL BUSINESS AND DESIGN CONFERENCE", OCTOBER 25—27, 2002

UNDER THE SCRUTINY OF "MARKETPLACE" HOST DAVID BRANCACCIO, DESIGNER-CLIENT TEAMS PRESENTED CASE STUDIES, WORKS-IN-PROGRESS AND NEW OPPORTUNITIES FOR THE STRATEGIC POTENTIAL OF DESIGN IN DRIVING MARKET DEMAND IN COMPETITIVE RECOVERY. TAKING AS ITS THEME THE CONCEPT OF "BEYOND BRANDING," THE CONFERENCE LOOKED AT HOW THE STRATEGIC INTEGRATION OF DESIGN, MARKETING, COMMUNICATION AND PRODUCT DEVELOPMENT IS CRITICAL IN MOVING BEYOND THE UNIVERSAL BRANDING CONCEPT THAT DEFINED THE LAST ECONOMIC CYCLE. SPEAKERS INCLUDED: TOM O'GRADY, VICE PRESIDENT AND CREATIVE DIRECTOR OF NBA PROPERTIES/NBA ENTERTAINMENT; LILLIAN SVEC, DIRECTOR OF USER EXPERIENCE AT WALMART.COM; AND KEITH YAMASHITA, FOUNDING PRINCIPAL OF STONE YAMASHITA PARTNERS.

GAIN: AIGA JOURNAL OF DESIGN AND BUSINESS

UNDER THE EDITORSHIP OF GONG SZETO, *GAIN: AIGA JOURNAL OF DESIGN AND BUSINESS*, A LIVELY ONLINE RESOURCE THAT CONSIDERS THE ROLE OF DESIGN IN BUSINESS STRATEGY, EXPANDED WITH NEW FEATURE ARTICLES AND INTERVIEWS WITH DESIGN AND BUSINESS LEADERS.

aiga 2002 activities

november

"365: AIGA ANNUAL DESIGN EXHIBITION 23," PART 1, NOVEMBER 14–DECEMBER 28, 2002
THE EXHIBITION OF THE WINNERS OF AIGA'S ANNUAL DESIGN COMPETITIONS IS THE
BELLWETHER OF DESIGN EXCELLENCE AND EFFECTIVENESS FOR WORK PRODUCED
IN THE PRECEDING YEAR. DESIGNERS AND THE PUBLIC CAME TO AIGA NATIONAL DESIGN CENTER
GALLERY ON NEW YORK'S FIFTH AVENUE TO DISCOVER THE MOST CREATIVE,
SMART AND WELL-EXECUTED EXAMPLES OF THE PROFESSION'S CONSIDERABLE ACHIEVEMENTS IN
THE YEAR 2001. IN AN EFFORT TO HIGHLIGHT THE PROCESS OF DESIGN, EACH
EXHIBITED SELECTION WAS FRAMED BY THE JURORS' COMMENTS AND THE DESIGNER'S
PROJECT STATEMENT PLACING THE PIECE WITHIN THE CONTEXT OF ITS PURPOSE,
CONTENT, OBJECTIVE, AUDIENCE AND RESOURCES.
PRESENTING SPONSOR: AQUENT

december

"GROW: AIGA PROFESSIONAL DEVELOPMENT SEMINAR SERIES"
THROUGHOUT THE YEAR AIGA CHAPTERS IN SAN FRANCISCO, WASHINGTON, DC,
MINNEAPOLIS, CLEVELAND, LOS ANGELES AND NEW YORK HOSTED A SERIES OF "GROW"
SEMINARS WITH DAVID C. BAKER FROM RECOURSES, INC. THE SEMINARS WERE SPECIFICALLY
TAILORED FOR DESIGN MANAGERS, STUDIO PRINCIPALS, SENIOR DESIGNERS,
ART DIRECTORS AND BUSINESS DEVELOPMENT PEOPLE, AND TOPICS INCLUDED: TAKING
CARE OF CLIENTS; POSITIONING AND MARKETING YOUR SERVICES; BEING A GOOD
MANAGER; AND MONITORING AND BENCHMARKING YOUR PRACTICE.
PRESENTING SPONSOR: SAPPI

AIGA EDUCATOR SERIES
AIGA CHAPTERS IN BOSTON, MINNEAPOLIS, SEATTLE, LOS ANGELES, SAN FRANCISCO AND
CHICAGO HOSTED REGIONAL CONFERENCES ON DIFFERENT ASPECTS OF DESIGN EDUCATION.
PRESENTING SPONSOR: MEADWESTVACO

POSTSCRIPT, A SPECIAL ISSUE OF TRACE: AIGA JOURNAL OF DESIGN
THIS SPECIAL ISSUE OF TRACE: AIGA JOURNAL OF DESIGN, BUILDS UPON THE FIRST
THREE ISSUES OF THE PUBLICATION AND EXPANDS AND DEVELOPS THE THEME OF "VOICE,"
AIGA'S MOST RECENT NATIONAL DESIGN CONFERENCE. POSTSCRIPT ASSEMBLES ARTICLES
AND VISUAL ESSAYS—GERMINATED AT THE CONFERENCE—CONCERNING THE SOCIAL
AND POLITICAL AGENCY OF DESIGN AND THE CONCEPT OF THE "VOICE" OF THE DESIGNER.
CONTRIBUTORS INCLUDE THE CONFERENCE SPEAKERS, CRITICS AND INFLUENTIAL
DESIGNERS. THIS ISSUE OF THE JOURNAL SHARES CONFERENCE CONTENT WITH
ALL OF AIGA'S MEMBERSHIP AND CONTINUES THE WORK OF THE CONFERENCE IN CONSIDERING
THE CRUCIAL ROLE DESIGN PLAYS AS AN AGENT OF CHANGE.
PRESENTING SPONSOR: MOHAWK

aiga leadership and staff

BOARD OF DIRECTORS

CHAPTER PRESIDENTS

STAFF

aiga board of directors

2001—2002

PRESIDENT
CLEMENT MOK

SECRETARY/TREASURER
SAM SHELTON

EXECUTIVE DIRECTOR
RICHARD GREFÉ

DIRECTORS
DANA ARNETT
JOHN BIELENBERG (STARTING JULY 2002)
JOHN CHUANG
MARC ENGLISH (ENDING JUNE 2002)
PETER GIRARDI (ENDING JUNE 2002)
BILL GRANT
NIGEL HOLMES
TERRY IRWIN
JOHN MAEDA
JENNIFER MORLA (ENDING JUNE 2002)
STEFAN SAGMEISTER (STARTING JULY 2002)
TERRY SWACK
GONG SZETO
PETRULA VRONTIKIS
ANN WILLOUGHBY (STARTING JULY 2002)
MARGARET YOUNGBLOOD

CHAPTER PRESIDENTS' COUNCIL REPRESENTATIVE
NOREEN MORIOKA (STARTING JULY 2002)
AMY STRAUCH (ENDING JUNE 2002)

aiga chapter presidents

2001—2002

ARIZONA
LAURA VON GLUCK (ENDING 2002), AMY LONG (STARTING 2002)

ATLANTA
KATHI ROBERTS

AUSTIN
SHERRI WHITMARSH

BALTIMORE
BRIGITT THOMPSON (ENDING 2002), JOE WAGNER (STARTING 2002)

BIRMINGHAM
BETH SANTORO (ENDING 2002)
RACHEL CRUTCHFIELD & CRAIG HYDE (STARTING 2002)

BOSTON
LEIGH MANTONI

CHARLOTTE
PATRICK SHORT

CHICAGO
MARCIA LAUSEN

CINCINNATI
RONDI TSCHOPP

CLEVELAND
LINDA BROWN

COLORADO
STUART ALDEN

DALLAS
BILL FORD (ENDING 2002), WENDY WALKER DAVIS (STARTING 2002)

DC
GERETTE BRAUNSDORF

DETROIT
BRUNO HOHMANN & ALLISON MILLAR

HONOLULU
STACEY LEONG MILLS

HOUSTON
DYLAN MOORE

INDIANAPOLIS
LORI LONG (ENDING 2002)
TRACY NELSON-ALBERTSON & MARTIN SCHLIESSMANN (STARTING 2002)

IOWA
ANTJE GRAY

JACKSONVILLE
BONNIE BARNES (ENDING 2002), MARY ANN ROSENTHAL (STARTING 2002)

KANSAS CITY
JOSEPH LACRUE

KNOXVILLE
DAN LIPE

LAS VEGAS
VICTOR RODRIGUEZ

LOS ANGELES
NOREEN MORIOKA (ENDING 2002), MATT PASHKOW (STARTING 2002)

MIAMI
JONATHAN GOUTHIER (ENDING 2002), ANNETTE M. PISKEL (STARTING 2002)

MINNESOTA
JOELLE ANDERLIK (ENDING 2002)
SCOTT GEIGER (STARTING 2002)

NASHVILLE
VALERIE SLOAN

NEBRASKA
CATHY SOLARANA

NEW ORLEANS
RODERICK LEMAIRE

NEW YORK
JANET FROELICH (ENDING 2002), EMILY OBERMAN (STARTING 2002)

OKLAHOMA
MARC BOSTIAN (ENDING 2002), ANNE RICHARDSON (STARTING 2002)

ORANGE COUNTY
YAMINI PRABHAKAR

ORLANDO
JENISE OBERWETTER DAVIS

PHILADELPHIA
GILMAN HANSON (ENDING 2002), STEPHEN SHACKLEFORD (STARTING 2002)

PITTSBURGH
LARKIN WERNER & TED WILLIAMS (ENDING 2002)
ELLEN AYOOB & TED WILLIAMS (STARTING 2002)

PORTLAND
RON DUMAS & CATHERINE HEALY

RALEIGH
CHRISTY WHITE (ENDING 2002), DAVID BURNEY (STARTING 2002)

RICHMOND
JASON BURTON

ST. LOUIS
RIA SHARON

SALT LAKE CITY
RYAN MANSFIELD

SAN DIEGO
JOHN DENNIS

SAN FRANCISCO
BRIAN JACOBS

SANTA FE
JOEL NAKAMURA

SEATTLE
TAN LE & LAURA ZECK (ENDING 2002), BROOKE MACKAY (STRATING 2002)

UPSTATE NEW YORK
MARJ CRUM (ENDING 2002), JAMES WONDRACK (STARTING 2002)

WICHITA
NONA CLARK

WISCONSIN
KEN HANSON

aiga staff

2001–2002

DIRECTOR OF PRODUCTION
PAMELA AVILES

DIRECTOR OF EVENTS
KELLEY BEAUDOIN

CHAPTER AND COMMUNITIES COORDINATOR
MOLLY BEVERSTEIN

MEMBERSHIP COORDINATOR
GEORGE FERNANDEZ

EXECUTIVE DIRECTOR
RICHARD GREFÉ

EDITORIAL ASSOCIATE
ELINOR HUTTON

CUSTOMER SERVICE ASSOCIATE
MELISSA LUM

DIRECTOR OF COMPETITIONS AND EXHIBITIONS
GABRIELA MIRENSKY

MEMBERSHIP AND CONFERENCE REGISTRATION ASSOCIATE
JENNIFER PHILLIPS

DIRECTOR OF CORPORATE AND PUBLIC PARTNERSHIPS
BROOKE SMITH

EDITOR AND PROGRAM ADVISOR
ALICE TWEMLOW

PROGRAM COORDINATOR
STEPHANIE UHL

FINANCE AND ADMINISTRATION ASSOCIATE
MARC VASSALL

FACILITY ASSISTANT
JOHNNY VENTURA

DIRECTOR OF NEW MEDIA
DAVID WOMACK

CHIEF EXPERIENCE OFFICER
DENISE WOOD

aiga
50 books/5
of 2001

aiga national design center

164 FIFTH AVENUE
NEW YORK, NEW YORK
212 807 1990

aiga national design center
164 FIFTH AVENUE
NEW YORK, NEW YORK
212 807 1990

2002 aiga national sponsors

AQUENT
OFFICIAL CAREER DEVELOPMENT SPONSOR

MEADWESTVACO
OFFICIAL EDUCATION SPONSOR

SAPPI
OFFICIAL CORPORATE SPONSOR

INTERNATIONAL PAPER
365: AIGA YEAR IN DESIGN 23 PAPER DONOR

AQUENT IS THE OFFICIAL AIGA CAREER DEVELOPMENT SPONSOR, PROVIDING AN ARRAY OF SUPPORT SERVICES AND PROFESSIONAL TRAINING OPPORTUNITIES FOR AIGA MEMBERS NATIONWIDE. THROUGH THIS MULTIYEAR PARTNERSHIP, AQUENT SPONSORS NUMEROUS AIGA NATIONAL CONFERENCES, EXHIBITIONS AND EVENTS.

AQUENT'S 45 DOMESTIC OFFICES ARE COMMITTED TO WORKING WITH AIGA'S LOCAL CHAPTERS TO SUPPORT ACTIVITIES THAT EDUCATE AND INFORM DESIGNERS ABOUT PROFESSIONAL ADVANCEMENT AND CAREER-PLANNING ISSUES.

THIS PARTNERSHIP, LIKE ALL THAT AIGA PURSUES, IS GEARED TOWARD EXPANDING AND ENHANCING MEMBER BENEFITS AS WELL AS INCREASING THE VALUE OF THE PROFESSION TO THE PUBLIC. TO THAT END, AQUENT, AS UNDERWRITER OF THE *AIGA|AQUENT SURVEY OF DESIGN SALARIES*, HELPS AIGA EXPAND THE SCOPE OF THE SURVEY AND MAKE IT MORE READILY AVAILABLE NOT ONLY TO AIGA MEMBERS, BUT ALSO TO COMPANIES THAT HIRE DESIGN PROFESSIONALS ACROSS THE COUNTRY.

AQUENT

MEADWESTVACO'S PARTNERSHIP WITH AIGA AS THE OFFICIAL EDUCATION SPONSOR IS A NATURAL EXTENSION OF ITS POSITION IN THE EDUCATION COMMUNITY. MEADWESTVACO PROVIDES NEW SERVICES, SUPPORT, INSPIRATION AND GUIDANCE FOR AIGA STUDENT MEMBERS, EDUCATORS AND ALL AIGA MEMBERS WHO ARE COMMITTED TO THE FUTURE OF DESIGN.

MEADWESTVACO'S COMMITMENT AS THE OFFICIAL EDUCATION SPONSOR INCLUDES ITS SUPPORT OF AIGA'S ENHANCED STUDENT ACTIVITIES AT THE NATIONAL DESIGN CONFERENCE, THE BUSINESS AND DESIGN CONFERENCE AND THE AIGA EDUCATOR SERIES. THE COMPANY'S SUPPORT ALSO HELPS TO MAINTAIN AND GROW AIGA ONLINE OUTREACH TO STUDENTS, AND INCREASE ACTIVITIES WITH DESIGN EDUCATORS AND SCHOOLS ACROSS THE COUNTRY.

MEADWESTVACO PROVIDES HIGH-QUALITY PRODUCTS AND SERVICES THAT HELP CUSTOMERS COMMUNICATE EFFICIENTLY AND EFFECTIVELY. MEADWESTVACO MANUFACTURES COATED PRINTING PAPERS IN A WIDE VARIETY OF GRADES, FINISHES AND WEIGHTS SUITABLE FOR VIRTUALLY EVERY PRINTING NEED.

MeadWestvaco

paper donor
international paper

INTERNATIONAL PAPER IS PROUD TO DONATE CUSTOM-WATERMARKED PAPER FOR *365: AIGA YEAR IN DESIGN 23*. WITH MORE THAN 150 YEARS OF EXPERIENCE IN PRODUCING NOTABLE BRANDS OF PAPER SUCH AS STRATHMORE®, BECKETT® AND VIA®, INTERNATIONAL PAPER HAS A LONG HISTORY OF SERVING THE NEEDS OF THE GRAPHIC DESIGN INDUSTRY.

INTERNATIONAL PAPER IS THE WORLD'S LARGEST PAPER AND FOREST PRODUCTS COMPANY. AS ONE OF THE MAJOR PRIVATE FOREST LANDOWNERS, INTERNATIONAL PAPER MANAGES ITS FORESTS UNDER THE PRINCIPLES OF THE SUSTAINABLE FORESTRY INITIATIVE (SFISM) PROGRAM, A SYSTEM THAT ENSURES THE PERPETUAL PLANTING, GROWING AND HARVESTING OF TREES WHILE PROTECTING WILDLIFE, PLANTS, SOIL, AIR AND WATER QUALITY. HEADQUARTERED IN THE U.S. IN STAMFORD, CONNECTICUT, INTERNATIONAL PAPER HAS OPERATIONS IN 50 COUNTRIES AND EXPORTS ITS PRODUCTS TO MORE THAN 130 NATIONS. VISIT WWW.INTERNATIONALPAPER.COM FOR MORE INFORMATION.

index

a

b

c

d

e

f

g

h

i

j

k

l

m

n

O

P

q

r

s

t

u

v

W

x - y

Z